International Political Economy Series

Series Editor
Timothy M. Shaw
University of Massachusetts
Boston, MA, USA

Emeritus Professor
University of London, UK

The global political economy is in flux as a series of cumulative crises impacts its organization and governance. The IPE series has tracked its development in both analysis and structure over the last three decades. It has always had a concentration on the global South. Now the South increasingly challenges the North as the centre of development, also reflected in a growing number of submissions and publications on indebted Eurozone economies in Southern Europe. An indispensable resource for scholars and researchers, the series examines a variety of capitalisms and connections by focusing on emerging economies, companies and sectors, debates and policies. It informs diverse policy communities as the established trans-Atlantic North declines and 'the rest', especially the BRICS, rise.

More information about this series at
http://www.palgrave.com/gp/series/13996

Chang Kyung-Sup

Developmental Liberalism in South Korea

Formation, Degeneration, and Transnationalization

Chang Kyung-Sup
Seoul National University
Seoul, South Korea

International Political Economy Series
ISBN 978-3-030-14575-0   ISBN 978-3-030-14576-7   (eBook)
https://doi.org/10.1007/978-3-030-14576-7

Library of Congress Control Number: 2019935536

This Palgrave Macmillan imprint is published by the registered company Springer Nature Switzerland AG.
The registered company address is: Gewerbestrasse 11, 6330 Cham, Switzerland

Research for this work has been supported by
Seoul National University Asia Center (SNUAC)
through its Basic Asian Studies Research Fund (2013-202).

CONTENTS

ACRONYMS

ADB	Asian Development Bank
AIIB	Asian Infrastructure Investment Bank
APEC	Asia-Pacific Economic Cooperation
EU	European Union
FKI	Federation of Korean Industries
FKTU	Federation of Korean Trade Unions
GDP	Gross domestic product
GNI	Gross national income
ICT	Information and communications technology
IMF	International Monetary Fund
KCTU	Korean Confederation of Trade Unions
KDI	Korea Development Institute
KFTC	Korea Fair Trade Commission
KIHASA	Korea Institute for Health and Social Affairs
KLI	Korea Labor Institute
KOSIS	Korean Statistical Information Service
KOTRA	Korea Trade-Investment Promotion Agency
NGOs	Nongovernmental organizations
NPOs	Non-profit organizations
NSO	National Statistical Office
OECD	Organisation for Economic Co-operation and Development
OJTs	On-the-job-trainees
PPP	Purchasing power parity
PSPD	People's Solidarity for Participatory Democracy
SI	Socialist International
TFR	Total fertility rate
UN	United Nations
WHO	World Health Organization

LIST OF FIGURES

LIST OF TABLES

FOREWORD

Over a long period, during which South Korea attracted attention as the leading developmental state in the wake of Japan's initial success, its system of welfare provision (with the possible exception of education to furnish an appropriately developmentally skilled labor force) was subject to neglect and, where it did draw attention, perceived to be negligible. Over the past two decades, this situation has changed significantly, not least with the most welcome work of UNRISD on Asian development welfare states, which has served to begin to correct both the neglect and the misperception of what are (differentiated) Asian welfare states. In this light, this volume is both a continuation of such invaluable research and, in some respects, a constructive break with it.

One way to see this is in terms of the location of social policy, and welfare provision more generally, within the much broader contextualized framing of economic and social reproduction. The question then changes from what social policies by comparison to those of the west to what forms are taken specifically by economic and social reproduction in the South Korean context. This is, across a number of respects, a much bigger and more demanding enquiry with the following elements. First, social policy of whatever kind and degree must be situated in the broader developmental experience of South Korea, something that is addressed in the book chronologically in terms of specifying the country as having journeyed from developmental liberalism to neoliberalism. The need for and contours of social policy look very different across when there is a rapidly industrializing economy, under the coordinated expansion of *chaebols*, with lifetime guaranteed employment and benefits for the many, than when jobs are insecure and more fortunate family members no longer exist to be relied upon to support those less favorably situated. As a result of what I have termed the variegated and volatile vulnerabilities of neoliberalism, South Korean society has experienced extreme distress in terms of rising rates of suicide and deprivation across different areas of (social) provisioning.

In short, and second, social policy in this volume has appropriately been situated in what might be termed the neoliberal condition with South Korean features, the latter themselves dependent upon an earlier history of (industrial) developmentalism. Some of these features are not unique to the country, not least the pressures on employment (through two major crises, one Asian and the other global if less Asian), on the family, on working conditions, on labor movements and the self-confidence of social democratic political parties, and the increasing reliance upon financialized credit to sustain levels of consumption.

Third, though, some features of the contemporary landscape are shared in common with, and mutually determined by, what is termed an Asianized industrial capitalism although this gives rise to specific South Korean parameters. In this respect, the rising influence of China (more or less overlooked during the classical development phase) is paramount and raises those longstanding issues of how dominant capitals exploit economic alongside social reproduction and what allows for a more progressive and harmonious embedding. How does social policy fit into the regional let alone the global context?

Fourth, then, this is to raise the issue of how progressive forces, labor and more, participate in the making of social policy. This has been unduly neglected in examining South Korea's developmental success if less so more recently, but it is of vital interest to the current author, alongside the ideological discourses that accompany the making of social policy.

Finally, put this mix together and we are offered a refreshingly new and interdisciplinary take on social policy, one far from the straitjacket of the hegemonic welfare regime approach that I have argued has long exceeded its use-by date. This volume may not be the last word on the nature and determinants of South Korean social policy, but it does offer an admirable lesson in how social policy should be studied.

School of Oriental and African Studies   Ben Fine
University of London
London, UK

PREFACE

After spending so many years in life as a social scientist, I am increasingly anxious about the (im)practicality of the conventional disciplinary division of labor. With all massively accumulated bodies of "scientific" knowledge in separate disciplines, social realities appear, at least to myself, more and more elusive. I believe this is in a great part due to the rapidly increasing complexities of contemporary social phenomena that badly defy both conventional sectoral and institutional boundaries and academic disciplinary divisions supposedly reflecting them.

In South Korea, a society characterized by what I call *compressed modernity*, academic development has generally been governed by a modernization regime of compartmentalized institutional simulation. Although most academic disciplines have been housed in *univer*sities, each of them has pursued a highly compressed mode of institutional advancement by independently emulating, if not outright copying, the supposedly best practice in the corresponding disciplines of the hegemonic West. Through this process, the already rigid disciplinary boundaries have become even more stiffened, leaving university in an institutional state of total mutual dislocation. Perhaps some neologism like *departmentry* could be a more relevant word than university for describing an un(der)coordinated aggregate of disciplinary departments.

Most of South Korea's historical and social realities, on the other hand, have chronically been plagued with contaminations and compoundings among supposedly separate spheres of the social world. Economy, politics, society, and culture are rarely independent of each other. In particular, virtually everything has been politicized as modernization and development have been pervasively state-driven and even state-framed. Thus, everyone is struggling, whether through action or imagination, for preferential or, at least, fair access to state power. At least, media have long noticed this fact, with most of their news coverage politically framed. In fact, they consciously and unconsciously intensify the politicization of economy, society, and culture as a strategy of political self-aggrandizement. To many social scientists, such politicized realities are felt very unpleasantly. To them, what deserves condemnation is not their social sciences under the assumption of neat intersphere separation and autonomy but the corruptly complex (and undermodernized) realities.

Paradoxically, it has been through such complicated realities that South Korea has achieved economic development, political and social democratization, and even sociocultural prominence. Moreover, the particular manners, processes, and consequences with which South Korea has arrived at the current economic, political, and sociocultural status has helped critically revamp global social sciences. The wide popularity and influence of the so-called Korean studies are in a large part thanks to such general social scientific significance of Korean experiences. Solid and innovative studies on South Korea's economic development, democratization, labor politics, popular culture, and technological innovation have helped invigorate many disciplines in research and education, however, in significantly different ways from conventional approaches in orthodox social sciences. Broadly speaking, many of highly successful overseas and domestic analysts of South Korean development and modernity have systematically dealt with the interfaces between the state, society, economy, and/or culture.

Following such scientific lead, this book pays analytical attention to another critical interface—namely, the interface between developmental politics and social policy. One of the popular characterizations of South Korea in social welfare is "welfare laggard" (vis-à-vis its superb economic capacity and robust political democracy). Relatedly, conservative developmental politics is often condemned as the key culprit. On the other hand, it is an ordinary scholarly practice to explain whatever social welfare exists in South Korea either as a certain type of welfare state or in terms of differences or distances from prototypical Western welfare states. To me, as a believer in the fact that South Korea has been ruled by a "developmental state", both of these condemnations and explanations remain quite unsatisfactory in scientifically making sense of what South Koreans have gone through socially under developmentalist state rule.

I would agree with many scholars of social welfare when they appraise that South Korea has remained "liberal" (reads limited) in the scope and level of social welfare. But, instead of condemning developmentalist politics for limited social welfare, I propose to acknowledge that South Korea has been *developmentally liberal* in social welfare and, in fact, in a long series of other social affairs such as health, education, labor relations, environment, and so forth. In this way, we will be able to systematically discern South Korea's many on-surface similarities in social conditions to prototypical liberal societies like the United States. If the United States has been liberally liberal, South Korea has been developmentally liberal.

During my very short career as a journalist of economic affairs in the mid-1980s, I felt both intellectually puzzled and politically disturbed about the government's "meetings of ministers of economic policy" in which ministers of social affairs attended practically as subordinate or accessorial participants. (My political disturbance was due to the fact I had become social democratic mostly through personal experiences, encounters, and relationships.) In such meetings, ministers of social affairs were expected to discuss or present policy measures for promoting economic growth and industrial development by organizing, mobilizing, or even constraining social policy concerns. Not unrelatedly, there were no separate meetings of ministers of social affairs. (Even the formal concept of social policy did not exist until the mid-2000s when the supposedly progressive government of Roh Moo-Hyun was put under mounting criticism for neglecting social welfare and other social policy concerns.) More fundamentally, the developmental liberal state nearly refused to acknowledge its citizenry as its social policy constituency. Most South Koreans were not angered about such political line and instead kept focusing on economic opportunities and benefits, for instance, during presidential and parliamentary elections.

When South Korea's developmentalist governance came under abrupt interruption and damage due to an unexpected and unprecedented national financial crisis, the crisis-led social confusions and impairments were further amplified in proportion to the significance of developmental liberal order. Curiously, despite South Korea's continually strong industrial economic basis and swift macroeconomic recovery, its citizenry expressed much stronger frustrations than those of other financially troubled Asian countries. Such frustrations soon turned into a sort of developmental nostalgia as South Koreans chose Park Chung-Hee marketers, Lee Myung-Bak and Park Geun-Hye, in two successive presidential elections.

Unfortunately, these opportunistic (and opportune) leaders failed to prevent South Koreans from showing, "for economic reasons", some of the world's most extreme levels of suicide and low fertility.

This book is presented both as a theoretical/conceptual reformulation on social governance under developmentalist state rule and an empirical account of a series of socioeconomic trends during South Korea's turbulent transition from developmental liberal to neoliberal order. Theoretical/conceptual ideas have been developed and empirical observations made all along the lengthy process of South Korea's late- and post-developmental transformations. It means this book has taken almost two decades in research and writing.

Naturally, I feel extremely relieved about its final completion with all numerous remaining shortcomings. In fact, I have almost simultaneously prepared and published another book (in Korean) on an essentially related topic of *familial liberalism* and also stand on a half way into completing still another related book (in English) on *democratic neoliberalism*. The first book, entitled *The End of Tomorrow? Familial Liberalism and Social Reproduction Crisis* (2018), explains that South Korea has been more *familially liberal* than individually liberal due to the developmental liberal state's wide and intense mobilization of familial norms, relations, and resources for maximum national capitalist accumulation and private citizens' frequently proactive accommodation of familialized social responsibilities and economic functions. Under the national financial crisis and concomitant neoliberal restructuring, however, these institutional and behavioral mechanisms have similarly helped familialize various socioeconomic risks stemming from the macroeconomic turbulences and ultimately induced South Koreans to become highly cautious and reserved about family formation and expansion.

The second book, tentatively entitled *The Paradox of Democratic Neoliberalism: South Korea's Transition in Developmental Politics*, addresses the puzzling question of South Korea's nearly instantaneous neoliberal socioeconomic transformations precisely along the political courses of democratic restoration and stabilization. For diverse reasons yet to be explicated, the self-congratulatorily democratic administrations, intellectually activist civil society, socially entrenched trade unions, ordinary citizens as habitual developmental aspirants, as well as economically mighty but politically vulnerable *chaebol* all have converged, albeit not always consciously and cooperatively, on the ultimately neoliberal paths of socioeconomic transformations. My intention behind writing these ambitious

PREFACE xxi

books together is to analyze—instead of condemning—South Korea's liberal order in its historico-social actualities and systemic entireties.

Some parts of the current book have incorporated revised versions of earlier published articles as follows: Chap. 3 has been thoroughly rewritten and updated from "Social Ramifications of South Korea's Economic Fall: Neo-Liberal Antidote to Compressed Capitalist Industrialization?" (*Development and Society*, vol. 28, no. 1, 1999); Chap. 4 has partially reflected various revised parts of "The End of Developmental Citizenship? Restructuring and Social Displacement in Post-Crisis South Korea" (*Economic and Political Weekly*, vol. 42, no. 50, 2007); Chap. 5 has partially incorporated various revised parts of "Financialization of Poverty: Proletarianizing the Financial Crisis in Post-Developmental Korea" (*Research in Political Economy*, vol. 31, 2016); Chap. 7 has partially drawn from various revised parts of "Predicaments of Neoliberalism in the Post-Developmental Liberal Context" (*Developmental Politics in Transition: The Neoliberal Era and Beyond*, edited by Chang Kyung-Sup, Ben Fine, and Linda Weiss, Palgrave Macmillan, 2012).

It is simply impossible to list all scholars to whom I owe enlightening feedbacks, constructive suggestions, and collegial encouragements in preparing the current book. Nonetheless, I would like to thank Ben Fine, Pietro Masina, C. P. Chandrasekhar, Jayati Ghosh, Kong Tat Yan, Alvin So, Hagen Koo, Eui-Hang Shin, Pieter Boele Van Hensbroek, Hiroshi Kojima, Emiko Ochiai, Raymond Chan, Gu Shengzu, Zhang Yi, Zsombor Rajkai, Linda Weiss, Elizabeth Thurbon, John Matthews, Susanne Soederberg, Peter Abrahamson, Chua Beng Huat, Shen Hsiu-hua, Teo Youyenn, Bryan S. Turner, Göran Therborn, Laurence Roulleau-Berger, Stevi Jackson, Lynn Jamieson, Sven Hort, and many other overseas colleagues for offering various useful inputs through scholarly gatherings and collaborations. I am also thankful to Kim Taekyoon, Chang Dae-oup, Seol Dong-Hoon, Lee Seung-yoon, Lee Cheol-Sung, Lee Hyunok, Kim Se-Kyun, Chin Meejung, Lee Jaerim, Sung Miai, Kwon Hyeong-ki, Gong Suk Ki, Cho Heungsik, Kim Hye-Lan, Kwon Huck-ju, Chin Seung Kwon, Kim Chul-Kyoo, Kim Hung Ju, Shin Kwang-Yeong, Kim Myong Soo, Kuk Min Ho, Yoon Sang-Woo, Lim Woon Taek, Kim Hyun Mee, Eun Ki-Soo, Lee Keun, and many other Korean colleagues in the same vein.

The International Development Economics Associates (IDEAs), the International Initiative for Promoting Political Economy (IIPPE), the Society for the Advancement of Socio-Economics (SASE), and the Korean Association of Comparative Sociology have served as essential scholarly platforms for presenting various parts of the current work and exposing myself to crucial scientific advances made by other participants in related issues. Let me express cordial thanks to those colleagues who have devoted themselves to promoting global intellectual scholarship through these organizations. I also wish to indicate that my intellectual indebtedness to Dietrich Rueschemeyer, Paget Henry, Sidney Goldstein, and Louis Putterman at Brown University and to Kim Kyong-Dong, Lim Hyun-Chin, and Kwon Tae-Hwan at Seoul National University has been indispensable in exploring an academic career as a sociologist of development issues.

Finally, I am much grateful to Timothy Shaw, the academic editor of the International Political Economy (IPE) series of Palgrave Macmillan, and Christina M. Brian and Anca Pusca, the publisher's formerly and currently responsible editors of the IPE series, for their great enthusiasm and patience offered to me despite a long delay in delivering the book manuscript. Also, Katelyn Zingg's careful assistance at the final stage of preparing all materials for the book and the wonderful effort of the copyeditors at SPi Global are cordially appreciated. I regard this book as a companion volume with *Developmental Politics in Transition: The Neoliberal Era and Beyond* (2012) that I coedited with Ben Fine and Linda Weiss also for the IPE series. It is my sincere wish that this book can make meaningful intellectual and practical contributions like many books published earlier in the same book series.

Seoul National University   Chang Kyung-Sup
South Korea

PART I

Developmental Politics
and Social Policy

CHAPTER 1

Introduction: Developmental Social Governance in Transition

After a brief period of a self-congratulatory mood which began with the democratic restoration in 1987 and the Seoul Olympic Games in 1988 and culminated in terms of South Korea's acceptance to the Organisation for Economic Co-operation and Development (OECD) in 2006, both the everyday livelihood of ordinary people and the national economy have been subjected to extreme instabilities and uncertainties. This tendency was radically dramatized in late 1997 by a national financial crisis, which forced millions of South Koreans to instantly lose jobs, incomes, and/or families amid unprecedented scales of corporate bankruptcies and labor reshufflings. The Kim Dae-Jung government managed to orchestrate an impressively quick recovery of the South Korean economy at the macro level, but the instabilities and uncertainties in grassroots livelihood have not been clearly alleviated in spite of the globally prominent performance of several industrial conglomerates locally called *chaebol*.[1]

For these chronically jeopardous conditions of grassroots livelihood, the neoliberal ideology and policies have often been to blame in intellectual and political debates. It is true that some of the troubles South Koreans have confronted are quite analogous to those of many developed and undeveloped societies that have undergone drastic neoliberal transitions. However, the contents, conditions, and consequences of neoliberalism should be appraised in the specific political economic context of South Korea since the mid-1980s. In particular, the historical relationship between neoliberalism and the country's pre-neoliberal developmental

© The Author(s) 2019
Chang K-S, *Developmental Liberalism in South Korea*,
International Political Economy Series,
https://doi.org/10.1007/978-3-030-14576-7_1

politics should be systematically analyzed as the most critical determinant of the socioeconomic conditions of South Koreans' work and life in the twenty-first century.

In this book, I characterize South Korea's pre-neoliberal regime of social governance as *developmental liberalism* and analyze the turbulent processes and complex outcomes of its neoliberal deformation since the mid-1990s. Instead of repeating the politically charged critical view on South Korea's failure in socially inclusionary and sustainable development, I closely examine the systemic interfaces of the economic, political, and social constituents of its developmental transformation. Developmental liberalism is the developmental state's (both explicit and implicit) regime of social governance, under which a wide range of social policies have been strategically harnessed for facilitating capitalist industrialization and economic growth as the nation's prime purpose. South Korea has turned and remained *developmentally liberal,* instead of liberally liberal (like the United States among others), in its economic and sociopolitical configuration as to social security, labor protection, population, education, and so forth. Ordinary South Koreans have not necessarily been resistant to the state's developmental liberal position as they have tried to organize their own lives according to a sort of private developmentalism attuned to the socioeconomic opportunities engendered by the nation's aggressive capitalist development. Such developmental symbiosis, if not collusion, between the state and citizenry was not evenly beneficial to South Koreans even during the heydays of developmental governance. Furthermore, South Korea's neoliberal transition, initially conceived since the late 1980s, ironically along its democratic transformation, and radically accelerated during the national financial crisis in the late 1990s, turned out incomparably volatile and destructive crucially due to its various distortive effects on the country's developmental liberal order. The main purpose of this book is to examine the basic attributes of South Korea's developmental liberalism as the developmental state's regime of social governance and analyze the conditions, processes, and consequences of the country's neoliberalization as a post-developmental liberal transition.

1   SOCIAL LIMITS OF DEVELOPMENT AND DEMOCRACY: DEVELOPMENTAL LIBERALISM AND ITS NEOLIBERAL TRANSITION

The South Korean experience of late modernization (or catching-up modernization) has attracted a wide international approbation not just because of its enviable economic result alone. More crucially, South Korea's vibrant democratization in tandem with its explosive capitalist industrialization and economic growth has led the world to suddenly acknowledge the country's full modernity. Not surprisingly, South Korea's acceptance into the OECD in 1996 was taken in South Korea as evidence of its status of an advanced industrial democracy and accompanied by a fervent self-congratulatory mood. The economic and political dynamism of South Korea, however, implicated a structural political economic instability, which kept spawning societal emergencies. Such structural instability has been further intensified by neoliberal globalization, in which South Korea has aggressively, but often clumsily, participated. The self-congratulatory period indicated above turned out to be rather short as compared to the protracted period of back-to-back political economic crises beginning with the national financial crisis in late 1997.

When the country stumbled into the Asian financial crisis as a result of its injudicious participation in (or incorporation by) the global neoliberal financial system, Western neoliberals wasted no time in loudly branding the economic calamity as a pitfall of "crony capitalism". In fact, it was a disguised ideological attack on the East Asian model of developmental political economy as epitomized by the so-called developmental state. Despite (or because of) a decade of its haphazard subscription to neoliberal ideologies and policies, the South Korean government did not try to openly refute the deceitful neoliberal framing of the economic crisis. Nor were South Korean grassroots (*seomin*) particularly defensive of their country's past of developmental political economy. In fact, an awakening was spreading among them that national economic development might not ultimately enhance the material welfare of those social groups who had sacrificed or had been forced to sacrifice their interests under the patriotic slogan of "national regeneration" (*minjokjungheung*) and that their arduously won democracy might not be usable in rectifying such political economic betrayal.

In spite of such awakening, South Korean grassroots were being told to sacrifice themselves again in order to rescue their national economy from a supposedly impending collapse. This time, the slogan of "pains-sharing" (*gotongbundam*) replaced the previous nationalistic ones, suggesting that they would not be subjected to lopsided sacrifices. More specifically, they were persuaded to trust the political pledge that state and business elite would equally share whatever sacrifices required for the emergency relief of the national economy. Before the crisis, the slogan of "growth first, distribution later" under the military-led authoritarian developmentalist regimes had been rather straightforward in demanding asymmetrical sacrifices from grassroots, whereas the renewed developmental drive by the democratically elected governments had continued, though deceptively, to subject them to uneven losses. The unfair nature of the developmental political economy, as it had long been critically recognized by grassroots, was nothing new. But the inefficacy of the democratic polity in rectifying the unfair political economy was deeply disappointing. The neoliberal developmental drive of the Kim Young-Sam government—in particular, economic expansion on the basis of internal and international financial deregulation—only pushed the national economy into a financial calamity, and the next democratic government under Kim Dae-Jung had to exhort South Korean grassroots (along with state and business elite) to go through still another stage of self-sacrificing. The neoliberal formula for economic restructuring was not conducive to pains-sharing at all, and even a "Latin Americanization" of South Korea began to be frequently hinted at in media reports and intellectual debates. The beginning years of the twenty-first century have been marred by pervasive grassroots discontents about their developmental alienation, while a handful of corporate conglomerates are strengthening their dominant position in the national economy and many sectors of the world economy.

The South Korean experience of modernization and development presents a fundamental question as to the ultimate goal of national advancement or social progress in the modern era. On the national political level, economic development and democratization have been upheld as almost universal targets of national advancement. Neither of these two targets has been easy to achieve, so that the South Korean performance has attracted widespread international envy. However, the South Korean industrial economy and democracy have become subjected to deep-seated popular disenchantments from inside. And, as indicated above, South Korean grassroots seem to have due reasons for such discontents in their everyday life. There is a pressing need to formulate an appropriate analytical framework for comprehending such grassroots discontents.

For such grassroots citizens' despair, the country's defective welfare system has frequently been to blame. The limited efficacy of South Korean democracy in channeling the outcomes of national economic development into the equitable and sustainable socioeconomic benefits of the general citizenry has been deplored not only among South Koreans themselves but also by the broad international community, including the United Nations (Chang, K. 2012a). In domestic and international scholarship, South Korea's failure in a political evolution into an effective welfare state has often been analyzed as an outcome of a relative deficiency of social democratic impetuses such as broadly organized labor activism, an influential working-class party, progressive civil society, and so forth. Such observations may not be irrelevant but the existing conditions and structures of the developmental state's (non-social democratic) social governance have remained largely unexplored. Some scholars of social policy have tried to highlight some developmentalist nature of South Korean, and East Asian, welfare systems under the concept of the "developmental welfare state" (Kwon, H. 2005). Such approach is apparently flawed by hastily classifying South Korea/East Asia as a welfare state while offering no convincing clue to their "welfare laggard" reality even at the stage of advanced industrial economies.

We should closely examine the systemic interfaces of economic management, political rule, and social policy in South Korean (and East Asian) development in order to reveal the specifically extant regime of social governance in this part of the world. That is, instead of dwelling on separately practiced scholarships on (developmental) industrial policy, (procedural versus substantive) democratization, and comparative welfare states, I propose developmental liberalism as an actual regime of developmental social governance placed on the interfaces of economic, political, and social constituents of South Korea's developmental transformation. Under developmental liberalism, a wide range of social policies have been strategically harnessed for facilitating capitalist industrialization and economic growth as the nation's prime purpose. I do not deny that South Korea has been a "welfare laggard" or "liberal" as evinced by its problematic conditions in labor protection, income distribution, social security, and so on, but intend to emphasize that it has been *developmentally liberal*, not liberally liberal like the United States. The developmental state was not simply antagonistic against social welfare but proactively managed popular interests and resources so as to developmentally redefine and subordinate otherwise social policy concerns. In effect, it did not even epistemologically allow social policy (and social citizenship) to exist as an independent political agenda except residual measures for poverty alleviation.[2] It should be indicated that most of grassroots citizens have not necessarily opposed the state's developmental liberal position and instead endeavored to manage their own lives according to a kind of private developmentalism attuned to various socioeconomic opportunities generated along their nation's expeditious capitalist industrialization and economic growth. There has been a sort of developmental liberal alliance between the developmental state and its political economic constituencies.

Developmental liberalism, both as the developmental state's regime of social governance and grassroots South Koreans' political economic culture, was as much beset with crucial social risks as instrumental to utmost material gains. All kinds of differential endowments in financial, human, and sociopolitical capital have been developmentally amplified into socioeconomic inequalities that are as intense as South Korea's economic growth itself. All structural instabilities and vulnerabilities embedded in the country's aggressive capitalist industrialization and global economic expansion have been directly translated into ordinary citizens' privatized risks in livelihood. Most critically, South Korea's slapdash neoliberal transition, firstly conceived since the late 1980s and radically accelerated during the national financial crisis in the late 1990s, turned out incomparably volatile and destructive because of its crucially distortive impacts on the country's developmental liberal order. If the political economic processes and social ramifications of South Korea's neoliberal transition are examined in the immediate historical context of its hitherto developmental liberal conditions, we will be able to much more systematically understand why so abrupt, so pervasive, so perplexing, so disruptive, and so painful are South Koreans' symptoms of neoliberal social dislocation.

2   Summary of the Chapters

The main purpose of this book is to examine the basic attributes of South Korea's developmental liberalism as the developmental state's regime of social governance and analyze the conditions, processes, and consequences of the country's neoliberalization as a post-developmental liberal transition. The following pages of this book are divided into three parts which, respectively, cover: (1) a general introduction to developmental liberalism and its historico-political backgrounds (Chap. 2), (2) socioeconomic conditions and consequences of neoliberalization in the developmental liberal context (Chaps. 3, 4, 5, and 6), and (3) double-layered neoliberal transitions of South Korea in the domestic and global (Asian) boundaries (Chaps. 7 and 8).

Chapter 2. Developmental Liberalism: The Developmental State and Social Policy

This chapter appraises the South Korean developmental state with regard to its distinct social policy characteristics and the sociopolitical conditions and effects of such characteristics. Particularly notable, among others, are the following five characteristics that render the social policy orientation of the developmental state *developmental liberal*: (1) depoliticization/technocratization/developmental obfuscation of social policy, (2) developmental cooptation of social policy constituencies ("growth first, distribution later"), (3) state-business entrepreneurial merge and direct state engagement in labor relations, (4) familial reconstitution of social citizenship, and (5) welfare pluralism and demobilization of civil society. I present contextual and substantive details of each of these characteristics and explain the broad conditions of grassroots life as critically shaped by them. In lieu of a conclusion, I briefly compare developmental liberalism with other major regimes of social policy such as (liberal) liberalism and social democracy (in various versions).

Chapter 3. Coping with the "IMF Crisis" in the Developmental Liberal Context

South Korea's economic collapse of 1997 was no less dramatic than its earlier economic success for three and a half decades. Obviously, South Koreans overstretched their economic ambitions in the 1990s, so that suicidal investment for economic expansion using short-term foreign loans was destined to cause a major balance-of-payment crisis. Institutionally, hasty neoliberal liberalization of the financial governance and industries critically accelerated such a self-destructive path. As analyzed extensively by various scholars, the developmental state's financial institutional arms (i.e., virtually state-directed banks servicing its industrial policy in terms of risky loans to state-designated export firms) and corporate regulation practices (i.e., tolerating—and even practically underwriting—private firms' excess borrowing-based industrial investment) always harbored structural possibilities of national financial meltdown under any significant

economic slowdown. The unprecedented economic—and, for that matter, social—crisis, however, seems to have rooted in many more ills of the
South Korean model of development. Particularly menacing were social
problems emanating from the psychological bubble concerning material
betterment, the welfare-suppressive accumulation strategy, and the
authoritarian treatment of labor. These practices and habits were often
considered instrumental to achieving rapid industrialization and economic
growth, but their social costs remained unpaid. Incidentally, various risky
social conditions which had been built up under the South Korean development strategy and concomitant developmental liberalism in social policy began to hurt South Koreans at the grassroots level, with the
International Monetary Fund (IMF) programs working as a crucial catalyst. In this sense, the IMF could (and should) have been much more
careful about the local social contexts in which its economic restructuring
programs would take effects (and side effects).

Chapter 4. Developmental Citizenry Stranded: Jobless Economic Recovery

During the three pre-crisis decades, South Koreans had been enfranchised
by the successive developmentalist governments in *developmental citizenship*. Then the South Korean developmental state managed to industrialize
and expand the national economy at a pace that could incorporate almost
all economically motivated individuals through increasing jobs and better
incomes. South Koreans responded to this dynamic economic process by
fully mobilizing private material and human resources as economic investment. The economic crisis of 1997 and its emergency rescue measures—in
large part recommended by the IMF—dealt a fatal blow to this state-
grassroots interactive developmentalism. As clearly shown in formal statistics, labor shedding was the most crucial measure for rescuing South
Korean firms, a big part of which were on the verge of bankruptcy. Even
after the breathtaking moments were over, most of the major firms continued to undertake organizational and technological restructuring in an
employment-minimizing manner, and thereby got reborn as globally
competitive leading exporters. The sustained economic growth buttressed
by phenomenal increases of export by a handful of major *chaebol* firms has
not been accompanied by meaningful improvements in grassroots employment and livelihood. Instead, temporary and underpaid jobs have become
normal, and on-the-job poverty has increased sharply. Income inequality

has kept expanding continuously, and even those under absolute poverty lines have drastically increased in numbers and proportions. Under the sudden evaporation of developmental citizenship, South Koreans have attempted various actions of exiting or wishing to exit the jobless industrial capitalist system.

Chapter 5. Financialization of Poverty: Consumer Credit Instead of Social Wage?

In post-crisis South Korea, the loss or lack of stable and decent jobs among ever-increasing numbers of South Koreans has inevitably led to the stagnation and even decline of wage income across society (in a stark contrast to the phenomenally swelling corporate dividends and financial transaction profits accruing to foreign investors). Poverty has seriously expanded both in absolute and relative terms, but the notoriously ungenerous and underinstitutionalized social security system has failed to alleviate the inequalities and destitution to meaningful extents. Even after struggling to reduce consumption, South Korean households in rapidly growing numbers and proportions have been entrapped into heavy indebtedness to banks, credit card companies, private usurers, kin members and friends, and even the state. Within a decade since the crisis, the total debts of South Korean households nearly tripled. In particular, the first few years of the twenty-first century saw South Koreans' household debts literally exploding. Considering that this was also the period of remarkably fast post-crisis economic recovery, such economic recovery seems to have been in part sustained by South Koreans' borrowing-based consumption. The extent of South Korea's household indebtedness, vis-à-vis both disposable income and financial assets, now far surpasses those of most developed countries (including the much troubled United States). Not surprisingly, the poorest group shows a particularly high debt-service burden. (For them, even the quality of debt service is most horrendous because they are often denied by regular banks and thus forced to rely on exploitative private usurers.) In sum, behind the rosy pictures of the South Korean economy as an internationally conspicuous case of prompt recovery from the recent global financial crisis, grassroots South Koreans in rapidly growing numbers are confronted with their own financial crisis of heavy personal and familial indebtedness. This is another, increasingly crucial, component of the so-called financialization trend in the contemporary world political economy.

Chapter 6. Demographic Meltdown: Familial Structural Adjustments to the Post-Developmental Impasse

The South Korean government has done everything to (re)define social policy—or, for that matter, social citizenship—in terms of private familial responsibilities for mutual support and protection. In no coincidence, the developmental state long kept staging political campaigns for exhorting its citizens to faithfully fulfill the supposedly traditional duties for familial support and care. South Koreans' acceptance of familial(ized) duties for social welfare, however, does not necessarily imply that their private sphere is focused upon personal well-being and security. Most South Korean families are interestingly analogous to the developmental state in prioritizing (personal) developmental purposes in value assignment and resource allocation. The primacy of familial engagement and investment is widely prevalent in education, housing (real estate investment), finance (familial lending or giving), economic production and management (including self-employed services, mainstream industries (*chaebol*), and constitutionally stipulated family farming), as well as human care and protection. The national financial crisis and attendant neoliberal economic restructuring have led South Koreans into a situation where all such familial(ized) socioeconomic functions and duties remain unreduced despite the radical developmental disenfranchisement of laboring citizens. Accordingly, family relationships could become and have actually become a conduit for a highly complicated set of social risks accompanying the radical neoliberal perversion of the developmental liberal system of political economy and social policy. South Koreans have tried to cope with this dilemma by carefully, if not desperately, managing the effective scope, magnitude, and duration of family relationships. Increases in divorce and separation, delay and avoidance of marriage, less or no fertility, and even pervasive suicide—all at historically unprecedented levels—are manifest symptoms of such familial structural adjustments to the post-developmental liberal context. In a sense, it is the outcome of a sort of *self-imposed structural adjustment in social reproduction* by a developmentally disenfranchised citizenry.

Chapter 7. From Developmental Liberalism to Neoliberalism

The world before global neoliberalization was a complex of disparate ideologies, political economies, and social structures. In South Korea, as explained in Chap. 1, the active political pursuit of industrial catching-up and export promotion was backed up by *developmental liberalism* in social policies that required systematic sacrifice of labor and welfare. The dual sacrifice of grassroots through repressive work conditions and minimal social welfare became untenable when the dramatic democratic transition significantly empowered industrial workers and other grassroots citizens vis-à-vis authoritarian developmental bureaucracy and its business allies. It was during this crisis of developmental liberalism that Western neoliberalism in social policy was politically embraced (now by the supposedly democratic political regimes) in order to fend off grassroots political challenges to developmental liberal policies. Furthermore, and ironically, the neoliberal economic crisis of 1997 necessitated sweeping neoliberal social policies and economic practices including indiscriminate lay-offs and pay-cuts, generalization of casual contractual jobs, practical annulment of social securities through employment casualization, as well as unrestrained overseas relocation of industrial jobs to China, Vietnam, and so on. These radical changes added up to critically damage the developmental basis of the social policy regime, whereas its social democratic nature is yet to be consolidated.

Chapter 8. The Rise of Developmental Liberal Asia: South Korean Parameters of Asianized Industrial Capitalism

In South Korea's twenty-first century, neoliberal economic globalism has been manifest both inbound (global financial capital's appropriation of South Korean industries) and outbound (South Korean industries' overseas relocation, particularly across Asia), exposing the country to all such factors for post-democracy as explained by Collin Crouch. However, the historical sociopolitical nature of the South Korean state, the industrial capitalist system it has led as a national collective bourgeoisie, its developmental liberal regime of social governance, and its contribution to Asianized industrial capitalism and developmental liberal governance all add to critical complexities and particularities in the country's post-democratic transition (or degeneration). Most critically, a sort of public bourgeois consciousness of the South Korean state (and other Asian states) is blended with the logic of neoliberal economic globalism, so the neoliberal prioritization of corporate interests and prerogatives is even more intensified while social democratic demands of the working population are more and more disregarded. All such social detriments and political predicament accompanying the country's post-developmental and post-democratic transition are widely shared among those other Asian countries similarly industrialized under the respective developmental states. The transnationalized regime of developmental liberal social governance consciously and unconsciously constructed on the basis of capitalist industrial integration between these industrialized countries and those other Asian countries which aspire to dependently industrialize by hosting foreign industrial capital from them is quite likely to help assimilate the latter countries with the former countries in respect to the long-term difficulty in politically evolving into genuine social democratic polities.

CHAPTER 2

Developmental Liberalism: The Developmental State and Social Policy

1   INTRODUCTION

South Korea used to be hailed as an exemplary success case of the developmental state by numerous institutionalist and political economic analysts of development (Amsden 1989; Wade 1990; Evans 1995; Weiss 1998). By contrast, neoliberals and their liberal predecessors in Western academia, governments, and media had rather tried to deny any meaningful operation of entrepreneurial statism in South Korea and other rapidly developing Asian economies by attributing their economic achievement to a supposed adherence to liberal principles in domestic economic management and international economic relations (Mason et al. 1981). This position was turned around overnight during the Asian financial crisis in the late 1990s. The crisis was taken by many Western observers as evidence of the supposed structural pitfalls of Asia's mercantilist states in nurturing "crony capitalism". In particular, the engulfing of South Korea by the Southeast Asia-originated financial turmoil seemed to vindicate neoliberals' claim on the danger of interventionist statism in a capitalist industrial economy. Western neoliberals relentlessly blamed interventionist state elite and their "crony" business partners in Asia for allegedly causing financial frauds and industrial mismanagements. By doing so, in effect, they came to acknowledge that the hitherto Asian industrial dynamism had been driven by non-liberal, if not illiberal, impetuses. The neoliberal reform coercively demanded to South Korea and other Asian countries by

© The Author(s) 2019
Chang K-S, *Developmental Liberalism in South Korea*,
International Political Economy Series,
https://doi.org/10.1007/978-3-030-14576-7_2

the International Monetary Fund (IMF) was crucially targeted at developmental statist programs and practices in the region.

Barely had a year passed since the outbreak of the region-wide economic crisis when the neoliberal financial rescuers headed by the IMF found themselves in a self-contradictory position of acquiescing—and sometimes even encouraging—active state policies to resuscitate industries.[1] In South Korea, President Kim Dae-Jung even had to call back economic administrators of the Park Chung-Hee era (the Third Republic) in order to cope with the economic slump. (Park Chung-Hee was the helmsman of developmental statism in South Korea during his politically controversial reign in the 1960s and 1970s.) It was not a neoliberal state but a developmental, if reformed, state that ushered in an economic recovery no less dramatic than the economic downfall, popularly dubbed in South Korea "the IMF crisis" (see Chap. 3).

However, still another crisis awaited South Koreans. The swift economic recovery did not function to stabilize the critically damaged conditions of economic life for a majority of South Koreans. In fact, the economic recovery was accompanied by the permanent sacrifice of grassroots South Koreans because the IMF and the South Korean government concurred on brutal labor reshuffling in many ailing industries. A social crisis was virtually programmed for the neoliberal measures for economic recovery. The magnitude of this social crisis cannot be explained without examining the pre-crisis conditions of grassroots life as affected by the social policy attributes of the South Korean developmental state.

Before the economic crisis, the only broadly significant component of South Koreans' social citizenship used to be the availability of work predicated upon sustained economic growth. Unemployment had never been a fatal social problem ever since South Korea embarked on rapid industrialization in the 1960s. The economic crisis of 1997–1998, as was diagnosed by the IMF or evinced by realities, dictated the end of such era. The so-called structural adjustment policy, as well as the sheer financial insolvency of innumerable industrial enterprises and financial institutions, virtually deprived South Koreans of their *implicit entitlement to work*, and thereby of the only meaningful basis of collective material survival. When desperate jobless South Koreans and their dependents across the country continued to astound society through such shocking incidents as inflicting grave injuries on own and family members' bodies for scam insurance compensation, deserting children and elderly parents, taking up various forms of prostitution jobs, and, not least importantly, committing *bingonjasal* (poverty-driven suicides) often involving the killing of little children unaware of their fate, the state was simply unprepared to tackle with such social troubles (Chang, K. 2018). For instance, it was only after the outbreak of the economic crisis that the government rushed to institute a public (yet non-Pay-As-You-Go) unemployment insurance program, whose effect by nature would not materialize until many years after.

The wrongdoing of the developmental state did not simply consist in neglecting social welfare but more critically in driving the entire population into an almost blind pursuit of material aggrandizement and thereby making them so vulnerable to any risk of economic downturn. Instead of persuading its citizens that they should prepare individual safety nets because the state was unable or unwilling to maintain social safety nets, it kept seducing them to bet all private resources entrepreneurially—whether in education, skill training, small business, stock investment, or even real estate speculation.[2] It was a strategy of mobilizing all social resources into economic growth and ironically resembled the stalemate of the socialist states that had exhausted all national and social resources in politically promoted industrialization and thereby deprived their citizens of any effective means of material security against their (impending) economic collapse. Most South Koreans gladly responded to such "developmental" prompts from the experienced basis of explosive economic growth since the mid-1960s. The developmental state enjoyed the strong support from a sort of *developmental citizenry*.

Such alliance came to an end under the "IMF economic crisis". Grassroots South Koreans could not hide a grave sense of betrayal when the government—though now led by Kim Dae-Jung who had fought strenuously against *gaebaldokjae* (developmental dictatorship)—embarked on a crisis management program which would not only refuse the protection of their basic living conditions but also flatly ignore their entrepreneurial and occupational preparations by inducing a bifurcated economic structure almost exclusively in favor of big business (dubbed *chaebol*) in a few internationally competitive sectors. Kim Dae-Jung left his presidency just at that stage, so that his successor Roh Moo-Hyun was instantly beset with "ten million potential demonstrators" suffering from poverty and/or joblessness.[3] Unfortunately, the self-consciously progressive Roh spent most of his presidency in ideological controversies with the conservative forces in politics and media during a critical historical period in which the neoliberal measures for economic restructuring and the accompanied social displacements became firmly congealed into the long-term features of the South Korean economy and society.

Roh practically assisted two supposed political heirs of Park Chung-Hee—namely, Lee Myung-Bak, a famous entrepreneur during the Park era, and Park Geun-Hye, Park's daughter—to easily capture presidency because ordinary South Koreans felt political progressivism to be obsolete in improving their economic fate and thus got attracted to neo-developmental slogans and expectations.[4] Instead of entering a genuine neo-developmental era under the two political beneficiaries of people's "Park Chung-Hee nostalgia", the country had to witness even its political democracy to be degenerated into rampant kleptocracy. In fall and winter of 2016, South Korean citizens staged "the candlelight revolution", involving more than ten million protesters in total, which led to the impeachment of Park Geun-Hye and, later on, the imprisonment of both Park and Lee on corruption charges. Moon Jae-In, the late Roh's political ally, was elected into presidency in May 2017 and has been struggling in devising and implementing socioeconomic reforms that had been delayed nearly two decades since the "IMF crisis". South Korean citizens praise his sincerity but remain confused about the nature and feasibility of Moon's reforms (as of winter 2018).[5]

The above situation in South Korea—and in other economic crisis-hit Asian countries—should serve no less an intellectual and political prompt to a serious assessment of social conditions and consequences of the developmental state than a rationale to debate its utility and cost in developmental economic management. The national economic crisis in the country unmistakably divulged various perilous social risks pertaining to the state-directed developmental drive under which not only the corporate management of business elite but also the economic and social life of almost all grassroots citizens had been governed. It is imperative to question the social sustainability of developmental statism as much as its economic sustainability.

While the developmental state has been studied by diverse groups of social scientists (in economics, political economy, political science, as well as sociology), their academic concern has frequently excluded social dimensions in which developmental statism is practiced onto the everyday life of workers and other ordinary citizens. This tendency seems above all due to an overwhelming theoretical interest in the nature of state-business relationship in industrial development and management.[6] As an unfortunate outcome in this regard, research on the developmental state has even spawned an implicit nuance that economic development is basically a high-level achievement of the authoritative state leadership and its compliant partners in the industrial economy. On the other hand, while innumerable studies have been carried out on various social problems and groups under the rapid capitalist industrialization of Asian countries, these tend to constitute a research genre separated from the developmental state. While abundant studies have investigated state policies on such crucial social issues as labor, gender, and income inequality, the main theoretical characteristics of the developmental state have not been systematically linked to the concerned social issues. Likewise, the relationship between the state and social groups has usually been characterized by all too familiar political sociology concepts such as "authoritarianism" and "corporatism".

2   DEBATES AND RESEARCH ON SOCIAL POLICY

In exploring social conditions and consequences of developmental statism, we may raise a fundamental question on whether the developmental state is (or should be) accompanied by a distinctly identifiable social policy regime. If not, can the developmental state rely on many different types of social policy regimes in accordance with diverse local conditions and situations? If a distinct social policy regime is identified as a systemic component of the developmental state whether in a specific country or in general, it will allow us to much more methodically analyze the concrete relationship between the state and various social groups in the process of state-led capitalist economic development. It will furthermore enhance the classification of social policy regimes (states) in the world as most of the Asian countries currently or previously under developmental statism remain vague according to conventional categories of social policy.[7]

Regardless of its association with developmental statism, however, the nature of social welfare and other social policy concerns in South Korea has been fervently discussed among scholars, activists, and politicians. Such discussions seem to have been propelled as much by a political motivation as by a scientific interest. From the early 1990s, South Korean intellectuals, who wanted to channel their arduously won democracy into a viable socioeconomic system, saw a great practical as well as moral value in European social democracy. The sudden collapse of state socialist regimes in Russia and Eastern Europe, not to mention the dismal realities in North Korea, deterred them from any open allegiance to a Marxist socioeconomic system, whereas the hyper-conservative nature of South Korean capitalism along with the atrocious political suppression of civil causes for economic and social justice pressed them to explore alternative models of development. In this context, social democracy began to be envisaged as a sort of South Korean "third way" by many intellectuals and even by ordinary citizens in rapidly growing numbers and proportions.[8] A number of scholars from sociology, political science, and social welfare studies even embarked on serious firsthand research on European social democracies, making Sweden, among others, one of the world's most thoroughly studied countries in South Korea.[9] This political motivation induced South Korean scholars to appraise their country's situation on the basis of implicit and explicit comparison with European social democracies—a practice evidently and ironically reminiscent of conservative developmentalists' frequent reference to American and Japanese economies in their evaluation of the South Korean economy. Consequently, they have been more critical than analytical in explaining social problems and policies while prescribing the South Korean situation as something to be overcome in political praxis rather than as something to be conceptualized and theorized.

Likewise, most South Korean scholars do not hesitate to utilize the categories of social policy regimes that have been devised to portray Western societies—most notably those presented by Esping-Andersen (1990). Borrowing from Esping-Andersen's typology, many South Korean scholars have placed the social policy regime of their country at various positions on the liberal-conservative continuum. According to them, broadly speaking, South Korea has displayed a liberal orientation in the level of financial (and, for that matter, political) commitment to public protection of people's livelihood, whereas the overall institutional development of social policies and programs has taken on a resemblance to the (Continental European) conservative regimes.[10] The former is a different way of branding the country as a "welfare laggard". The latter reflects the deceptive political gestures for worker protection through various social insurance schemes conditioned upon formal employment—deceptive because the number and proportion of regularly employed (and thus protection-eligible) workers have dramatically declined since the economic crisis and because non-Pay-As-You-Go social insurance schemes are more a political lip service than an actual act of protection until many years after. These seemingly complex and dubious characteristics of South Korea's welfare programs and policies tend to discourage South Korean scholars from putting forward a clearly demarcated model of social policy for the country's experiences.

Further complications have been brought about by various strands of culturalist propositions and criticisms associated with the supposedly Confucian ethics of work and support. The propositions in this regard include a family-centered "Korean model of social welfare", *yeonbokji* (relational welfare) of various social and cultural groups (such as extended kin, hometown network, and alumni organization), paternalistic, if not communitarian, company welfare, and so forth. These components of social welfare have been praised by two groups of outside observers, that is, (neo)liberals and "positive Orientalists" (White and Goodman 1998). Liberals have extolled the culturally mandated private responsibility of South Koreans (and other East Asians) for social care and protection as an integral element of capitalism, whereas pro-Confucianism East Asianists have further proceeded so as to suggest a superior social quality in the traditional East Asian arrangement for communitarian and/or paternalistic welfare. (Since most of these pro-Confucianism scholars willingly accept the hegemony and/or utility of the liberal economic order, they may be called *liberal Confucianists.*) There is no denying that these components of welfare provision, whether ideologically driven or pragmatically devised, have constituted an indispensable condition for the basic livelihood of most South Koreans. However, it is equally factual that they have been far from stable resorts for protection to which South Koreans can regularly turn to alongside their turbulent life courses and family life cycles. Likewise, the culturalist propositions and praises have met with various internal and external criticisms.[11] These criticisms concern the political abuse of culturalist discourse in welfare suppression, the abstract or ideational nature of any culture-driven social policy regime, the asymmetrical burden and undemocratic treatment of women, and so on. A systematically designed Confucian regime of social policy may well have been an integral asset of traditional Koreans (and other East Asians), but this does not enable their modern offsprings to do without a serious modern social policy regime of their own.

The above review of major threads of scholarship on the South Korean social policy regime seems to endorse more wide-scoped inquisitions that will allow for a comprehensive yet systematic analysis of the relationship between the nationally dominant force of state-led industrialism and various social policy concerns. At least during the Park Chung-Hee era—and even until the very day of the national financial breakdown in the late 1990s—South Korea was governed by a renowned developmental state. The main concern of this developmental state was without doubt rapid industrialization and economic growth, but social policy was not delegated to a different political body. It was this developmental state that was accountable for the basically liberal doctrine of social policy partially coated with culturalist ideologies and, more recently, covered up slapdashly with (Continental European-type) conservative programs of social insurance. Perhaps we may not have to recall the elementary production function of neoclassical economics—in the case of South Korea, labor was the most crucial economic input in the early stage of labor-intensive industrialization and is still considered to be the most crucial in the current age of "knowledge economy"—in realizing that (labor-related) social policy could not but be a crucial element of developmental statism. Then, the remaining task is to document any systematic relationship between economic developmental goals and liberal social policies both of which have been attributes of the developmental state. Such documentations will serve an empirical basis for proposing what I suggest to call *developmental liberalism* as a distinct social policy regime.

This chapter intends to construe the particular characteristics of the South Korean social policy regime as have been shaped by the developmental(ist) doctrine of the successive governments since the early 1960s. The so-called developmental state in the country has been well known for its comprehensively organized and aggressively implemented policies for industrialization, export promotion, and so on, whereas its social policy orientation has often been simplified as one of brutal conservatism against those in need—be they workers, women, the poor, or a host of other disadvantaged and alienated social categories. While such appraisal has much validity, there is a pressing academic as well as practical need for more systematically analyzing the structural relationship between economic developmentalism and social policies and practices than dwelling on the implicitly suggested zero-sum relationship between them (i.e., social policies have been *sacrificed* in favor of economic developmental goals). To begin with, the extent of the zero-sum relationship itself has varied over time. Even with regard to the sacrificing of social policies, the conditions, manners, and outcomes of such sacrificing should be systematically documented. Instead of simplifying all these tendencies as liberal, it is necessary to scrutinize any possibility that they are *developmentally liberal*, as opposed to being liberally liberal like the United States. For instance, *if a liberally liberal polity prefers to restrain public welfare for the sake of minimized taxes and maximized private interests, a developmentally liberal polity may choose to do so for the sake of maximized industrial investment.* As the natural resource-barren and war-destroyed country's "economic miracle" is widely believed to have been buttressed almost exclusively by human resources, a simple neglect or single-minded suppression of social welfare would not have sufficed to achieve its national economic goals.

The necessity of researching developmental liberalism or any other systems for linking developmental goals and social policies is aptly exemplified by the German experience under Bismarck. According to Alexander Gerschenkron (1962), the German state in the nineteenth century intensely aspired to catch up with the neighboring rival states in economic buildup and therefore found it necessary to directly organize social groups and mobilize national resources into comprehensive and condensed industrialization. It was no coincidence that the Bismarck government devised and implemented some classic social insurance schemes in order to exhort main groups of labor and bureaucracy into the developmental process and contain leftist revolutionary sentiments in society. These schemes were later termed a "Bismarckian welfare system" by Esping-Andersen (1990). Thus, it is essential to decipher the origin and nature of the German social policy regime in the context of state-led late development.[12] In a similar vein, a proper understanding of the South Korean social policy regime requires its contextualization in the process of state-led capitalist industrialization and economic development.

In the remaining parts of this chapter, I will overview the historical contexts, political conditions, and structural characteristics of developmental liberalism as the distinct social policy regime of the South Korean developmental state. The subsequent chapters in Part II will discuss how developmental liberalism has been protracted in a neoliberal disguise in spite of the formidable torrent of democratic demands since 1987 and what social consequences have been generated since South Korea stumbled into a national financial fiasco after decades of developmental liberalism.

3   HISTORICAL AND POLITICAL BACKGROUNDS OF DEVELOPMENTAL LIBERALISM

The dramatic twists and turns in the South Korean social policy regime reflect the complex historical circumstances and transformations in polity, economy, and social structure. In particular, the seemingly paramount hegemony of a liberal order in South Korea as the world's last bastion of the Cold War against communism has in fact been a clutter of historical discontinuities of its political, economic, and social dimensions, intra-dimensional abnormalities, and inter-dimensional temporal inconsistencies and interactive changes. In this perplexing context, developmentalism has served not merely a provisional and partial adjustment to the country's liberal order but a forceful melting pot for dissolving endless internal contradictions of the liberal order. The developmental state has as much harnessed as revised the liberal order, particularly in the economy. Its social policy regime of developmental liberalism has been an indispensable instrument for that function. This section will systematically explain historical and theoretical conditions for the rise of developmental liberalism and then examine the institutional and financial configuration of the South Korean social policy regime in the 1960s to the mid-1980s as its proto-typical instance.

Let me begin with historical complexities of the liberal order in South Korea. It was the economic sphere in which Koreans were for the first time exposed to the liberal order in a broad sense. Japan's colonial policy was above all to advance its own capitalist interests through various coercive measures for incorporating Koreans into a world-regional capitalist division of labor. America's military's occupation of South Korea, accompanying its victory against Japan in the Pacific War and engagement in the Korean War, was intended to broaden and fortify the international boundary of capitalism by containing communist influences beyond an arbitrarily set fault line of the 38th parallel. Ever since, the South Korean economy has remained basically a liberal market capitalism although its sustenance and growth have necessitated various politically driven measures such as the American foreign aids, the local state's developmental engagement, and even a few IMF-led financial bailouts.

In a historical paradox, most of the political promoters for capitalism (or capitalist exploitation) have been illiberal political actors, at least, to grassroots South Koreans (Chang, K. 2019). The colonial governments of both Japan and the United States could institute themselves in the Korean Peninsula only by exercising brutal physical forces against local populace. The American military occupation authority nevertheless arranged a liberal democratic system for the Southern half of the divided nation, but before long its de facto political appointee, Syngman Rhee, began to distort legal democratic procedures for his hoped permanent reign. Rhee's political departure forced by the popular uprising in 1960 did not lead to a sustained period of liberal political order but was soon followed by an outright authoritarian military rule of General Park Chung-Hee, albeit in a flimsy disguise of legal democracy for most of his almost two-decade leadership. He openly aired a view that South Koreans had better swap political democracy for economic betterment, on which he focused his leadership. Nor did Park's political departure by his controversial assassination in 1979 lead to a liberal democratic order. Park's protégé, General Chun Doo-Hwan ushered himself into political power through a military coup claiming hundreds of civilian lives atrociously. After seven years of perhaps the most violent post-independence political leadership, the nationwide civil uprising in 1987 by students, activist intellectuals, workers, and middle classes forced Chun to accept constitutional amendments for a direct presidential election and other democracy-safeguarding measures. This set a course for the so-called democratic consolidation thereafter through relatively strict and stable democratic procedures.

The liberal social order, on the opposing side, may date back to the immediate post-liberation period in which the sudden removal of the authoritarian Japanese colonial state spawned a brief period of civil liberty and activism. Civil society at the grassroots level, however, was organized and led under a strong socialist influence, which was not to be tolerated by the American military occupation authority and its client rightwing Korean politicians. Anti-socialist armed rallies were staged wherever and whenever necessary, while land reform was carried out to economically pacify the predominantly agrarian population (Cumings 1981). Syngman Rhee's assertion of Cold War dictatorship in the post-Korean war period managed to politically silence most of the hunger-stricken population. But civil society was not dormant altogether and ultimately erupted to oust (in 1960) the contentious political leader who delivered neither better livelihood nor democratic advancement. However, the democratic struggle of civil society was not staunch enough to deter any reactionary attempt by political aspirants from military—Park Chung-Hee in particular. Nor was Park able to politically demobilize civil society through coercion or bribe. Park's reign was paradoxically a double-sided process of (re)creating a civil society which is now internationally hailed for its vibrancy and activism. First, Park's unreserved resort to physical coercion, ideological tyranny, and legal distortion throughout his rule constantly enraged educated groups including intellectuals, students, and many white-collar workers, who never stopped actions of resistance and thereby kept stimulating civil society politically. Second, the explosively rapid processes of industrialization and urbanization accompanied by a virtually overnight universalization of high education led to the expeditious formation of urban civil spaces in which organized civil and class consciousness mushroomed. When Park's de facto political heir, Chun Doo-Hwan, intended to enthrone himself against these social trends, he had to resort to unprecedentedly atrocious violence against protesting citizens, including the army's carnage of hundreds of Gwangju citizens in May 1980. When civil society erupted again in 1987 against Chun's arbitrary power succession scheme, it was no more suppressible by physical force alone. Ever since, a highly liberal but well organized civil society has always mobilized itself against any reactionary political attempts—its latest instance being the "candlelight revolution" against Park Chung-Hee's daughter in 2016.

Even a very sketchy retrospection like above allows us to appreciate the complex nature of the liberal order in South Korea—that is, historical discontinuities of political, economic, and social dimensions, intra-dimensional abnormalities, and inter-dimensional temporal inconsistencies and interactive changes. Among these complexities, further elaboration on the inter-dimensional interactive changes in the liberal order is essential in order to comprehend the emergence of developmental liberalism as a social policy regime of the developmental state from the 1960s to the mid-1980s. This was a prototypical period of developmental statism under Park Chung-Hee and Chun Doo-Hwan. In this period, the distortion of the liberal order was particularly problematic in politics as the constitutional foundation of liberal democracy was openly ignored by the very holders of state authority. It was this deformation of the liberal political order for and by which developmental statism in economic policy and developmental liberalism in social policy rose as the dual stands of the governing paradigm. The chronic political illegitimacy of the self-enthroned state leaders had to be mitigated by their performance in social and economic domains. Unlike the political liberal order (i.e., democracy), economic and social liberal orders themselves were not, and did not have to be, justified for their own sake. The Cold War served a formidable pressure to deny socialism and collectivism, but it fell short of becoming a self-contained rationale for liberal capitalism and individualism. What fundamentally mattered to both state leaders and ordinary citizens were national economic strength and better material life—the objectives shared even by illiberal societies.

These two goals can be both mutually competing and complementing according to various circumstances and ideologies. The better material life for a majority of citizens may require economic growth, social redistribution, or both. A classic liberal proposition may be that social redistribution deters economic growth and consequently hurts national economic strength and, due to decreased national wealth in the long run, public material well-being as well. A progressive counterproposition may be that the capitalist economy cannot grow without causing inequality and/or even impoverishment to low classes and thus requires redistributive measures which in the long run stimulate economic growth by improving labor quality and augmenting demands for commodities. In a very poor capitalist economy where little redistributable wealth or natural endowment—not to mention national economic strength—is available, it is rather normal for both state elite and citizens to initially focus on national economic growth.[13] The potentially competing relationship between economic growth and social redistribution itself may not be conceived seriously because the former is broadly considered as an indispensable condition for the latter. Thus, Park Chung-Hee's slogan of "growth first, distribution later" did not immediately meet with serious intellectual criticisms or popular resistances.

However, a politically illegitimate leader like Park Chung-Hee could not afford to stick to a purely liberal position of declaring material welfare as a personal matter, especially before hunger-stricken political constituencies. He needed to convince South Koreans that his government would deliver material betterment to everyone and that no one would be left out in the process of national economic development. (Of course, national economic development itself was a collectively cherished wish of South Koreans after a series of atrocious external encroachments associated with their national powerlessness.) In political mottos like "Let's live affluently!", *economic development was communicated to people as a long-term social policy*. The public slogan of "growth first, distribution later" was not merely a deceitful catchphrase improvised to deflect social demands for fair livelihood but a theory of equating economic and social policies. It was under this equation of economic development and social justice that both economic and social policies were shaped into draconian state interventions into private economic and social activities. Economic development was not left to be an aggregate outcome of private economic activities because it was a precondition for the state's delivery of collective welfare in the long run—that is, a long-term social policy. Thereby was the forceful developmental state justified politically. (Another political justification for the developmental state was that rapid economic development was indispensable for national security against the ever-hostile international political environments as well as possible North Korean aggressions.) Economic development as a long-term social policy, in turn, dictated short-term social policies. Restraining popular demands for material redistribution—that is, classic laissez-faire regarding public livelihood—was in no way a sufficient social policy for economic development. Social policies were to facilitate economic development by mobilizing, preserving, and improving social resources for production and by reducing and controlling social factors obstructive to production. Thereby arose *a liberal yet developmentally proactive social policy regime* in South Korea which would survive into the twenty-first century.[14]

Developmental statism in economic policy and developmental liberalism in social policy as the two mutually reinforcing stands of governance reflected the desperate effort of a basically illiberal political regime to overcome its illegitimacy through rapid national economic development. Interestingly, it was also the illiberal nature of the political regime that facilitated the mobilization and regimentation of private actors (such as industrial corporations, workers, peasants, and women) for state-set industrial projects and social programs in a "bureaucratic authoritarian" manner (Im, H. 1987; Cotton 1992). State elites including Park Chung-Hee himself were openly aware of this instrumentality of state authoritarianism and did not reserve its exercise wherever and whenever deemed necessary.[15] It was more often in the social policy side than in the economic policy side that state authoritarianism was resorted to in policy formulation and implementation. Developmental liberalism was meant to extract maximum resources and efforts from grassroots South Koreans and use them as conditions and incentives for entrepreneurial activities.

Unfortunately, to many South Koreans concerned about sheer daily subsistence, no matter how many of them would enjoy, in the long run, material progress amounting to upward class mobility, developmental liberalism must have been at best a social policy regime of deferred gratification and at worst one of inverse resource allocation. As owners of big industrial capital were, and are, bluntly called "thieves" because of their wealth accumulation through recurrently revealed collusion with bribed state elites, developmental liberalism very often became an unpopular social policy regime for supporting such thieves. However, despite the authoritarian implementation of such unpopular social policies, grassroots South Koreans could not but comply with the state, hoping that at least its developmental side would benefit them. Practically, there was no political outlet for demanding otherwise.

Epistemologically, it is arguable if Korean capitalism has ever been a liberal construct based upon social liberalism. In and for national(ist) development, capitalism has not only been an institutional system for private economic activities but also a collective political project for national economic ascent in which the nation itself assumes the status of collective bourgeoisie. Koreans had been subjected to Japan's capitalist exploitation as a sort of collective proletariat. Against this historical experience, postcolonial capitalist development was conceived as a process of national rebirth into collective bourgeoisie, accommodating Korean citizens in all occupations and sectors (Chang, K. 2019). Helping make the nation an internationally powerful collective bourgeoisie was politically defined as a citizenship duty for all South Koreans. As components of this collective bourgeoisie, South Koreans have had to internalize a sort of *patriotic liberalism* by which capitalist rules in social relations and economic activities have been universalized and even essentialized as civic codes.

Furthermore, the Cold War both as an international and inter-Korean affair permitted the already authoritarian state to monopolize on political ideology as the basic framework for social and economic policy.[16] No ideology or policy explicitly endorsing socialist values and principles was left unpunished. Equality was, and still is, not supposed to be used in open public discourse, whereas reducing serious inequality would be a nominally acceptable point. Even the demand for basic social welfare or social rights protection has often been branded as socialist. Consequently, not only socialism but also social democracy used to be de facto prohibited.[17] On the political front, for instance, Kim Chul—the internationally recognized leader of South Korean social democracy and national representative to the Socialist International (SI)—was constantly harassed by intelligence and police agencies and kept from free political activities throughout the Park Chung-Hee era. Such political order meant that the Cold War ideological rivalry between South and North Korea prevented both sides from inter-systemic learning.[18] Socialism, including its social democratic variant, was to be negated, not emulated in South Korea.[19] This presented a fundamental contrast to Bismarckian Germany where a growing socialist influence on industrial proletariat was contained by progressively inventive social policies of the early developmental state.

4   MAIN SOCIOPOLITICAL ATTRIBUTES
OF DEVELOPMENTAL LIBERALISM

In the following, let us examine the main sociopolitical attributes of developmental liberalism as have been manifested in the South Korean context, namely, (1) depoliticization/technocratization/developmental obfuscation of social policy, (2) developmental cooptation of social policy constituencies, (3) state-business entrepreneurial merge and direct state engagement in labor relations, (4) familial reconstitution of social citizenship, and (5) welfare pluralism and demobilization of civil society.

4.1   Depoliticization/Technocratization/Developmental Obfuscation of Social Policy

State autonomy has been a focal issue in research on the developmental state in East Asia. In South Korean development, it has usually been achieved through a depoliticization of administrative work. The hard authoritarian political leaders, who had established themselves in state leadership by wrecking due political procedures, were not interested in restoring normal political order. They created their own (nominal) political parties and manipulated elections to ensure a parliamentary majority status for these personally controlled parties. The lawmaking function of the parliament was practically annulled as even the supposed ruling parties were denied any autonomy in ideological debate and policy formulation. The everyday organizational basis of state leadership was confined to technocrats and administrative offices whose work in both economic and social policy was considered tantamount to an absolute prerogative entrusted by their absolutist presidents. They were only responsible to each incumbent president, whose main concern was not formal political procedural legitimacy but instrumental legitimacy through economic development. The supposed ruling party under each administration was instead autonomous from people, and the bureaucracy was autonomous from people and the ruling party (as well as the opposition parties).

The government bureaucracy as a whole was a developmental institution, and its collective performance was measured in terms of growth rates of export, national income, and so forth. Officials and offices in charge of social policy concerns were not allowed to envisage or emphasize the importance of their duties as separated from economic developmental goals. Even these officials' personal ambitions often lay in a transfer to economic policy organs. In fact, ministers formally in charge of welfare, health, labor, education, environment, and other social policy concerns were often required to attend the regular "meetings of economic ministers" and present measures to (ab)use and compromise social policy for economic development (Chung, C. 1988). Social policy was a purely technocratic and, for that matter, technical matter whose efficiency was to be appraised in terms of its contribution to improved economic indicators.

The depoliticization and technocratization of social policy were not seriously challenged by opposition parties and politicians. As a matter fact, there was no political party or ideology in the formal political arena seriously representing social policy concerns. In the immediate postindependence period, Americans superimposed not only their liberal political system but also their liberal ideology onto South Koreans, whose sentimental and political subscription to socialist causes were apparent and thus had to be purged violently. The Korean War made the US-backed Syngman Rhee government (along with its accessory Liberal Party) a staunch anticommunist regime on its own. Rhee created a state system in which no alternative to liberal political and economic order was allowed in formal political discussion (Hong, Y. 2007). Even social policy-centered versions of socialism such as Fabian socialism and social democracy were not tolerated (Chae, O. 2014). Rhee practically assassinated Cho Bong-Am of the Progressive Party in his personally controlled court. Later, Park Chung-Hee politically incapacitated and physically tortured Kim Chul of the Innovation Party. The removal of the political leaders and parties representing bourgeois versions of socialism resulted in a mono-ideological political system in which the liberal capitalist order was never to be challenged even in social policy, not to mention in economic policy (Chae, O. 2014). Such vacuity of social security was occasionally and minimally complemented by American aid to South Korea (Yoon, H. 2018), which nevertheless dwarfed those offered to Latin America, Africa, and so on. Even the basic notion of social citizenship rights remained absent in South Korean politics, at least until the late 1980s.[20] Social policy, without a coherent political doctrine or a seriously devoted party for its advancement, continued to remain an area of lack-lust bureaucratic improvising in response to impromptu political directives. Government changes usually resulted in a wide neglect of previous commitments and efforts in social policy even when the basically same bureaucracy was in charge.

The abolition of progressive politics in social policy did not imply that not too many serious social problems accrued to South Korean capitalism, nor that the authoritarian rightwing regimes were politically able to dispense with social policy altogether. Grassroots South Koreans never stopped erupting when confronted with miserable life situations deemed meshed with political unfairness. Social policy in the form of interest group politics was not infrequently resorted to in managing immediate political crises and securing minimum political legitimacy. But physical suppression was usually prioritized to and at least combined with social policy under a supposedly developmental pretext that social and political stability was essential for sustained economic development.[21] Also, the doctrine of "growth first, distribution later" was financially upheld only by physically abusing those underclass South Koreans who showed defiant intent or behavior against their seemingly indefinite material hardship. Besides, any organized expression of grassroots social interests, particularly under activist intellectual intervention, was subjected to McCarthian manipulation and purge, which sometimes involved death sentences for alleged or fabricated espionage for North Korea. Social programs and benefits, if any, were usually narrow-based to cater to people in exceptional miseries (such as war orphans and widows, wounded veterans, leprous patients, etc.) as well as state functionaries (such as civil servants, career military personnel, and teachers).

Such political basis and limit of social policy do not fundamentally deviate from the American approach. American liberalism lacked, and still lacks, a serious interest in progressive social policy for safeguarding social citizenship rights of the general public.[22] So did, and does, its copycat state's liberalism in South Korea.[23] In the United States, strategic assistance to certain target social groups specified by politico-military situations has been the historical pivot of the national social policy regime (Skocpol 1992). The earliest specific target groups were soldiers (veterans) and their left-behind mothers, who were subjected to particularly generous protection benefits in livelihood, health, and so on. The plentiful American aids to South Koreans, particularly after the Korean War, may be understood in a similar vein. When the South Korean government gradually took over the relief responsibility for its people, it simply replicated the American practice into a sort of *internal aids*.

4.2   Developmental Cooptation of Social Policy Constituencies

The emergence of a developmental statist regime in the 1960s induced South Korea to seriously depart from its earlier duplication of the American approach to social policy. As widely known, the South Korean industrial miracle was primarily based upon abundant and talented human resources. The preparation, mobilization, and regimentation of South Koreans for industrial production were as much a social as an economic policy. However, the core aim of such social policy was not social protection of citizenry but economic utilization of population. A social policy regime in the direct service of economic development was gradually forged and would then survive into the twenty-first century. Grassroots South Koreans were not against the economic developmental subordination of social policy. Lacking even an elementary notion of social citizenship rights, they rarely conceived themselves as serious political constituencies of social policy. They instead related their citizenship status to fair economic (and educational) opportunities as hopefully expanded and improved by the successive developmentalist governments. Political leaders and technocrats welcomed such economic or developmental orientation of the otherwise burdensome constituencies of social policy. A sort of developmental cooptation of citizenry was pursued without any significant social resistance.

The successful developmental cooptation of social policy constituencies—and, for that matter, the suppression and postponement of earnest social citizenship politics—should be appraised not only against the rapid industrialization and sustained high economic growth in the following decades but also against the complicated political and social context in the latter half of the twentieth century. First, the virtual elimination of civil society in the postliberation period through relentless armed attacks on grassroots in various provinces, who were then under a notable influence of socialism, lessened an urgency of winning over the otherwise politically challengeable populace through (re)distributive social policy.[24] Civil society was further debilitated by the Korean War and the ensuing domestic and international Cold War that allowed the state to exercise nearly absolute political power over its citizenry. Land reform, of course, was a social as well as an economic policy offered to console and enfranchise the dominantly agrarian population. However, after having allocated a seemingly fair share of land, individual peasant households as well as their rural communities became the bulwark of economic individualism and political passivity (Cho, O. 1998).

Second, it was from this politically pacified, but economically motivated, peasantry that labor power, capital, and entrepreneurship would be mobilized for industrialization.[25] Rural families opted to become an active subject of national economic transformation and thereby remained largely indifferent to their disadvantaged status as a social policy object. It needs to be pointed out that South Korean peasantry had always been a producer class with a sustained high level of agricultural productivity by the international standards and continued to be so, particularly after land reform (Cho, S. 2015). Such economic performance was indispensable not only for their material survival but also for the initiation of industrialization without any significant prior accumulation of private or public capital. The role of the peasant economy in industrial capital accumulation, however, mostly took on an indirect nature—that is, through qualified but cheap labor force. The stable supply of affordably priced foods for urban industrial workers enabled industrial capitalists to maintain low wages and, consequently, high profits. More importantly, rural families heavily allocated their human and financial resources for new economic opportunities associated with capitalist industrialization. They unmistakably foresaw a lopsided development of the urban economy and society at the sacrifice of rural interests, so no hesitation was shown in their active participation in urban economic and social activities. An explosive rural-to-urban migration stream ensued as the pursuit of urban employment and education became basically a universal objective of rural families. What I elsewhere described as "social transition costs of industrialization"—costs for city-headed family members' education, training, business initiation, residential relocation, foodstuff, emergency livelihood, and so forth—were willingly borne by rural families. Instead of demanding village-centered welfare protection, rural families themselves acted as a quasi-social policy instrument for the industrial economy and urban society.

Third, the instant formation of a heavily urbanized industrial society was not accompanied by a comparable construction of the political constituency for a serious urban social policy regime. Even after its initial overnight success in export-oriented industrialization, the South Korean economy has kept radically restructuring to date. Only a tiny minority of the urban population have found certain industrial work as lifetime career, whereas an overwhelming majority of them have had to struggle in securing livelihood through incessant shifts between wage labor and self-employment (Choi and Chang 2016). Thus the political organizing of industrial proletariat at the national level has been an inherently baffling task to labor leaders and intellectual activists. Trade unions—mostly company-based ones—have functioned, at most, to promote individual company-level negotiations for better wages and fringe benefits. The urban proletariat class, as it has remained socially ambiguous and politically underorganized, has failed to form a clear political constituency for a serious social policy state. A social democratic future has not even been conceived as an ideological possibility by a majority of grassroots urban population, so that any progressive political party has had to battle for sheer institutional existence in national politics. Their recurrent petty-bourgeoisie status attached to informal service sector self-employment has even induced them to turn extremely conservative and express antagonism against progressive political causes upheld by some unions, leftist parties, and progressive civil activists (see Chap. 4). Besides, as discussed in Chap. 3, a sort of false middle class consciousness used to engulf their social and political outlook as most of them, in social surveys, categorized themselves as middle class by comparing their present socioeconomic status not with that of their better-off contemporaries but with their own "cold and hungry days" not long ago. Even when confronted with obvious destitute, many poor South Koreans would hope the conservative developmental policy line to continue, at least until they themselves could achieve some success in job, business, investment, and/or speculation. The actual middle class have remained no less conservative as they have attributed their relatively better-off status mainly to the economic developmental policy and managed to maintain livelihood without resorting to state-organized social services and protections. Instead of politically expecting the state to develop policy measures and public programs for stabilizing their decent existence against economic uncertainties and social risks, many of them have actually feared that redistributive social policy would damage their class interests. Their own measure for risk hedging and future indemnity has often involved real estate investment (or speculation) and, more recently, stock ownership, so that their political conservatism has become even more stiffened.

Surrounded by apparently conservative and opportunistic members of rural petty-bourgeoisie and urban proletariat and petty-bourgeoisie, South Korean capitalists have lacked any serious motivation for voluntarily adopting redistributive measures for rescuing underclasses in cities and villages or persuading the state to devise comprehensive social policies and programs for stabilizing the general conditions of work and life for laboring population in a Bismarckian framework. In fact, the class identity of South Korean bourgeoisie has remained complex, contradictory, and unstable. If any, a handful of families governing major business conglomerates (called *chaebol*) in controversial manners have disproportionately represented the capitalist community (Kang, M. 1996). These oligarchic families have accumulated strong public antipathy owing to continual financial scandals and managerial malpractices, while many of their extra-business organizations and activities have been strategically deployed as patronage for strategically chosen social groups (such as journalists, politicians, and so on). South Korean bourgeoisie have been a negligible entity in the social and political shaping of the social policy regime whether in a conservative or progressive direction. They have only depended on the successive authoritarian governments in order to control proletarian resistance within the narrow confine of each enterprise.

Given this across-the-board conservatism of society, the most critical political constituency of the social security system has been the state itself. For many years, officials in various state organs, teachers and professors, and military officers were the only groups subjected to meaningful social security programs (including pension, educational allowance, etc.). This is no exceptional phenomenon in the general Third World context. But it had a special significance in the South Korean context in which the so-called developmental state exercised a decisive role in leading national economic development through various ingenuous industrial policies and financial programs (Kim, K. 2012). An *internal social policy regime* within the state was indispensable to lure talented people into state offices and induce devotion and asceticism in public duties. As the access to such state offices (and public welfare benefits) has been determined by meritocratic criteria—that is, mostly, written examinations—class differences in society have not been directly translated into officialized inequalities in social welfare. In fact, the examinations for entering state offices or related university disciplines used to be considered a crucial opportunity for children from poor families to overcome material disadvantages in joining the rank of elites in society.

4.3   State-Business Entrepreneurial Merge and Direct State Engagement in Labor Relations

While international scholarship on the developmental state has mainly focused on the unique developmental nature and cooperative interaction patterns of the state-business relationship, the formation of such corporate entities as would be strategically suitable for the national targets of industrial and trade growth has often been a mission of the developmental state itself.[26] By definition, industrialization as the growth of manufacturing industries in aggregate proportion and volume was initially a social project of creating modern industries as well as channeling workforce from farming to such industries. Private (and public) enterprises the developmental state thereby helped create have been treated as dear instruments for national development, and their corporate interests have often been protected as if they belonged to the state (or the whole nation). It was in this political economic context that the labor policy in South Korea began to assume an inherently anti-labor orientation.[27]

In the early stage of South Korea's export-oriented industrialization, wage suppression and abusive working conditions in sweatshop factories were practically considered indispensable conditions of international competitiveness, so that any organized resistances to such corporate practices were often directly quelled by the state (i.e., riot police).[28] In a sense, police functioned as an *instrument of industrial policy* to the extent that its anti-labor actions were intended to help strengthen corporate international competitiveness by low labor cost and spartan laboring. Even the state regulations for protecting the health, safety, and basic human rights of workers were widely neglected or arbitrarily distorted by their employers under the tacit support of the government.[29] Paul Krugman's (1994) critical observation that many Asian countries' industrial success has been largely "inputs-driven" may be elaborated on concerning the stern sociopolitical conditions for mobilizing and regimenting the most essential input of labor. In fact, South Korea's advancement to less labor-intensive sectors did not necessarily soften the state's authoritarian engagement in labor relations because it had a new usage for constant labor reshuffling along radically rapid industrial restructuring. That is, the developmental state's asymmetrical labor policy was sustained into more mature stages of economic development, but the oppressed class would grow in its organized power and social influence so as to gradually, if not fully, counterbalance the anti-labor developmental coalition. In fact, the democratic transition of 1987 was substantially fueled by organized labor movements as workers considered democratization an indispensable condition for rectifying the skewed industrial labor relations under the authoritarian developmental state. As an ironic consequence of this democratic transition, organized workers often found their employers unequipped with independent mechanisms and resources for labor control, so that the politically necessitated withdrawal of direct state engagement in labor disputes led to unprecedented compromises and concessions by the employers.

While the apparent class bias of the developmental state's labor policy has instrumentally reflected the necessity of helping industries, particularly in export sectors, to strengthen their price competitiveness and maximize production, such technocratic bias has been ideologically and epistemologically bolstered under the country's unique historical context of multilayered anti-proletarianism. It began with Japan's colonial capitalist suppression of Koreans as its proletarian subjects, which would be repeated after liberation by Korean industrialists with experiences of colonial collaboration. The Cold War order in the Korean peninsula accompanying the American military occupation of South Korea (with brutal crackdowns on suspected socialist influences) and then the devastating inter-Korean War coercively enforced anti-communist politics in South Korea, which in turn would demonize any political or ideological effort for promoting proletarian causes. In Park Chung-Hee's promotion of national(ist) economic development, the nation—rather than individual entrepreneurs— was conceived as the core subject of capitalist modernity, with the state assuming the status of grand bourgeoisie against whom any proletarian challenge would be branded as disloyalty. Most recently, South Korea's proactive engagement in neoliberal global capitalism has gradually infused a sense or identity of global bourgeoisie into the mindset of economic and politico-administrative elites, who have been thereby emboldened to curse local workers and unions as anachronistically parochial. All these anti-proletarian orientations, assertions, and practices have coalesced to constitute a grand hegemonic episteme of South Korean elites in political, administrative, judicial, journalist, educational, as well as industrial establishments. In this context, the developmental state's class-biased intervention in labor relations has not required any detailed scientific or technocratic justification in securing cooperation from such establishments. Conversely, workers and unions have been institutionally locked up all around except their last resort to street demonstrations.

4.4   Familial Reconstitution of Social Citizenship

No matter how successful the economy-centered developmental policy functions, a society cannot operate without proper institutional arrangements for meeting various material, physical, and cultural requirements of the so-called social reproduction. Social policy, if defined as public means, programs, and regulations for stable social reproduction of individual citizens and, ultimately, of the nation, is not merely an optional or conditional function of the modern state but its most essential and universal requirement. Thus, even when citizenry are willingly incorporated into economy-centered politics and remain content primarily with the economic performance of the developmental state, its operation still needs to be complemented by various public means, programs, and regulations for stable social reproduction. For a welfare state, social policy is the central political objective; for a developmental state, it is at least a complementary yet indispensable technocratic instrument.

In its actual administrative practice, however, the developmental state has done everything to redefine social policy—or, for that matter, social citizenship—in terms of private responsibilities for mutual support and protection. Above all, the openly publicized policy principle of "familial protection first, social welfare later" has remained virtually intact to date. Accordingly, families have been summoned in order to meet various public necessities in social reproduction. The developmental state has coincided with the early modern liberal state of the West in articulating various social problems accompanying industrial capitalism as individual and familial responsibilities and in morally regimenting individuals and families for cultivation of qualities and attitudes suitable for industrial work and life (cf. Donzelot 1979).[30] In so doing, the developmental state in South Korea used to be equipped with two distinct advantages—namely, its developmental appeal and the Confucian family culture.

To the extent that South Korean citizens concurred with the developmental state on the urgency of economic development and thereby became a sort of developmental citizenry (see Chap. 4), the minimal state commitment to social policy and the concomitant private shouldering of social reproduction were nothing opposable. More critically, South Koreans have managed to maintain Confucian values and norms in private life, under which mutual support duties have been heavily emphasized among members of (extended as well as nuclear) families and other nepotistic groups (Chang, K. 1997, 2018; Kim, D. 2002).[31] In particular, filial support for aged parents and meritorious upbringing of children have been universally upheld as supposedly Korean characteristics. The developmental state could not wish for more when its citizens voluntarily relieved it of the daunting burdens of protecting elderly livelihood and health and covering children's educational expenses (Chang, K. 2018; see Chap. 6). Such familial arrangements for elderly welfare and youth education have remained still normatively binding to most South Koreans to date. However, the century-end economic crisis has meant a growing impracticality of the family-dependent system of care and support, so that rampant poverty has plagued the lives of aged people in rapidly increasing numbers and class-based educational inequalities have become a chronic factor for social conflict and division.

It is no coincidence that the Asian value debate has been most strongly staged in societies that used to be governed under the (successful) developmental state regimes—Singapore, Taiwan, Malaysia, as well as South Korea. For instance, Singapore has moved as far as to enact the "filial piety" law, whereas South Korea has implemented the same policy line in various indirect ways (i.e., applying a strict means test for adult children before providing welfare benefits for their aged parents). A political discussion of the filial piety law did take place in the country, but the South Korea state (after democratization) has not been as authoritative as the Singaporean counterpart in social policy (Park, K. 2007). A potential societal backlash has prevented any further political move for the morality-based welfare law. Nonetheless, the Asian value debate appeared tantamount to the family value debate in the Anglo-American West under neoliberalism in that both ideological drives were meant to articulate many social problems accompanying industrial capitalism as private responsibilities (Chang, K. 1997) and thereby reinforce the conservative pro-capitalist social order and political economy.

While the developmental state's formal mobilization of family has mostly focused on otherwise social security concerns such as care provision, educational support, health care, and housing, South Korean families have not necessarily confined their social functions to such nonbusiness matters. Just like traditional peasant families combining agricultural production and familial social reproduction, modern urban families have tried to flexibly organize their familial resources and relationships in such ways to developmentally maximize socioeconomic outcomes from their various activities. This has been somewhat indispensable in that South Korea's dynamic yet unstable developmental capitalism has necessitated virtually all citizens to continually cope with macroeconomically derived financial uncertainties. Under this circumstance, whenever possible, South Koreans used to developmentally manage both their everyday livelihood and long-term familial assistance, leading to the world's highest levels of household saving, private educational spending, and so forth.[32] Such developmentalist management of family life, in turn, has strengthened South Koreans' almost generalized subscription to the developmentalist political rule well into the twenty-first century (Chang, K. 2012a, b).

4.5   Welfare Pluralism and Demobilization of Civil Society

Family welfare, whether codified culturally or obliged politically, is a self-contradictory doctrine. The main function of social protection is expected of least capable social groups—namely, families in destitute. This means that, in a capitalist society where the self-protection of families and individuals is politically emphasized, various types of actors and institutions need to step in to make up for the structural lacuna in social protection. Thus, welfare pluralism (in terms of the social diversity in welfare services and providers) has been a common attribute in liberal (including developmental liberal and neoliberal) societies. In South Korea, the mobilization of every thinkable type of (non-state) welfare provider has been a consistent policy of the developmental liberal state.[33]

The complementary players in welfare provision would take on diverse ideological and organizational characteristics resulting from their social and political origins, but a paternalistic attribute is commonly shared among them. That is, they would pose themselves as a kind of *quasi-surrogate families* that take the place of the moral duty of private families, not the political right to state-organized social benefits. In South Korea, private philanthropy, religious social work, corporate welfare, welfare NPOs, nepotistic support networks, and media-based fundraising for emergency relief have usually been deployed in a pseudo-familial ideological and/or organizational framework. On the other hand, a dominant majority of the actors and organizations involved in these welfare activities have been keen to keep distance from specific political lines and groups. In that way, they have in effect sided with the conservative political line of preempting or subduing social democratic politics.

Under South Korea's welfare pluralism, many of civilian welfare institutions and groups have made welfare-receiving disadvantaged citizens become clients of narrow paternalism and thereby turned these innocent beneficiaries into hostage to divisive or sectarian interests they represent. Such hidden prices of welfare benefaction have included religious affiliation or conversion, divisive corporate loyalty, as well as outright violation of basic human rights (Kim, M. 2006; Park, J. 2014). Also, just like the developmental state's role of helping to form industrial entrepreneurial class for national economic development, the developmental liberal state, under an absence of sufficient non-state welfare providers, has helped form certain types of civilian actors and organizations in welfare provision. Of these state-backed welfare entities, many have behaved entrepreneurially, under a tacit endorsement of the budget-conscious bureaucracy, as if in profit sectors (Kim and Park 2012). On the other hand, most of them have kept distance from those progressive political lines and voices that advocate civil activism. As welfare provision has been conceived not as an active expression of civil social solidarity but often as a clientelistic bene-faction for narrowly targeted groups, it has paradoxically contributed to segmenting and demobilizing civil society.[34]

Thus, welfare pluralism in South Korea has been much more a situa-tionally contingent institutional phenomenon than a sociopolitical ideo-logical trend. Besides, the plurality (or diversity) of welfare providers itself has contributed to worsening the political ambiguity of social welfare. Among others, corporate welfare and welfare NPOs are particularly indic-ative of the sociopolitical nature of welfare pluralism under the develop-mental liberal state.

Generous and comprehensive corporate welfare (often accompanied by lifetime employment) used to be considered a core material basis of the paternalistic labor relations in East Asia. This supposedly explains the exis-tence of the "company human" who seems wholeheartedly devoted to work and identifies his/her company virtually as own family.[35] From a societal perspective, however, corporate welfare shares the self-contradictory nature of family welfare because needy workers are more likely to belong to destitute companies that are less capable of welfare provision. Nevertheless, corporate welfare has been a significant instru-ment for the developmental liberal state, particularly in the following two senses. First, it has helped allow the social protection of urban industrial workers to remain as a non-state responsibility. Among urban workers, furthermore, those who enjoy richer corporate welfare are more likely to be employed in such large companies and factories as to enable an effective organizing of labor interests (Song, H. 1995). Therefore, the potentially more defiant part of industrial proletariat with regard to national politics has often been co-opted through corporate welfare schemes. The strong tendency of company-based unionization in South Korea has reinforced such tendency. Second, corporate welfare is a mode of welfare provision under which the specific human capital needs of each enterprise can be directly incorporated into welfare programs and extra-industrial welfare expenses can be automatically minimized in accordance with the expira-tion of job tenure. From a societal perspective, corporate welfare is by nature a type of *productive welfare*. Above all, the corporate support for employees' education and training (sometimes toward a doctoral level) has been a crucial part of the corporate welfare system of major South Korean companies. Likewise, even within a same company, the human capital differentials among employees have been finely linked to different levels and scopes of corporate welfare.

As in most other societies, welfare protection of dependent and/or handicapped persons, medical service, and education, among other human and social services, have been defined as non-profit sectors in South Korea.[36] However, the everyday institutional practice of the concerned organizations and their relationship with the government often confuse the public as if they were commercial business. Non-profit hospitals have practically been allowed to refuse medical service to those who are unable to pay, and prices for medical service have been high enough to enable most physicians to join the upper income class. Most of private universities have financially survived mainly on the basis of tuitions (which are now among the world's most expensive), with the financial contribution of the governing foundations often remaining minimal or negligible.[37] Numerous non-public care institutions have operated on the basis of government subsidies, and some of them even have exploited inmates' labor for commercial production and construction.[38] In frequent instances, furthermore, the supposedly non-profit foundations for these social services organizationally resemble industrial/commercial enterprises in terms of familial control of management (and de facto ownership).[39] Not coincidentally, the governing families often control a complex mix of social service foundations and industrial/commercial enterprises simultaneously. The rampant illicit internal trades between their non-profit institutions and for-profit enterprises have served a core mechanism for the phenomenal growth of their private wealth.[40] The state regulation of these social service entities have virtually ensured their profitability through a liberal price policy permitting fully profitable prices for the concerned services and a legal leniency to various illegitimate or illegal practices for amassing private wealth. In recent years, the state has openly taken the notion of industrial policy for developing and/or restructuring these social services into globally competitive and profitable sectors. Among others, the possibility of commercial medical service by specially licensed hospitals, for foreign visitors at the beginning, has engendered a huge societal controversy (Lee, P. 2015).

5   DEMOCRATIC CHALLENGES TO DEVELOPMENTAL LIBERALISM

As a broad implication from the functionalist thesis of developmental authoritarianism upheld by Huntington (1968) and innumerable followers, it is understandable that developmental liberalism as a state policy paradigm has been crucially predicated upon authoritarian political power.[41] Developmental liberalism is supposedly a rule of "carrot and stick", but grassroots South Koreans used to be continually exhorted or coerced to keep receiving material rain checks (i.e., delayed carrots) while continually threatened of physical oppression (i.e., immediate sticks). With their national economy already highly developed, the delayed carrots became increasingly intolerable to ordinary people, including overworked and underpaid workers. Such widespread material discontents themselves served a crucial social basis for immediate political upheavals, whereas their gradual acknowledgment of the autocratic state as the main basis for the socioeconomic injustices helped bolster the societal alliance for democratization led by progressive intellectuals and civilian professional politicians. When the civil social struggles for democratization finally forced the dictatorial regime to agree on restoration of the democratic political procedures in 1987, the developmental liberal approach to social policy could not but be subjected to serious political challenges from below (and increasing second thoughts by policymakers).

First, social policy—social welfare in particular—began to take on independent political significance as the post-authoritarian governments tried to bolster their political legitimacy through protective and/or redistributive social programs and services (Kwon, H. 1999).[42] The democratically elected government of ex-general Roh Tae-Woo, confronted with mounting social pressure and political challenge against him, even declared that it would do its best in order to establish "the welfare state" as early as possible. It was more a lip service for securing his own political safety than a serious politico-ideological transition to anything resembling social democracy. Nevertheless, welfare expenditure increased substantially and social services and insurances were augmented significantly. An especially notable affair was the overnight construction of mammoth bed towns for coping with the extreme shortage of urban housing. Social policy became no more reducible to an auxiliary part of national economic development in the minds of both political elite and grassroots citizens. Social rights—

or socioeconomic components of modern citizenship—gradually began to help define the state-citizen relationship.

Second, the political rise of social policy was closely linked to a political rebirth of citizenry as social policy constituencies. The political eruption of organized labor, along with various groups of middle class citizens, was a critical determinant of the democratic transition of 1987, and their political yearning for democratic rights was immediately succeeded by the practical demands for improved wages and working conditions, basic housing, nutrition, and education, and a host of other components of decent livelihood (Kim, D. 1995). The struggle of unions and other organized social groups for social rights turned out quite effective as manifested in terms of rapidly enhanced wages, social welfare benefits, and so on.

Third, and relatedly, the politico-legal purge of the corruption chains between industrial capital and the deposed autocratic politicians and the reform of the *chaebol* system as a whole, no matter how limitedly these were implemented, were quite consequential for social policy as well. Since the inherently illicit nature of *chaebol*'s corporate control and management was judged to be a chronic structural factor for legal as well as economic distortions, their foul history of relying on the military-based autocratic regimes for politico-legal safety and business expansion constituted a direct political concern to the public.[43] A majority of *chaebol* heads (*chongsu*) ended up being convicted of grave criminal charges with some being sentenced to prison terms along with military-turned politicians. Apart from such legal punishment of *chaebol*'s specific instances of political bribing and corporate embezzlement, the reform of *chaebol*'s corporate governance, financial structure, and industrial monopoly became a main agenda in national politics. Even without any formally declared setback in the state-business developmental alliance, the legal punishment of *chaebol* heads and the political pronouncement of *chaebol* reform induced a gradual, if not full, political balancing of the state-business-grassroots relationship and ultimately helped strengthen the political significance of social policy vis-à-vis economic development. As a more immediate process, the lopsided relationship of state offices to employers (vis-à-vis workers) in industrial and labor policies had to be seriously rectified. The politically softened state began to restrain its physical interference with labor relations, leaving employers directly confronted with workers' demands and challenges (Choi, J. 2002; Koo 2001). The resulting corporate concessions to workers in wage levels, employment conditions, and fringe benefits, in effect, significantly relieved the burden of the state in welfare provision. Nevertheless, the state itself had to undertake its own political work of reconfiguring grassroots citizens as beneficiaries of new social services, protections, and insurances.

Fourth, women's role for democratization and labor struggle, while much less conspicuous than that of men, was succeeded by a strong feminist movement for women's human, cultural, and social rights.[44] As most women's hardships were closely linked to their familial duties, roles, and positions, the feminist movement came to serve a powerful initiative for socializing the familial functions of social support and protection for elderly, infants and children, handicapped, and so on. To the extent that the developmental orientation of the state had required its institutional dependence on patriarchal family relations for welfare provision, the democratic repositioning of women implied a political reconfiguration of private welfare provision into a public duty of the state.[45]

Finally, the (above-mentioned) political affirmation of the social rights of citizens was soon accompanied by various civil initiatives and struggles for actually realizing such social rights. Whereas developmental political economy defined the state-society relationship mainly in terms of corporate roles (and proletarian duties) for realizing national economic goals in exchange for preferential business support (and improved incomes), democratic polity involved the proactive engagement of civil society (i.e., NGOs, community initiatives, intellectual movements, etc.) for realizing various humanitarian, communitarian, and socioecological concerns as public goals or state duties. Besides the hitherto existing philanthropic, religious, or politically minded providers of welfare and relief, many broad-based civil social organizations and movements arose as crucial counterparts or watchdogs to the social policy bureaucracy of the state. These civil society actors, on the one hand, purported to ensure political pledges and legal (constitutional) stipulations for social rights to materialize into actual enhancement of people's livelihood and security and, on the other hand, attempted to propose new or better social policies and programs for augmenting social rights.[46]

Given the above social pressures and corrections on the developmental liberal state, democratization became a very uncomfortable experience to conservative state elite and their developmental allies in business. Under the state leaderships sensitively responsible to, if not morally responsible for, popular opinions and demands, their reactionary temptations would not be easily facilitated through direct political and administrative instruments anymore. Instead, they began to seek various extra-state mechanisms for maintaining or reinforcing the developmental liberal framework for socioeconomic governance. Some industrial elite tried to establish their own sociopolitical platform for national, not to mention corporate, developmental management by closely (and secretly) communicating with incumbent government officials, hiring resigned officials with potential influence on incumbent ones, creating economic research institutions and journalism foundations, and so forth (Song et al. 2016; Chang, J. 2014; Hong, D. 2006; Lee, S. 2010). In this process, *chaebol* and their practical auxiliaries in political, administrative, journalist, and academic sectors came to find the West-derived neoliberalism as a highly convenient ideological instrument for renewing business-friendly developmentalist governance (see Chap. 7).

6   Conclusion

This chapter has tried to construe the particular sociopolitical attributes of South Korea's developmental liberalism as has been historically manifested under the successive developmentalist governments since the early 1960s. The so-called developmental state in the country has been well known for its comprehensively organized and aggressively implemented policies for industrialization, export promotion, and so forth, whereas its social policy orientation has often been simplified as one of brutal conservatism against those in need—be they workers, women, poor, or a host of other disadvantaged and alienated social categories. While such appraisal has much validity, there is a pressing scholarly as well as practical need for more systematically analyzing the structural relationship between economic developmentalism and social policies and practices than dwelling on the implicitly suggested zero-sum relationship. To begin with, the nature and extent of the zero-sum relationship have varied over time. Even with regard to the sacrificing of social policies, the conditions, manners, and outcomes of such sacrificing should be systematically documented. As the natural resource-barren and war-destroyed country's "economic miracle" is widely believed to have been buttressed almost exclusively by human resources, a simple neglect or single-minded suppression of social policies would not have sufficed to achieve its national economic goal. On the other hand, the tenacious conservatism of politico-bureaucratic as well as economic elites against social policy well into the twenty-first century (which has put South Korea at a rank of notorious "welfare laggard" even as compared to much poorer countries) should be analyzed more in terms of structurally interwoven interests associated with decades-old developmental statism than of political backwardness or fundamentalist conservatism. In sum, a new line of theoretical and empirical investigation is urgently called for in order to systematically analyze whether and how South Korea—and other nations under developmentalist rule—has been developmentally liberal rather than liberally liberal in its social policy configuration.

PART II

Post-Developmental Restructuring and Social Displacement

CHAPTER 3

Coping with the "IMF Crisis" in the Developmental Liberal Context

1 INTRODUCTION

South Korea's economic collapse of 1997 was no less dramatic than her earlier economic success for three and a half decades. Obviously, South Koreans overstretched their economic ambition in the 1990s, so that suicidal investment in heavy industries using foreign loans was destined to cause a major balance-of-payment crisis. The economic, and social, crisis, however, seems to have rooted in many more ills of the South Korean model of development. While South Korea's then elected president Kim Dae-Jung managed to persuade the International Monetary Fund (IMF) and foreign commercial lenders into emergency relief lending and debt renewal, his real challenge was to impose radical reforms on business (*chaebol*), labor, as well as bureaucracy that would undo various entrenched privileges and instead demand *gotongbundam* (pains-sharing) accruing to strict market principles. Kim was achieving what he could achieve with direct administrative orders. But *chaebol* heads were still demanding old preferential treatment for their restructuring programs, labor unions were refusing to drive workers into unprotected unemployment and poverty, and many government officials were simply trying to buy time until President Kim ran out of energy and zeal for reform.[1] The addiction of business leaders and bureaucrats to the so-called crony capitalism, however derogatory this term may have sounded, did pose a serious impediment to Kim's neoliberal reforms.

© The Author(s) 2019
Chang K-S, *Developmental Liberalism in South Korea*,
International Political Economy Series,
https://doi.org/10.1007/978-3-030-14576-7_3

A much more fundamental dilemma arose from the very social conditions and mechanisms with which the South Korean economy had grown explosively, mobilizing grassroots resources and energies. Such conditions and mechanisms closely reflected some of the structural features of developmental liberalism (as explained earlier in Chap. 2), namely, state-business entrepreneurial merge, minimization of public social security (and maximization of familial responsibilities), and developmental cooptation of social policy constituencies. First, the successive authoritarian governments had allied with business to quell labor demands, thereby creating a highly spoiled industrialist class that was reluctant to prepare material and social conditions for conciliatory labor relations. As a result, the corporate structural adjustment programs were more difficult to implement, because employers had difficulty securing cooperative responses from extremely suspicious and angry workers. Second, the developmentalist regimes had refused to invest in social and economic protection measures for workers and other needy groups in order to maximize the allocation of national resources in economic projects and corporate subsidies. The cost of lacking any meaningful social safety net against economic fluctuations became evident as massive unemployment instantly created a completely helpless population of fired workers and their families. Third, even under the hostile governmental and corporate policies concerning labor rights and welfare, grassroots people—most of whom had experienced war and extreme poverty in their immediate past—were largely satisfied with their material betterment, remained optimistic about their economic futures, and continued to mobilize individual and familial resources into education, job training, and entrepreneurship. However, the sudden loss of work at unprecedentedly massive scales amid the bleak economic forecast came to demolish the psychological underpinnings of grassroots participation in capitalist industrial development.

None of these crisis tendencies were necessarily the inevitable consequence of the balance-of-payment crisis of late 1997 itself, but nonetheless aggravated by the supposed economic cures coerced by the US-masterminded International Monetary Fund. As many international figures began to criticize, the Fund's flat indifference to the particular local social and economic situations of the countries under its financial rescue programs served to exacerbate social pains and economic conditions. Unfortunately, this was the case in South Korea more clearly than anywhere else. Kim Dae-Jung's loyal subscription to the IMF doctrine, and to neoliberalism in general, was certainly instrumental in persuading

Western governments and international lenders to participate in debt renewal and new lending, but none of his reform programs concerning business conglomerates (*chaebol*), labor relations, or government work were shown to be very effective in the long run. As a former democracy fighter, Kim tried to enfranchise labor unions into the formal political process through the labor-business-government agreement framework. This seemingly social democratic political arrangement, however, was (ab)used only to justify massive lay-offs as the core of corporate structural readjustment. Labor unions could not but feel betrayed and thus vowed to struggle instead of pursuing compromise. In the meantime, the unemployment rate continued its steep hike, and the downward leveling of the middle and poorer classes was increasingly apparent. Despite the gradual recovery of macroeconomic indicators, the symptoms of the social crisis were accumulating. In fact, the core condition for the economic recovery was the plundering of the classic social foundations of South Korea's "economic development primarily dependent upon human resources". South Korea's developmental liberalism was the crucial local context under which the national financial crisis and its neoliberal rescue measures would cause particularly serious social devastations. Understanding what South Koreans then called "the IMF crisis" in the specific structural context of developmental liberalism is critically important because the country's socioeconomic conditions in the subsequent two decades would be decisively shaped by the supposedly tentative (but indefinitely effectuated) neoliberal rescue measures and accompanying social displacements of various grassroots groups.

2   Social Conditions of South Korean Development

Up until the sudden financial crisis of late 1997, South Korea's experience with economic development had served as a main arena for new theories and concepts in development studies. Neoclassical economists, political economists, sociologists, political scientists, and historians joined the forum on the country's "developmental miracle". All conceivable factors for development had been introduced: laissez-faire and free trade, state initiative, human capital formation, Confucian work ethic, state-business nexus, international product cycle, international political structure, colonial legacy, and even sheer abundant labor. Some saw the utility of the scientific tools already existing in their respective disciplines, whereas others invented new models and concepts to highlight various unique aspects of the South Korean developmental experience. In either way, the stunning speed of economic growth and industrialization in South Korea compelled these scholars to verify their ideas (and ideologies) against perhaps the most notable developmental achievement in the latter part of the twentieth century.[2]

One line of debate drawing particular attention along the Asia-wide economic crisis was triggered by Paul Krugman (1994), an American Nobel laureate in economics. He characterized the developmental experience of South Korea (and other Asian countries) as "input-driven" economic growth as compared to the supposedly "efficiency-driven" growth of Western industrial economies. Many (neoclassical) economists followed his view, albeit without presenting systematic research outcomes. With Krugman's perspective extended, the Asian economic crisis may well have been an inevitable outcome of what could be termed *debt-driven growth*.[3] However, there were already serious case studies of South Korean industrialization—for instance, by Alice Amsden (1989), Peter Evans (1995), and John Matthews (1995)—which had evinced how South Korean bureaucrats and entrepreneurs successfully strove to achieve a technically advanced industrial system.[4]

I do not intend to side with either one of these opposing parties of thought. In my observation, there is no denying that South Korea's *chaebol* conglomerates, under the tacit encouragement of the previous president Kim Young-Sam's *Singyeongje* (New Economy) administration, relied more on debt for their growth than on technological and organizational innovation. Still, these South Korean enterprises came to compete successfully against Japanese, American, and European enterprises in many of the most advanced industrial sectors. Since their overexpansion was accompanied by increasing competitiveness, it was certain to create worry, if not fear, among Western and Japanese enterprises in this age of global overproduction.[5] In the 1960s and 1970s, the South Korean economy took off through the utilization of nearly "unlimited supplies of labor" (cf. W. Arthur Lewis 1954). The simple fact was that the economy grew too fast to hang on continuously in the primitive labor-intensive sectors. Thus, in the late 1970s, the South Korean government decided to undertake an ambitious transition from labor-driven growth to technology and capital-driven growth, and *chaebol* leaders successfully rode on the tide to receive various preferential governmental support in building up their industrial kingdoms in the government-suggested direction. In this process of cease-less industrial transitions, South Koreans proved themselves to be exceptionally capable OJTs (on-the-job trainees) in capitalist industrialization.

Given that the South Korean economy developed through both maximum input mobilization and substantial technological progress, my question is how South Koreans were able to drive maximum amounts of social and economic resources into the industrialization process. It has to be acknowledged that even input-driven economic development is a highly difficult task, at which only a handful of non-Western countries have had success. I do not think that South Koreans had some magical ability in this regard. Material sacrifice, political suppression, and self-consoling optimism on the part of grassroots South Koreans were the basic social requirements for the economic growth strategy centered on the concentration of material and human resources in state-selected industrial enterprises. Such requirements closely reflected some of the structural features of developmental liberalism—namely, state-business entrepreneurial merge, minimization of public social security, and developmental cooptation of social policy constituencies.

First, the successive South Korean administrations exhausted their public budgets on economic development projects, whose benefits were immediately monopolized by private industries. They therefore had to minimize state programs for protecting and improving the everyday lives of ordinary citizens. Until then, social security had not been a significant component of national politics or government policy. Moreover, an integrative framework for social policy had not existed. Second, military-turned political leaders did not hesitate to support exploitative private industrialists, often using brutal physical force, when they were challenged by workers for decent wages and work conditions. Labor had to be suppressed supposedly for the sake of international (price) competitiveness, and South Korea's hegemonic conservative politicians' deep confrontation with the Labor party in North Korea intensified their hatred against the proletariat. Under such political auspices, a heavily spoiled capitalist class arose in South Korea which continued to deal with labor mainly on the basis of state-provided physical suppression.[6] Third, no South Koreans opposed the national industrialization project even when they were alienated or adversely affected by it. Even under these hostile conditions, many workers did experience increasing income, although such increases were usually far behind the profit growth of their employers. More importantly, most grassroots people motivated or hypnotized themselves to become loyal supporters of the national industrialization project. Their "today" did look better than their "yesterday", whereas their "tomorrow" would be even better than their "today". Their "yesterday", without too many exceptions, had been filled with poverty, hunger, confusion, and war. This mentality induced them to accept personal austerity measures voluntarily and to allocate all financial resources for education, savings, and other future-oriented social and economic investment.

These social conditions have not been exclusive to South Korea but widespread in rapidly industrializing capitalist economies. Poverty, suppression, and illusion are rather typical symptoms of unfair domination, and I would not expect that South Koreans could have enjoyed an exceptionally humane capitalist economic system. However, abusive social conditions cannot, and should not, be perpetuated too long if a sustainable social and economic system is to be established. The crucial mistake made by South Korean politicians, bureaucrats, and business leaders was that they had clung to an unrealistic premise that such conditions could be maintained endlessly. Even at the time South Korea faltered into the national financial crisis in the late 1990s, such problematic conditions had not been alleviated to any meaningful extent. The social pains triggered by the financial fiasco were much more acutely felt because of these conditions.

3   Economic Bubble, Psychological Bubble

The national financial crisis instantly put South Koreans in an entirely unfamiliar situation of drastic income decline and loss after three and a half decades of explosive economic growth. The national economy suffered a 5.8 percent decline in gross domestic product (GDP) in 1998. In US dollars, against which the value of the Korean won nearly collapsed, the same year recorded a devastating 32.5 percent shrinkage of the national economy. Once ranked as the 11th largest economy in the world, the South Korean economy was demoted to the 17th. Likewise, per capita gross national income (GNI) plummeted to 6823 US dollars, marking a 33.8 percent decrease from the previous year, or the same level reached seven years before. South Koreans became a less-than-affluent people whose income level was only the 42nd highest in the world. Other crisis symptoms were in line. Corporate and private assets were devalued at unprecedented scales, innumerable corporations went bankrupt or liquidated, and workers in almost every industry faced massive lay-offs and pay-cuts.

The values of stocks, houses, and land plummeted as well. According to a report by Samsung Economic Research Institute (quoted in *The Hankyoreh*, 18 September 1998), the total value of listed stocks decreased by 54.6 percent between May 1997 and July 1998; the total value of houses (including apartments) shrank by 11.8 percent between November 1997 and July 1998; and the total value of land dwindled by 20 percent between the fourth quarter of 1997 and the second quarter of 1998. Obviously, these value depreciations far exceeded the level of economic "bubble bursting". It may have appeared rather surprising to many outside observers that most South Korean firms survived the stock price collapse. Ironically, according to the apt analysis of Robert Wade (1998), this outcome should be attributed to the fact that the financial structure of South Korean firms had been sustained by borrowing, and not by stock prices.[7] The depreciation of housing and land values and the freezing of housing and land markets effectuated a finishing blow to many middle class families and small industrialists who had maintained their financial basis by investments in real estate.

The unemployment rate soared instantly—from 2.6 percent in November 1997 to 7.0 percent in June 1998 and 8.7 percent in February 1998 (Chang, K. 1999b). In fact, this was statistically mitigated by the sharp increase of those giving up job search which reduced the denominator of unemployment statistics. Official figures on employment, which counted unemployment still under ten percent by regarding even those working only a few hours per week or staying home on unwanted leave as employed, severely underrated the actual situation.[8] The number of people in unstable and/or tentative employment was considered even larger than the number of unemployed people. If these underemployed and practically unemployed people and those who had helplessly given up on the job search are taken into account, the actual number of unemployed people may well have reached three to four million, accounting for nearly 15–20 percent of the working-age population.

Because of these consequences, South Koreans became the second most damaged population in Asia amid the region-wide financial crisis. (The Indonesian economy, as widely known, suffered the greatest damage.) As shown in Table 3.1, the "misery index"—the pressure of unemployment and inflation beyond economic growth—increased most dramatically in South Korea among all Asian countries.[9] Since the pains from an economic crisis are relative to the pre-crisis conditions of life, South Koreans' sufferings appeared particularly severe.

Table 3.1   Misery index in 1997 and 1998

Country	1997	1998
Asian countries		
South Korea	1.5	20.9
Indonesia	6.8	96.5
Thailand	10.6	25.1
Malaysia	−2.4	10.8
China	−1.0	−0.1
Hong Kong	2.6	9.6
Taiwan	−3.2	0.7
Advanced countries		
United States	3.4	2.8
Japan	4.3	6.7
France	11.4	10.0
Germany	10.7	10.0
England	5.4	5.8
Sweden	7.1	4.8
Italy	12.5	11.8
Spain	19.4	18.1
Canada	7.1	6.7
Australia	5.6	6.7

Notes: Misery index is computed as unemployment rate plus inflation rate minus GDP growth rate; 1998 figures cover January to October

Source: Abridged from data in Daewoo Economic Research Institute, 1998, "The Phenomenon of Pain Transfer from Advanced Countries to Asian Countries and Its Implication for the South Korean Economy" (in Korean; an unpublished report)

The pains, however, were not felt evenly among different classes (see Table 3.2). The poorest segments of the working population were hit particularly hard. The richest group of workers was clearly an exception, as they experienced an *increase* in nominal income in the first half of 1998 (in part due to skyrocketing interest rates). These income disparities widened with time. It should be noted that these statistics omitted those at the extreme ends of the economic hierarchy (i.e., urban capitalist households, on the one hand, and unemployed and underemployed persons' households, on the other) and thus could not fully describe the actual extent of the existing inequality. On average, urban worker households suffered nominal income reductions between 1997 and 1998: by 2.8 percent between the first quarters, by 5.3 percent between the second quarters, by 14.4 percent between the third quarters, and by 3.8 percent between the

Table 3.2 Annual income changes among urban worker households between 1997 and 1998

Income group	Compared quarters (1998/1997)			
	1st	2nd	3rd	4th
All	−2.8	−5.3	−14.4	−6.7
Highest 20%	0.9	2.3	−8.0	−0.3
2nd high 20%	−3.1	−5.6	−15.2	−8.0
3rd high 20%	−4.4	−6.9	−18.3	−9.9
2nd low 20%	−5.5	−8.8	−19.6	−11.8
Lowest 20%	−12.0	−14.9	−24.4	−17.2

Source: Compiled from the database of the National Statistical Office

fourth quarters (National Statistical Office 1999).[10] The year 1998 as a whole showed a 6.7 percent decrease from the previous year.

As a consequence, every household was forced to reduce consumption. The consumption expenses of urban worker households decreased between 1997 and 1998, by 8.8 percent between the first quarters, by 13.2 percent between the second quarters, by 16.8 percent between the third quarters, and by 4.0 percent between the fourth quarters (National Statistical Office 1999). The entire year of 1998 showed a 10.7 percent decrease from the preceding year.[11] It was quite notable that South Koreans' consumption expanded rapidly until the very moment of their country's financial collapse. That is, the third quarter of 1997 marked an 8.2 percent increase in the consumption expenses of urban worker households over the previous year. Reductions in consumption were relatively small among the richest and the poorest groups, however, for diametrically different reasons (Cheil Communications 1998). The most destitute people did not have any room for cutting down on consumption any further. The most affluent people, with their cash assets bloated abruptly thanks to the IMF-set ultrahigh interest rates, may have had an interest in expanding their conspicuous consumption, but social rage and political pressure against them amid the national financial fiasco seem to have forced them to feign repentance by abstaining from lavish spending.[12]

Such forced austerity was far from over, as additional unemployment resulting from corporate structural adjustment and exhaustion of household savings were still in order for many subjectively and objectively middle class families. As shown in Table 3.3, about 40 percent of the

Table 3.3 Survivable months after the unemployment of household head by income groups in South Korea

Income group	Survivable months after unemployment of household head
1st (lowest 20%)	17
2nd (21–40%)	21
3rd (41–60%)	31
4th (61–80%)	36
5th (highest 20%)	122

Source: Bae, Jun-Ho, 1998, "Life Changes of Low Income Strata under Employment Uncertainty" (in Korean), paper presented at the National Statistical Office Seminar on *The Changes and Trends in the Living Conditions of South Korean Households*, 1 September 1998

South Korean population would lose all means of subsistence within two years, and the next 40 percent within three years. Even if the rapid economic recovery promised by the then incumbent government was to be realized, many of these demoted South Koreans would never be able to regain their earlier economic and social status.

The figures in Table 3.4 reveal that the economic crisis induced *hahyang pyeongjunhwa* (downward leveling) of income as the proportions in the lowest income groups increased drastically. The "collapse of middle class", which was talked about frequently in media articles and academic seminars then, did appear a serious possibility in any future. Class-specific patterns of income reduction were largely similar. Again, the poorer they were, the more seriously their income decreased in the course of the current economic crisis.[13] The bursting of a sort of *psychological bubble* accompanied the income reductions. South Koreans' self-perceived class status was falling substantially. On the eve of the economic crisis, 65 percent of South Korean urbanites classified themselves as "middle" class, 12 percent as "high middle" class, and 19 percent as "low middle" class. Six months into the economic crisis, those perceiving themselves as "high middle" or "middle" class decreased notably, if not dramatically.

In a sense, this psychological dejection was what haunted South Koreans most seriously and destabilized the social and political basis of South Korean development most critically. In the pre-crisis period, when the authoritarian developmentalist state had denied them social rights to humane living conditions, and when greedy industrialists had refused to give reasonable compensation for their work, grassroots South Koreans would still remain highly motivated and optimistic about their economic futures. An interesting ramification of this attitude was a sort of *false*

Table 3.4 Changes in monthly income and self-perceived class stratum before and after the "IMF crisis" in four largest South Korean cities (n = 2500)

	Pre-crisis (1997)	Post-crisis (1998)
Monthly income (in million won)		
401 and more	6.5	3.8
301–400	11.2	7.5
251–300	16.3	13.2
201–250	24.3	20.0
151–200	21.6	22.3
101–150	16.5	23.0
100 and less	3.6	10.2
Self-perceived class stratum		
High	1	1
High middle	12	6
Middle	65	60
Low middle	19	26
Low	3	7

Source: Compiled from data in Cheil Communications, 1998, "IMF Half Year, Self-Portrait of South Koreans" (in Korean; an unpublished survey report), pp. 6–7

middle class consciousness. At least before the economic crisis, as shown in Table 3.4, almost everyone thought of themselves as middle class. A nation-wide survey in 1994 by the South Korean Consumer Protection Board reported that 81.3 percent classified themselves as "middle class" as opposed to 7.1 percent and 11.7 percent who saw themselves as "upper class" and "low class", respectively (as reported in *Sisa Journal*, 11 November 1998). South Koreans' "workaholism" was largely fueled by such psychological self-aggrandizement. The sudden demoralization of grassroots South Koreans as developmentalist subjects (as opposed to welfare constituencies) could not but lead to a catastrophic constraint on socially sustainable development.

The precise factors generating the bloated self-perceptions of South Koreans in the social and economic hierarchy are yet to be analyzed, but the following three matters seem to have been critical.[14] First, most South Koreans had been enjoying better lives, at least as compared to their miserable existence in the pre-Park Chung-Hee era with a per capita GDP of less than one hundred US dollars. In locating their class positions, South Koreans seem to have used, as the basic reference category, their destitute past more importantly than the living standards of their domestic or overseas contemporaries. Almost everyone had been feeling gratified by recollecting their memory of "cold and hungry old days". Second, and relatedly, most South Koreans had been expecting even better lives in the future. Interestingly, poor latecomers in social and economic competition used to show particularly conservative attitudes about the national developmental situation. With hard proletarian work aside, educational certification, real estate investment (speculation), and small self-employed entrepreneurship had been the most popular conduits for class advancement. Under a sort of *makcha* (last train) effect, those underclass individuals who had just attained educational certificates, real estates, or business ventures were desperately hoping that the competitive, if not unfair, socioeconomic opportunity structures be maintained, at least until they could finally receive differential returns on their arduous investments. Third, South Koreans' material as well as psychological attachments to adult children, parents, and siblings used to induce them to tie their class status to those of their extended family members (in particular, successful ones). Poor old parents would consider the social and economic situation of their successful children, if any, more importantly than their own situation in evaluating their class status. Adult (as well as young) children, even when lacking educational, technical, and financial resources for independent living, would identify themselves as part of their rich parents' family, if any, in evaluating their class status.

For these and many other reasons, grassroots South Koreans used to maintain a highly positive and optimistic attitude about material advancement.[15] This attitude underlay the widespread political conservatism of the lower classes that had been apparent in parliamentary and presidential elections. More importantly, the same attitude used to induce them to adopt voluntary austerity measures and to allocate all of their financial resources for education, savings, and other future-oriented social and economic investments. Such future-oriented investments had customarily been made on a familial basis—that is, educational investment for children and siblings, savings pool for family business, and so forth (Chang, K. 2010a). As compared to the "social investment state" suggested by Anthony Giddens (1998) for the "renewal of social democracy" in the neoliberal West, what may be called *the social investment family* had socioeconomically characterized South Koreans (Chang, K. 2010a). International comparative statistics by the Organisation for Economic Co-operation and Development (OECD) concerning educational investment kept revealing that South Korea was far ahead of other OECD member countries in the family-provided proportion of the expenses for higher education during the pre-crisis period (and the post-crisis period).[16] Such parental devotion to children's extensive education is analyzed as a key factor for pervasive old-age poverty in South Korea (Park and Cha 2008).

The significance of this self-generated social and economic efficacy may be proved conversely by the fact that grassroots South Koreans had nevertheless been aware of the unjust and biased nature of the "crony capitalist" order.[17] That is, even acknowledging the highly corrupt nature of wealth and power in their society, South Korean people had striven to positively integrate their mental energy for the ongoing process of national development. As illustrated in Table 3.5, most (urban) South Koreans in the mid-1990s perceived the economic opportunity structure as skewed and unfair. Nearly a half also thought that law and order had been abused for the sake of injustice. Not surprisingly, such negative perception of social order got exacerbated since the national economic crisis of 1997–1998. Likewise, in Table 3.6, a 1998 survey conducted by the Free Enterprise Center—the official ideological apparatus of the *chaebol* community—revealed an embarrassing reality that ordinary citizens' perceptions of large corporations and business leaders were extremely negative. Obviously, grassroots South Koreans did not have much respect for the very kind of people they tried to emulate. In the past, they used to tolerate these "ruthless, dishonest, and greedy" business leaders and their political and bureaucratic supporters only because they thought wishfully about their own chances of joining the economic developmental parade and sharing its perks. Now, suddenly realizing that this possibility might well be unattainable in a foreseeable future, grassroots South Koreans found reason to accumulate psychological fuel for revolt.[18]

Table 3.5   Percent of agreement on the unfairness of social order in four largest South Korean cities ($n = 2500$)

	Only rich people can make more money	Success is not possible with honest effort alone	People obeying law and order get disadvantage
1994	75	70	39
1995	74	70	42
1996	74	71	44
1997	78	75	53
1998	80	75	56

Source: Cheil Communications, 1998, "IMF Half Year, Self-Portrait of South Koreans" (in Korean; an unpublished survey report), p. 18

Table 3.6   Images concerning corporations and business leaders (five most negative ones in percent)

Images	Percent
Corporations	
Voracious (*muneobalsik*) expansion	15.9
Sudden riches, greed	13.0
Exploitation of small enterprises	12.0
Government-business collusion	11.8
Insolvency	10.4
Business leaders	
Dogmatism, authoritarianism	21.3
Government-business collusion	11.8
Only profit-seeking	8.8
Immorality	7.4
Extravagant life	5.3

Source: Survey data released to the press by the Free Enterprise Center, the Federation of Korean Industries, covering 800 ordinary people and 200 professionals in 1998, as reported in *The Hankyoreh*, 25 September 1998

4   GROWTH FIRST, DISTRIBUTION LATER, AND STRUCTURAL ADJUSTMENT NOW?

What could the state offer for economically dislocated and psychologically dejected South Koreans? Interviews and surveys of unemployed individuals and their dependents reported unequivocally that most needy people did not receive any immediate public relief benefit, were not aware of any usable relief programs for them, and would not expect much help from the government anyway (e.g., Park, J. 1999; Kim et al. 1998; Korea Institute for Health and Social Affairs and Korea Labor Institute 1998).[19] Even those who received some assistance expressed very low satisfaction. For instance, according to a newspaper survey of July 1998, 19.4 percent of the respondents expressed satisfaction with relief assistance (*The Hankyoreh*, 31 July 1998). On the other hand, newspapers and televisions kept carrying almost daily reports of fraudulent use and even embezzlement of the special unemployment program budget by government officials and welfare contractors (e.g., *The Hankyoreh*, 30 September 1998; *Sisa Journal*, 13 August 1998). It was not unusual to hear candid confessions from government officials that they were simply inexperienced and did not know what to do in this kind of situation (*The Hankyoreh*, 6 August 1998).

Table 3.7   Government expenditure in the 1990s in selected countries

Country	Year	Gov't expenditure as % of GDP	% of Total gov't expenditure			
			Social security	Education	Economic affair	Defense
Australia	1995	27.9	33.8	7.6	7.1	7.6
Canada	1992	25.2	41.3	3.0	8.3	6.9
Chile	1994	19.7	33.3	13.9	15.4	8.8
Egypt	1993	35.7	11.0	12.3	8.0	8.7
France	1992	45.0	45.0	7.0	4.7	5.7
Germany	1991	32.5	45.3	0.8	9.7	6.4
Japan	1993	23.7	36.8	6.0	3.3	4.1
Kuwait	1994	56.2	16.6	10.9	8.0	22.3
Mexico	1990	17.4	12.4	13.9	13.4	2.4
South Korea	*1995*	*19.9*	*9.3*	*18.1*	*24.0*	*15.7*
Sweden	1994	48.5	48.2	5.0	13.2	5.5
Thailand	1992	15.0	3.9	21.1	26.2	17.2
United Kingdom	1992	43.1	29.6	3.3	6.6	9.9
United States	1994	22.0	29.6	1.6	6.4	18.1

Source: *Social Indicators in Korea*, 1997, p. 533

Simply speaking, few grassroots South Koreans had serious expectations for social protection and relief by the state against unemployment and poverty. They had seen the successive authoritarian developmentalist regimes either explicitly call for "growth first, distribution later" or make state work implicitly in that direction. As displayed in Table 3.7, before the national financial crisis, the South Korean state used to commit itself to social security far less than those of other late developing countries at similar levels of development, not to mention those of Western industrialized countries.[20] It was questionable whether any previous South Korean administration had developed an integrated conception of social policy per se.[21] As far as social security issues were concerned, the successive South Korean administrations had remained completely laissez-faire under the implicitly shared doctrine of *developmental liberalism*. Supposedly for the sake of sustained rapid economic growth, the state had shown a virtual indifference to social welfare.

The only social entitlement for grassroots South Koreans used to be work.[22] As most of the available national economic resources were allocated to economic development projects and corporate subsidies, South Koreans had to find work through which they could reap some benefit from the economy-centered system. Without work, therefore, they would be totally and systematically disenfranchised from the developmentalist economic system. Under the national financial crisis and its neoliberal rescue measures, this very situation came to surface in South Korean society. The most crucial dilemma of the incumbent South Korean administration was that it had to persuade workers to accept such total disenfranchisement. Even if South Koreans might not complain too noisily about not receiving social security benefits from the government, they would not tolerate bureaucrats and politicians demanding their resignation from work for the sake of "structural adjustments" in the national economy. Thus, at factories, offices, and other places of work, they did not hesitate to express their individual and collective anger at employers and government authorities whenever their *work entitlements* came under threat.[23]

Another, though not universal, factor contributing to the desperate resistance of workers to lay-offs was corporate welfare. Under the slogan of "company as family", many large companies used to offer employees such fringe benefits as housing, children's school tuition, medical protection, life insurance, child care, leisure and vacation facilities, and even graduate study opportunity, although these benefits did not constitute corporate legal responsibilities (Song, H. 1995). In particular, major *chaebol* conglomerates used to call themselves *gajok* (family), like Samsung Gajok and Daewoo Gajok, and provided workers with various paternalistic aid. Also, a crucial political reason had existed for bountiful corporate welfare, in particular, since 1987. The demise of Chun Doo-Hwan's military dictatorship paved the way for a sudden upsurge of workers against the government and its client industrialists. Roh Tae-Woo's next government tried to elude political confrontation with organized labor by leaving labor matters between business and labor. At large factories and offices where organized labor was able to exercise pressure and threat, employers had to reach compromise by offering various fringe benefits in addition to higher wages. With the government maintaining its abstinence from social welfare (even in times of huge budget surplus), corporate welfare became a significant tool for improving living conditions, at least for those lucky workers employed in large *chaebol*-affiliated companies. After the national financial crisis, such corporate welfare benefits evaporated as soon as workers were discharged from their companies in the process of personnel shake-up.

As massive lay-offs became an indispensable part of the structural adjustment program in an overexpanded but bankrupt economy, the South Korean government was at last realizing the true *social cost of lacking a comprehensive and functioning welfare system.* In this context, the so-called *sahoeanjeonmang* (social safety net) suddenly became a key word for public discourse. Without the social safety net, a democratic government such as Kim Dae-Jung's might not be able to persuade its people into massive unemployment, for it would mean nothing other than free fall to the ground. In this context, the South Korean government began an apparent struggle to reinvent itself as a *social policy state,* albeit at a fairly rudimentary level. The tragedy was that, while political leaders and government officials had to use most of their time in a trial-and-error process, thousands of grassroots South Koreans were losing their jobs and incomes every day.

Two factors in particular intensified the anger of grassroots South Koreans. As explained in detail below, in January 1998, labor unions reached a historical agreement with government and business leaders on how to overcome the current economic crisis in a cooperative and peaceful manner. The core tenet of the historically unprecedented tripartite compromise was *gotongbundam* (pains-sharing). As workers were supposed to accept lay-offs and pay reductions "under certain urgent managerial situations", the government and corporations should have embarked on thorough organizational reforms, expunging their entrenched and unjust prerogatives. Neither government offices nor *chaebol* corporations began to show any meaningful initiation of such reforms. In fact, their intention to implement such reforms itself came under question.

According to a 1998 survey of 1030 residents in the six largest South Korean cities, as shown in Table 3.8, as many as 50.6 percent of the respondents indicated that the occupation they most preferred for the spouses of their daughters or sisters was government official. *Sinbunbojang* (status guarantee) attached to these public jobs was an obvious reason for the overwhelming preference. This status guarantee began to be called "the iron rice bowl"—a term borrowed, ironically, from socialist China where urban workers, before reform, used to enjoy similarly secure employment conditions.[24] In early 1998, the government announced a plan to reduce the number of administrative personnel by ten percent, but not many were actually laid off. Natural retirement (by age) and some one-year-early retirement soon accounted for the promised ten percent reduction. Even the very intent of the political leadership to reform the

Table 3.8   Most favored occupations for spouse of daughter or sister (n = 1030)

Occupation	Percent
Official	50.6
Big restaurant owner	11.3
Big company employee	7.7
Professor	6.0
Physician	5.5
Businessman	4.4
Professional	2.3
Prosecutor	1.9
Technician	1.8
Foreign currency dealer	1.6
Reporter/producer	1.3
Judge	1.0

Source: A survey by *Weekly Chosun* of residents (aged 20 years and older) in the six largest cities, 28–30 September 1998 (*Weekly Chosun*, 22 October 1998)

government bureaucracy came under wide suspicion when it announced its government organizational restructuring plan on 23 March 1999 (*The Hankyoreh*, 24 March 1999). Contrary to the recommendations of the special committee which had carried out base studies, President Kim Dae-Jung adopted a plan which would require the addition of one ministry and one semi-ministry to the already bulky administrative bureaucracy, omitting any significant reduction in his administrative staff. The privilege attached to public occupations was manifest even in the process of the so-called structural adjustment. When employees were discharged from state-funded and/or state-run organizations (including banks), they were offered *wirogeum* (consolation money) amounting to hundreds of thousands of US dollars each. Not many private workers could have dreamed of saving that much amount, even throughout their entire careers. Popular outrage was intensified further when Kim Dae-Jung remarked, "as far as people's legal sentiment allows, it is necessary to generously forgive" the petty corruption of government officials in the past (*The Hankyoreh*, 26 March 1999). While this remark was intended as an offer of "carrot" to extremely resistant bureaucrats (whom Kim had not been able to discipline), the expectation held by ordinary citizens to see corrupt and incapable bureaucrats punished as part of the pains-sharing agreement and to be served by a clean and efficient government evaporated.

The resistance of *chaebol* leaders to structural reforms was even more problematic. Practically no one thought that *chaebol* conglomerates were undergoing serious reforms in ownership and management. Even from outside, the IMF, World Bank, international credit appraisal companies, and foreign political leaders considered *chaebol*'s sneaky disobedience as the most serious blemish of South Korea's otherwise satisfactory structural adjustment. At the first meeting between then president-elect Kim Dae-Jung and major *chaebol* leaders in December 1997, the late Chey Jong-Hyun, then president of the Federation of Korean Industries, remarked, "These days, we businessmen have no word to say. The economy got into this mess because of our fault. We are the worst among all sinners" (*Dong-A Ilbo*, 25 December 1997). This seemingly remorseful attitude, however, did not leave any clear imprint in terms of self-sacrificing corporate reforms. In fact, it appeared that the five largest *chaebol* conglomerates (Hyundai, Samsung, Daewoo, LG, and Sunkyung) were trying to expand their corporate bodies further, again through borrowing (Yun, Y. 1998). It was reported that these largest *chaebol* conglomerates monopolized the corporate bonds market, thereby accumulating operating funds in amounts large enough to counter governmental threats (or bluffs?) to withdraw bank loans in case of disobedience (*The Hankyoreh*, 22 October 1998). In the meantime, the government, under the unexpected but inevitable encouragement of the IMF and other Western authorities, declared on 9 September 1998 to embark on a program to boost the economy through expanded public spending, lowered interest rates, and so on. Even though Kim Dae-Jung would not likely agree, there was every indication that *chaebol*'s strategy of buying time was largely effective, nullifying the governmental initiative for corporate structural reforms.[25]

Grassroots people did not have as much freedom to refuse reforms as government offices and *chaebol* corporations. As indicated above, the unemployment rate continued to climb well in 1999. Moreover, an ever-increasing number of people were even giving up job search. The mighty *chaebol* firms did not lag behind smaller firms in resorting to massive lay-offs. Between January and September 1998, about ten percent of the employees of the five largest *chaebol* conglomerates lost their jobs (*Chosun Ilbo*, 28 October 1998). Among about 900,000 workers employed by the 30 largest *chaebol* conglomerates as of October 1998, still one third of them were expected to be eliminated through the process of corporate structural adjustment in the coming months.

As a result of relentless labor reforms, as shown in Table 3.9, South Korean companies were able to reduce the ratio of personnel expenses to total sales to 9.4 percent in the first half of 1998, marking a 2.6 percent point decrease from only a year before. Despite (or because of) such drastic reductions in personnel expenses, South Korean companies still enjoyed a 9.3 percent increase in the per worker amount of value-added and a remarkable 20.0 percent increase in the per worker sales volume in the first half of 1998. Largely due to labor reform effects, the operating profit rate of South Korean companies in this turbulent economic period reached 8.8 percent, achieving a 1.3 percent point *increase* from a year before. The trouble, however, lay elsewhere. The burden of debt service, in terms of the ratio of finance costs (interests, etc.) to total sales, increased drastically in the first half of 1998 to reach 9.3 percent, recording a 3.1 percent point increase from a year before. After paying huge finance costs which were nearly comparable to total personnel expenses, South Korean companies had to experience a current loss rate of 0.4 percent. The fruits of personnel lay-offs, pay-cuts, and harder work were all expended to deal with the financial mess created by the owners and managers of these companies. However, in the judgment of most South Koreans, these business owners and managers were not repentant about their wrongdoings.[26]

"Development with sizable structural unemployment" became a new saying since the economic shock (Chang, K. 1999b). However, though unrecognized previously, it had long been a hard reality. South Koreans now realized not only that economic depression and structural adjustment

Table 3.9 Analysis of corporate management performance in the first halves of 1997–1998 ($n = 2328$)

Performance item	1997	1998
Total sales increase rate	9.1	5.0
Sales profit ratio	7.5	8.8
Total profit ratio	1.4	−0.4
Per worker sales increase rate	13.9	20.0
Per worker value-added increase rate	11.4	9.3
Per worker expense increase rate	8.3	−4.7
Worker expenses to sales ratio	12.0	9.4
Finance costs to sales ratio	6.2	9.3
Total debt ratio (year-end for 1995–1997)	396.3	387.0

Source: The Bank of Korea, 1998, "The Analysis of Corporate Management in the First Half of 1998" (in Korean; an unpublished survey report)

necessitated massive lay-offs at various ranks and sectors of the economy but also that almost full employment, unlike their perception and governmental statistics, had never been a true reality. A large proportion of the officially employed population had actually been under chronic and severe underemployment and thus denied secure living. Temporary workers at construction sites, sales and service workers, and part-time home service workers constituted the very first group to experience unemployment (Nam and Lee 1998). Their transitory occupational status made it difficult to institute social security programs for them. The current economic shock hit these people most brutally as they were exposed to total unemployment with no personal or public means of relief.[27]

The newly unemployed were trying every possible self-help measure. Some decided to return to their home villages for farming, and others flew to foreign countries recollecting the years of the Middle East construction boom and the Vietnamese war.[28] Where possible, many workers attempted to resurrect their bankrupt companies by taking over ownership and management. People under on-spot unemployment—that is, new graduates from colleges and high schools—tried to evade their ill fate by applying for military service (which was already full!) and further schooling (usually at their parents' expenses).[29]

Most importantly, many unemployed people turned to their families (spouses, parents, children, and siblings) for such emergency relief measures as role switching, complementary wage earning, cash lending, bank payment guarantees, housing sharing, and so forth (Park, J. 1999; Chang, K. 2018; Chang and Kim 1999). These familial relief arrangements enabled many to earn time for preparing their comeback, and their family relationships, in turn, were further solidified (Cheil Communications 1998:32). Still more people, however, were seeing their families dissolve, as extreme material destitution placed them and their family members in uncontrollable stress and induced them to give up family support functions. A 1998 government survey of unemployed people in Seoul and Pusan revealed that separation and divorce were increasing rapidly due to the material and psychological distress of unemployment (*The Hankyoreh*, 26 September 1998). The numbers of children and youth in need of protection—such as deserted babies and out-of-wedlock babies, physically and mentally abused children, runaway youth, and students skipping meals—were also increasing seriously.

The misery of elderly, youth, children, and handicapped in poor neighborhoods, while simply taken for granted by the government and society, was likely to worsen as scarce public attention and support tended to dwindle even further under *the primacy of the unemployment issue*. In the near absence of public welfare protection, needy people used to depend for their sheer survival on generous family members and relatives with regular jobs and stable incomes (Chang, K. 1997). Under the economic crisis, these generous family members and relatives themselves were losing jobs and incomes without much hope for reemployment.[30] The pains of people in the poorest and most needy segments of society could not be concealed or contained within private support networks anymore, nor did they want to be institutionalized in notoriously managed (dis)welfare asylums.[31] Unemployment engendered a chain-reaction social disintegration for grassroots South Koreans.[32] In no surprise, newspapers were full of stories about the misery of these helpless groups, abandoned by the state and separated from generous but unemployed kin providers.

5   LABOR-BUSINESS-GOVERNMENT COMPROMISE, LABOR-BUSINESS BIGOTRY

South Korean workers may well have taken high pride in the political efficacy that had been achieved through decades of unbending struggles with ruthless employers and their authoritarian political patrons. Their rise as a politically and economically competent class within a surprisingly short period had been an outcome of the complex interplay between labor-capital class conflict and state-society political struggle (Koo, H. 1993; 2001; Chang, K. 1999a). The post-crisis structural adjustment of the South Korean economy also turned out to be a complicated sociopolitical process played out by the intrusive state, aggressive monopoly capital, and resolute organized labor.

Politically, the most significant achievement of Kim Dae-Jung's government was indisputably the *nosajeong* (labor-business-government) committee which began in early 1998. It did attest to Kim Dae-Jung's democratic inclination to incorporate various grassroots groups in national politics under the slogan of "participatory democracy". However, a more fundamental condition for the landmark tripartite agreement system was derived from the fact that, merely a year before (i.e., in early 1997), labor unions had successfully defeated the attempt of the Kim Young-Sam government to implement serious neoliberal labor reforms against workers' economic and political interests in an exclusionary manner.[33] Labor had fought its own way toward a full membership in Kim Dae-Jung's inclusionary state corporatist arrangement (Chang H. 1999; Lim, Y. 1997). However, South Korea's main bourgeoisie, that is, *chaebol* heads, were not accustomed to being treated equally with workers by state authorities. Even most bureaucrats were having difficulty reforming their high-handed approach toward labor.[34] The political economic order of what may be called *exclusionary developmentalism* seemed to have a strong inertia. The economic crisis, however, strengthened the normative social influence of labor unions vis-à-vis *chaebol* and bureaucracy, which were held jointly responsible for the national financial meltdown and accompanying social devastations.

The tripartite agreements, described in the "*Nosajeongwiweonhoe* (Labor-Business-Government Committee) Co-Declaration" of 20 January 1998, included (1) the government's acceptance of its responsibility for the economic crisis and duty to prepare serious protection measures concerning unemployment and living conditions, reform government organizations thoroughly, and supervise fundamental corporate restructuring; (2) corporations' obligation to pursue active structural adjustment, reform managerial practices, and avoid indiscreet lay-offs and unfair labor practices; (3) labor unions' obligation to cooperate with corporations in improving productivity and, under urgent managerial situations, adjusting wages and working hours; (4) workers' and employers' commitment to industrial peace through dialogue and compromise; and (5) the cooperation among labor unions, corporations, and the government to create an attractive environment for foreign capital (see Appendix).

Perhaps, it was this historical compromise among time-worn foes that built confidence in the minds of foreign creditors as well as ordinary South Korean citizens about the possibility of orderly economic recovery. In particular, the virtual acceptance by labor unions of lay-offs "under urgent managerial situations" was praised by foreign lenders and observers as a critical first step to a national economic comeback. South Korean employers should have felt blessed. However, a critical dilemma arose when employers and workers returned to their factories and offices and had to take concrete steps for economic structural reforms. When left to their own devices, little trust existed between labor and business, with each group resorting to tenacious suspicions and hard voices. The first test case concerned the Hyundai Motor Company. Ever since the company announced a plan for *jeongrihaego* (personnel shake-up), mutual accusations of breaching the labor-employer agreements prevailed, and even instances of serious physical violence were reported. Ultimately, the settlement of the feud required the intervention of major governmental and political figures including a vice president of the ruling party then and the Minister of Labor. By and large, the settlement of 24 August 1998 appeared more acceptable to labor. *Chaebol* and their client media, therefore, began to mobilize negative opinions on it (*The Hankyoreh*, 3 September 1998). This tactic paid off. The next major labor dispute at Mando Machinery Company was physically quelled by police on 3 September 1998, paving the way for liberal lay-offs (*Sisa Journal*, 17 September 1998). In this manner did the incumbent administration stay neutral between labor and *chaebol*.

As *chaebol* companies have continued to resist the national and international pressure for structural reforms in management, ownership, and financial structure, the rationale for the tripartite agreement system came under serious question.[35] After all, the agreements reached at the tripartite meetings were not legally binding. Workers seemed to have every reason for growing indignant although they still believed in the political values of the tripartite agreement system. But *chaebol* heads had never been sincerely interested in these multiparty consultation and compromise meetings. In their experience, secret manipulation and lobbying were much more effective means for realizing their business goals. An increasing number of South Koreans felt that *chaebol*'s such attempts were largely successful.

In the second year under the tripartite agreement, the feeling prevailed among labor leaders that the seemingly social democratic political arrangement had been (ab)used only to justify massive lay-offs supposedly for the sake of corporate structural readjustment. Minjunochong (the Korean Confederation of Trade Unions or KCTU), the progressive umbrella organization of labor unions, finally declared its withdrawal from the tripartite committee on 24 February 1999, vowing to stage street demonstrations and strikes (*The Hankyoreh*, 25 February 1999). On 28 March 1999, even the more moderate Hanguknochong (the Federation of Korean Trade Unions or FKTU) announced its possible withdrawal from the committee in early April, unless the government should agree to change its unfair reform policy (*The Hankyoreh*, 29 March 1999). While workers alone had difficulty mobilizing social and political support from the general public, the serious unemployment situation and the political weakness of the incumbent government were certain to prompt labor unions to stage forceful resistances in the coming months and years.

6   THE IMF ENIGMA: IMPERIALIST FINANCE AND LOCAL POPULATION

The Asian economic crises spilt over not only into Russia and Latin America but also into international financial regulators including the IMF. The IMF programs for austerity-based structural adjustments in Asia came to be harshly criticized by both neoclassical economists (e.g., Paul Krugman and Jeffrey Sachs) and progressive political economists (e.g., Robert Wade) for ignoring the unique characteristics of Asian economies. Even officials in the OECD and, subsequently, the World Bank began to express pessimism about the outdated IMF doctrine. Ironically, even George Soros came to join the IMF bashing by criticizing its lenient treatment of creditors (including himself?) at a congressional hearing in the United States (*The Hankyoreh*, 17 September 1998).

In particular, the 1997–1998 annual report of the OECD on the South Korean economy, prepared in mid-June 1998 (in a draft version), staged an outright attack on the mistakes of the IMF and instead suggested lower interest rates and expanded public spending on welfare as indispensable requirements for economic recovery (*Chosun Ilbo*, 27 July 1998). It did not take long for the IMF to modify its position, consciously or unconsciously, in the direction suggested by the OECD. As early as 28 July 1998, the director of the Seoul office of the IMF confessed in a media interview that the high interest rate policy had devastated the already troubled Asian economies and that more public spending would be necessary, in particular, for establishing an effective social safety net (*Sisa Journal*, 13 August 1998). At an international seminar on 14 September 1998, the director of the Asia-Pacific division of the IMF even called for the South Korean government to strategically boost the economy by expanding deficit spending (*The Hankyoreh*, 15 September 1998). Taking into account its failure to predict the Asian financial crises, the IMF seemed to have bungled its mission both for prediction and prescription.

In the South Korean context, however, the IMF mandate for remedying the "crony capitalist" structure of the South Korean economy received a heartfelt welcome from reform-minded local economists. Many of them in fact claimed that the IMF regulatory system could serve as an opportunity to redress all the inefficient and corrupt practices ensuing from state-*chaebol* collusion and unnecessary state intrusion into private economic activities.[36] Long before the IMF and Western observers began to criticize "crony capitalism" (as the supposed cause for the economic crisis in South

Korea and elsewhere), South Korea's reform-minded scholars had called for the dismantling of the government-business collusion. Without meaningful political influence, however, these scholars were continually frustrated by policy decisions and corporate activities which were going in the exactly opposite direction. When the "IMF occupation" began, they welcomed many of the Fund's prescriptions concerning financial, corporate, and administrative reforms. Kim Dae-Jung's ready accommodation of the IMF recommendations on *chaebol* reform could be understood similarly. At least on the urgent need for *chaebol* reform, the IMF, the OECD, international credit appraisal companies, and South Korea's domestic supporters for reform (i.e., the presidential office, labor, and both liberal and progressive economists) were all in agreement.[37] The staunch and sly resistance of *chaebol* further reinforced this agreement.[38] In addition, the increasing emphasis of the IMF and the World Bank on the establishment of a sound social safety net began to receive a warm welcome from reform-minded South Korean activists.[39]

Nevertheless, the liberal outlook of IMF officials (or their financial liberalism based upon contradictory state-interventionist austerity principles) reflected the spirit of the times, that is, US-dominated global economic laissez-faire underwritten by docile Third World states. After all, they *asked to be invited* in order to rescue the South Korean economy from bankruptcy and thereby ensure the repayment of South Korean debts to foreign lenders. Additionally, their later concern about the social safety net came far too late. The everyday existence of grassroots South Koreans used to be predicated upon paid work and occasional kin assistance, and their devotion to work buttressed by the satisfaction and optimism generated by the prospect of continual material improvement. These basic social conditions for South Korean development came to be pulverized by the austerity-based economic structural adjustment programs of the IMF which made massive and sudden unemployment inevitable in order to ensure the repayment of South Korean debts. By ignoring the fact that the entire social system in South Korea had operated on the basis of everyone's economic participation, the IMF's cherished panacea of austerity, requiring massive bankruptcy and unemployment, turned out wholly and fundamentally disastrous.[40] As Philip Golub (1998) aptly described, "what was really being asked for was a radical overhaul of traditional methods of institutional working and economic and social balances that had allowed development and social cohesion to be combined".

In sum, the IMF could (and should) have paid much more careful attention to the particular local social contexts in which its economic restructuring programs would take effects (and side effects). The initial IMF programs for structural adjustment through high interest rates, increased taxation, decreased public spending, comprehensive corporate reforms, and unconstrained lay-offs may well be criticized in terms of stifling the social conditions for sustainable development. More critically, there is no denying that various potentially hazardous social conditions which had arisen under the particular development strategy of South Korea's developmental liberalism began to generate actual pains to grassroots South Koreans with the IMF programs working as a crucial catalyst.

7   RECASTING THE STATE: NEOLIBERAL SOCIAL DEMOCRACY AS A SOUTH KOREAN ALTERNATIVE?

It was a truly unique phenomenon that the state corporatist arrangement of *Nosajeongwiweonhoe* (Labor-Business-Government Committee) functioned to facilitate supposedly neoliberal economic reforms in South Korea. In European political history, state corporatism was the political mechanism for establishing and maintaining social democracy. For South Korean labor, great political significance could be attached to the fact that the tripartite committee allowed their incorporation into national politics on a stable basis for the first time in South Korean history. Kim Dae-Jung, as a globally known democracy fighter, may have attached a similar political significance to this fact. More importantly, the historical utility of the so-called neoliberal economic reforms may have differed between South Korea and Western social democracies.

What was being reworked and undone in South Korean reform was not a dysfunctional welfare economic system with bloated state engagement in private life, but a *degenerated developmental state system* with unproductive state intrusion in private economic activities. Above all, the state-*chaebol* financial nexus mediated by defunct banks and corrupt bureaucrats had been criticized by South Korean opposition politicians, intellectuals, workers, and other citizens since long before Westerners suddenly identified it as the supposed cause of the national economic crisis of 1997–1998. At least since the late 1980s, the state-endorsed bank financing of *chaebol*'s audacious business expansion had been an unquestionable failure. Thus, everyone agreed on the need to dismantle the financial linkages between the state and *chaebol*. South Koreans' mistake in this regard was that they adopted a skewed and partial remedy, namely, liberalization according to market principles. That is, following foreign and domestic neoliberal advice, they concentrated reform efforts in rescinding state policies and regulations, leaving *chaebol* free to overexpand into suicidal business projects and distort social and economic order through their monopolistic status. Furthermore, the rash opening of South Korean financial markets, which had been advised and sometimes coerced by the IMF and Western political leaders, allowed *chaebol* to finance their risky projects liberally with direct foreign borrowing. If neoliberal reforms had also mandated the organizational restructuring and disciplining of *chaebol*, even workers and unions would have welcomed them with open arms. Workers wanted their employers to remain economically viable. The IMF and neoliberal observers suddenly discovered that *chaebol*'s restructuring should be a core part of neoliberal reforms and that they should encourage the South Korean government to take decisive action for it, even without being bothered by supposed "market principles". Thus a capable and autonomous regulatory—if not developmental—state has been called in to deal with *chaebol*.[41]

Labor reform was an entirely different matter. The successive authoritarian developmentalist governments in South Korea had never treated labor as a dignified partner for national development and politics. The paradoxical consequence was that the political weakening of the authoritarian regimes immediately led to a revolt by indignant workers against political leadership and business. Particularly in the late 1980s and the early 1990s, organized labor was able to pressure employers to make many concessions with the softened political regime looking on. In this context, the imported neoliberal slogan of "labor market flexibility" sounded quite appealing to South Korean business. Corporate leaders managed to make successful efforts to persuade the Kim Young-Sam administration for legal changes necessary for a flexible labor market. Incidentally, the Kim regime wanted not only a flexible labor market but also a politically contained working class. Neither was welcome on the part of workers and labor unions, that successfully fought back against his government's surprise attack to legalize labor market flexibility and political detainment of unions. Then, why did unions agree on liberal labor reform with the Kim Dae-Jung administration? It was because unions considered some labor reform indispensable for *chaebol* reform, particularly under this kind of national economic crisis. Basically, workers and unions were at best inimical to such neoliberal euphemisms as labor market flexibility, especially when it was virtually synonymous with the denial of their entitlement to work.

There was an unforeseen bonus from the consent of unions and workers to liberal labor reform. In the course of implementing labor reform, it became obvious that the macro-level tripartite compromise alone would not suffice in persuading workers actually to accept lay-offs, pay-cuts, and so forth. These concessions would mean nothing less than a free fall to the ground in the absence of any meaningful social relief programs. It did not require an ideological rebirth for notoriously conservative South Korean technocrats to accept the urgent need to establish a comprehensive and workable social relief system as a prerequisite for sustainable economic structural adjustment. Even neoliberal supervisors from the IMF and the World Bank began to encourage the South Korean government to prepare better social relief programs and expand public spending on them. Business leaders, even if not outspoken advocates for social security, saw the same rationale as far as new relief programs did not require immediate increases in corporate taxes.[42] However, the direct beneficiaries of the new relief programs—that is, unemployed/underemployed workers and other citizens under social displacement—were not impressed too much, because the inexperience, inefficiency, and even corruption of government offices and officials tended to prevent the new relief programs from generating meaningful effects. Nevertheless, social security needs and measures, as summarized under the concept of "social safety net", then constituted the very central political agenda for the first time in South Korean history. This political agenda had an obvious political constituency (i.e., underclass workers and disadvantaged neighbors) whose political power could no longer be ignored. Although it would not warrant the rise of a full-fledged *social policy state* within a short time, a crucial step was taken toward a long-term social democratic transition in South Korea.

An ironic repercussion of the inexperience, inefficiency, and corruption of bureaucracy in the provision of social relief was the rapid establishment of various civil society-based relief efforts. These civil efforts were provided by all types of voluntary and private organizations such as neighborhood groups, labor unions, religious institutions, welfare movement organizations, professional associations, unemployed self-help groups, student leagues, university organizations, intellectual associations, hometown associations, media, as well as individual families.[43] Many of these civilian relief programs did successfully assist unemployed and other devastated people in contrast to the largely ineffective public relief programs (e.g., *Sisa Journal*, 8 October 1998). Civilian social movement organizations also took lead in pressuring the government and the parliament to prepare better social relief programs as well as to implement stern measures for *chaebol* reform.[44] They also filed many *gongiksosong* (public interest suits) against *chaebol* and the government in order to protect the legal rights of grassroots citizens to basic economic justice.

On 8 November 1998, civil social movement organizations, labor unions, and other grassroots interest groups held the "People's Rally for Defending Survival Right, Dismantling *Chaebol*, and Opposing the IMF". At a press conference on 20 November 1998, these groups demanded ten important reforms to the Kim Dae-Jung administration: (1) an inquiry into the real cause of the economic crisis and the punishment of responsible persons; (2) the dismantling of *chaebol* and the resignation of dishonest and corrupt *chaebol* heads; (3) a revision of the IMF agreements and the writing-off of external debts; (4) the strengthening of the policies for women, job creation, and unemployment and the establishment of the social safety net; (5) the setting up of comprehensive anti-corruption measures; (6) the fixing of laws and institutions for media reform; (7) the improvement in fair taxation and realization of tax justice; (8) a reconsideration of large state public projects; (9) the execution of full-scale political reform; and (10) the upgrading of national competitiveness through governmental organizational reform (*The Hankyoreh*, 21 November 1998). In the long run, these civilian social movements, along with labor unions, would comprise the core sociopolitical force for sustainable democracy and progressive politics (Lee, C. 2016).[45]

The Kim Dae-Jung government openly tried to incorporate all these changes into its political doctrine for Jeigeonguk (the Second Foundation of the Nation) (*The Hankyoreh*, 14 August 1998; also see Choi, J. 1998). No one could dig out any coherent ideological or theoretical tenet in that doctrine. Kim Dae-Jung found himself swarmed by so many mutually contradictory historical necessities and thus was juggling them on a day-to-day basis. He kept making promises to bolster democracy, free market economy, a responsible and efficient state, welfare rights, industrial peace, civil society, human rights, and even globalism. His meetings with both neoliberal international financial supervisors and politicians and with European new left leaders were equally congenial. Regardless of Kim Dae-Jung's own political position, the social, political, and economic structures of South Korea were reshaping in every possible direction (except state socialism)—for instance, neoliberal, state mercantilist, social democratic, nationalist, and globalist.[46] The true ingenuity of Kim Dae-Jung—and of all South Koreans—should be proved by the skillful integration of all such contradictory historical necessities.[47]

8   CONCLUSION

This chapter has identified three major problems concerning the social devastations and confusions accompanying the "IMF crisis" as enmeshed with South Korea's developmental liberalism. During the Asian financial crises, South Koreans turned out to be the most severely damaged and frustrated people in Asia. This was accountable only by systematically analyzing the social consequences of the national financial meltdown and its neoliberal rescue measures in conjunction with the particular contextual conditions set by South Korea's developmental liberalism—namely, the developmental cooptation (or hallucination?) of all citizens, the neglect of a meaningful social security system based upon exaggerated familial responsibilities, and the state-business entrepreneurial merge at the cost of suppressed labor rights.

First, both material and psychological conditions for the renowned hard work of grassroots South Koreans were crumbling. Few could expect better income or maintain illusions about future material betterment when unemployment and bankruptcy began to leave them worried daily about food and shelter. In the past, even many of those South Koreans below the official poverty line used to classify themselves as middle class and remained optimistic about catching up with more affluent neighbors. Many of the poorer segments of society used to accept a competitive and unequal economic system, at least until they would finally have the opportunity to attain economic success through education, business, or even speculation. Since late 1997, the trials of dreadful everyday economic realities have been severely aggravated by the psychological distress emanating from unaccustomed expectations of a *worse tomorrow*. In persuading grassroots people to accept mass unemployment and poverty, the South Korean government could no longer replace immediate measures for material protection with empty propaganda for some affluent future. No sooner had South Koreans awakened from the hypnosis of future economic success than they fell into ever-deepening desperation and anger.

Second, South Koreans could not but realize the true costs of lacking a sound and comprehensive social safety net against mass unemployment and poverty. Under the slogan of "growth first, distribution later", their governments used to maintain an extremely conservative position concerning social welfare. Officials, whether in economic or welfare bureaucracy, had unequivocally viewed social welfare as unproductive. South Korean social citizenship consisted of (universalized access to) work, not of socially protected welfare. Even the growing political power of labor since the late 1980s failed to pressure the government to change its anti-welfarist orientation but instead forced many large business firms to implement various corporate welfare programs exclusively for their own employees. The family remained the only viable institution working for general welfare. It was only after the outbreak of the "IMF crisis" that the South Korean government came to understand the economic value of social security programs. After exhausting the abundant budget for irrational mega-size construction projects and highly questionable business subsidies, the government was no longer in a position to legitimately ask grassroots people to accept massive lay-offs—or, more fundamentally, an abrupt erosion of their developmental citizenship—as part of the structural adjustment program. In the meantime, all of the burdens of unemployment and poverty fell on individual families, so that widespread family dissolution was destined to threaten the essential fabric of this extremely *familialist* society (Chang, K. 2010a).[48]

Finally, the neoliberal ethos of a non-interventionist and non-authoritarian state was being defeated not only by politicians and bureaucrats who fed on state power but also by mutual suspicion on the part of business and labor. When the South Korean government tried to mobilize grassroots resources and energies for rapid industrialization and economic growth, it neither bothered to induce grassroots consent to unfavorable terms of economic exchange nor seriously persuaded business leaders to develop harmonious relationship with labor. Up until 1987, the military-*chaebol* alliance was politically invincible, and labor was simply disorganized. In 1998, *chaebol* heads (and numerous sympathetic bureaucrats) became extremely angry at Kim Dae-Jung for accepting labor as an equal political partner in the major decision-making process for economic restructuring. The landmark tripartite agreements among labor, business, and the government in early 1998 failed to have sufficient impact when business and labor had to take concrete steps in business offices and factories. Then Kim Dae-Jung's staff had to separately deal with (and inevitably lie to) labor and business, although the labor-business-government com-mittee would remain in formal existence. Lies, suspicion, and anger—instead of repentance and concession—tended to dominate the ongoing reform process. Once again, South Koreans (including both workers and employers), and foreign lenders, seemed to want decisive and determined, if not authoritarian, state leadership although their reasons may have dif-fered diametrically.

With all these complex predicaments, it did not take long before South Korea arose impressively in swiftly cleaning up the financial mess and sat-isfying IMF officials, Western political leaders, and potential investors through the adoption of quick reform actions. Has the most successful late industrializer of the post-WWII era become the most successful neo-liberal reformer?[49] Of course, at least within the South Korean context, Kim Dae-Jung's reform policy could be considered socially progressive in many aspects. The reduction of unemployment and the alleviation of pov-erty received no less emphasis than neoliberal economic restructuring in policy discussions. The pronouncements of Kim and his staff concerning labor, poverty, education, housing, and other social concerns closely resembled those of Western social democracies. At the same time, Kim did not hesitate to accept and implement those programs suggested by Western neoliberals as conservative reactions to their own social demo-cratic past. It still remains unclear whether these inconsistencies reflected his own indecisiveness or constituted a truly inventive doctrine for national development.

APPENDIX: "NOSAJEONGWIWEONHOE (LABOR-BUSINESS-GOVERNMENT COMMITTEE) CO-DECLARATION" OF 20 JANUARY 1998

1. The Government shall prepare the basis for sound economic devel-opment by sincerely accepting the responsibility for the current economic crisis and inspecting its causes thoroughly. In order to cope with the expected rapid increase of unemployment, the Government shall prepare a landmarking unemployment measure and a stabilization measure for workers' living including price stabi-lization, by the end of January and seek the measures for cutting the 1998 budget and reshuffling and reducing government organiza-tions by mid-February. Also, the Government shall prepare a master

plan for increasing corporate managerial transparency by the end of February, to include prohibiting the mutual payment guarantee between corporations, obliging the writing of integrated financial statements, etc. In addition, the Government shall make efforts to ensure the creativity and autonomy of corporate management and the basic labor rights of workers and to protect the living of low income strata by expanding social security measures.

2. Corporations shall pursue active structural adjustments and do their best to prevent indiscreet lay-offs and unfair labor practices in this process. Also, corporations shall take the lead for improving corporate managerial transparency, for instance, through the sincere disclosing of managerial information, and for the normalization of corporate management, for instance, through the improvement of corporate financial structures.

3. Labor unions shall do their best to improve productivity and quality for the resuscitation and competitiveness strengthening of corporations and, under urgent managerial causes, make strong efforts for the adjustment of wage and working hours in order to minimize unemployment.

4. Workers and employers shall try to maintain industrial peace by solving every problem through dialogue and compromise. Also, the Government shall strictly counter unlawful activities at industrial sites, which take advantage of the economic crisis.

5. We, *Nosajeongwiweonhoe* (Labor-Business-Government Committee) shall do our best to prepare environments for inviting overseas capital and, in consideration of the schedule of the provisional session of the National Parliament in February, reach a package settlement on the agendas agreed on and adopted by this committee as soon as possible through labor-business-government grand compromises.

CHAPTER 4

Developmental Citizenry Stranded: Jobless Economic Recovery

1   Introduction

A decade after what they called "the IMF crisis", South Koreans witnessed the neoliberal heartlands across the Atlantic Ocean fell prey to national financial meltdowns. The South Korean economy remained relatively unscathed by this sudden manifestation of neoliberal economic pandemonium, but the earlier social devastations from the Asian financial crises had barely been remedied for a large majority of ordinary South Koreans. On 19 December 2007, such protracted difficulties led South Korean voters to elect a neo-developmentalist candidate Lee Myung-Bak, mimicking Park Chung-Hee in political slogans and costumes, into presidency by a landslide margin. It became apparent by then that the supposedly emergency remedies for neoliberal reform during the financial crisis had become consolidated into the permanent structural conditions of the South Korean economy. Although they seemingly resuscitated their economy in a manner as impressive as their earlier industrial take-off, most South Koreans kept expressing increasing fatigue and hopelessness about their socioeconomic status. Where political progressivism failed to persuasively offer a post-neoliberal or post-developmental alternative in national economic management and public social protection, South Korean citizens—both aged and young ones—were desperately attracted to Lee's showy pledge of another developmentalist era.[1]

Chang K-S, *Developmental Liberalism in South Korea*,
International Political Economy Series,
https://doi.org/10.1007/978-3-030-14576-7_4

During the three pre-crisis decades, South Koreans had been enfranchised by the successive developmentalist governments with what I elsewhere conceptualized as *developmental citizenship* (Chang, K. 2012a, b). During that period, the South Korean developmental state managed to industrialize and expand the national economy at a pace that could economically integrate almost all economically motivated individuals. Its policy focus was to create jobs and improve incomes as rapidly as possible. However, South Koreans were denied comprehensive social security benefits that, in European welfare states, ensured "social citizenship" (T. H. Marshall 1964). South Koreans responded to this dynamic economic process by mobilizing private material and human resources for their own economic investment and advancement.

As explained in Chap. 3, the national financial crisis of 1997–1998 and the emergency rescue measures adopted in response, imposed in large part by the International Monetary Fund (IMF), dealt a fatal blow to this state-grassroots interactive developmentalism. As clearly shown in official statistics, labor shedding was the most crucial measure for rescuing South Korean firms, many of which were on the verge of bankruptcy. Even after the worst moments of the crisis were over, most major firms continued to undertake organizational and technological restructuring that involved significant reductions in employment, so as to reemerge as globally competitive leading exporters. The sustained economic growth in the new century buttressed by phenomenal increases in the exports of a handful of major *chaebol* conglomerates has not been accompanied by meaningful improvements in grassroots employment and livelihood. Instead, temporary and underpaid jobs have become normal, and on-the-job poverty has increased sharply. Income inequality has been increasing continuously, and even those under the conservatively set official poverty line have drastically increased in numbers and proportions. Such social polarization tends to worry major South Korean firms far less than before because they are not as much dependent upon domestic labor supplies now and because their ownership, if not their management, has been globalized at appalling speeds. Foreign corporate shareholders cannot but be happy with a situation where South Korea's economic growth is accounted for mostly by rapidly rising corporate income (as opposed to labor income).

The two arguably progressive governments under Kim Dae-Jung and Roh Moo-Hyun, respectively, tried to come to the rescue of grassroots South Koreans by implementing and strengthening various elements of the so-called social safety net. However, even after expanding social expenditure many years, South Korea's public budget for social security, not to mention direct social services, was far behind those of other advanced industrial societies. Income transfers through public welfare programs seemed to have only marginal effects on reducing inequality and poverty.

South Korea's organized labor, despite its international reputation for militant activism, has been surprisingly incompetent in resisting and redressing this proletarian crisis. As indicated in Chap. 3, their expressed willingness to cooperate with the government and business on the eve of the impending national economic crisis was only abused by the latter as a convenient pretext for unrestrained (neo)liberalization of labor markets, permitting massive layoffs and proliferating severely underpaid transitory employment across the economy. By contrast, pledges made by the government and business to provide workers with stable employment and reasonable livelihood and to undertake fundamental structural reforms in ownership and management have turned out to be permanent rain checks. Paradoxically, the rapid segmentation of labor markets between surviving regular employees in large *chaebol*-affiliated firms and public corporations (who constitute the core of union membership) and underpaid contractual and temporary workers (who constitute an overwhelming majority of the newly employed) has critically weakened the social sustainability of organized labor (Lee et al. 2017).

This chapter places an analytical focus on the immediate post-crisis decade as a critical period when the remedial government measures and adaptive corporate responses in neoliberal economic reform were ultimately congealed into the structural conditions of the newly appearing post-developmental economic system. This system has rapidly assimilated South Korea with postindustrial Western economies in such neoliberal conditions as pervasive "precariat" labor (Standing 2011) and even "deproletarianization" (Wacquant 2008).[2] While South Korea's post-crisis restructuring has spawned a new generation of underemployed young people largely comparable to Western precariat, their long-term socioeconomic prospect appears to be prone to a dismal possibility of becoming entirely disenfranchised from its mainstream capitalist economy.

2   EMPLOYMENT AS NATIONAL DEVELOPMENTAL
ENTITLEMENT

The economic and social calamities accompanying the national financial crisis of 1997–1998 paradoxically made South Koreans realize what kinds of social entitlements had been ensured for them during the previous few decades under the successive developmentalist governments. Apparently, such entitlements were not social security measures that would have stabilized living conditions in a volatile situation like the 1997 crisis. Whatever social programs of the state then existed failed to alleviate in any meaningful sense the material difficulties of ordinary South Koreans caused by the sudden and massive unemployment amid widespread corporate bankruptcies and turnovers. What came as a totally alien experience to most South Koreans was their sudden and irreparable exclusion from work. For almost three decades, almost all willing adults not only had been employed but also used to work more hours each week than most workers elsewhere in the world. All of a sudden, their willingness to work was no more respected by the market economy or the state.

South Koreans' entitlement to work had been a core element of the developmentalist rule of Park Chung-Hee and his political successors (Chang, K. 2012b), but it had not been legally codified as a political responsibility of the state. This reflected a fundamental difference of the capitalist developmental state from the socialist state, whose political constituency (i.e., the proletarian population) had a universal citizenship right to work. Nevertheless, the constant provision of abundant jobs and business opportunities through sustained economic growth was an undeclared responsibility of the South Korean developmental state that had only limited legitimacy from its historical origin and had to periodically turn to authoritarian measures for political control. In this respect, as a national case broadly in line with Therborn's (1986) argument, South Koreans' full employment reflected a conscious political negotiation between the authoritarian developmental state and its citizenry.

As shown in Table 4.1, the authoritarian developmental state may well have taken pride in guaranteeing its political constituencies with a de facto entitlement to work ever since the onset of industrialization—as compared to citizens' welfare entitlements in Western social democracies. The unemployment rate fell drastically from 8.1 percent to 2.6 percent during the 1963–1997 period, whereas the total number of those employed nearly tripled simultaneously. Most of the new jobs were of course created in the

Table 4.1 The size and sectoral composition of employment and the unemployment rate, 1963–1997

	Total number of employed persons (1000)	By sector (%)			Unemployment rate (%)
		Agriculture/ fishery	Manufacture/ mining	Services	
1963	7563	63.0	8.7	28.3	8.1
1970	9617	50.4	14.3	35.3	4.4
1980	13,683	34.0	22.5	43.5	5.2
1990	18,085	17.9	27.6	54.4	2.4
1997	21,048	11.0	21.4	67.6	2.6

Source: NSO (1988), *Fifth Years' Economic and Social Change Seen through Statistics*, p. 97

manufacturing and service industries, so that the proportion of rural population precipitously declined. At least on the economic front, one of the most rapid urbanizations in human history coupled with an explosive population growth ensuing from the post-Korean War baby boom was successfully managed by a political regime driven by single-minded developmentalism.

Although South Koreans—middle class citizens in particular—never stopped politically challenging the historical illegitimacy and undemocratic governance of the military-led state, they nonetheless positively responded to the developmental initiative of the same political regime. They did not bother to criticize the developmentalist bias of the state, neglecting and sacrificing social welfare. They even allocated most of their own private material resources to individual developmental causes, including education, training, own business, real estate investment, and so forth.[3] The undisputed dependence of the South Korean economic success on rich human capital and abundant savings, among various other factors, was crucially conditioned upon ordinary citizens' active response to the developmentalist initiative of the state.

In almost every opinion poll on politics, South Koreans used to choose economic performance as the foremost responsibility of each incumbent or incoming government. They believed that the government can determine the state of their economic lives. As a result, the persisting negligence of social welfare objectives by the state did not worry South Korean citizens. Ruled by a political regime *satisficing* (cf. March and Simon 1958) with occasional political reminders of the necessity for preserving Confucian values of family support, South Korean citizens were equally conservative in social issues and clang to an entrepreneurially biased life.

3   Financial Crisis Structurally Resolved Through Proletarian Crisis: Neoliberal Developmental Statism as Long-Term Remedy

As the Asian financial crisis enveloped South Korea defying all predictions otherwise, the developmentalist nature of the South Korean state became unevenly dissipated between the grassroots population and business (*chaebol*). Saving the economy was considered tantamount to saving industrial and financial enterprises. And, as explained in Chap. 3, so many industrial and financial enterprises were rescued by dumping their employees under a structural adjustment program adopted by the newly sworn-in government of Kim Dae-Jung under the pressure from the IMF. Even South Korea's powerfully organized unions had to compromise on this asymmetrical arrangement. The vague hope that a large number of discharged workers would be reemployed and brought back into the national economy after some growth recovery has been belied even after the national economy returned to a stable growth path.

The economic miseries and desperate social responses of grassroots South Koreans in the immediate wake of the economic crisis have been documented in the previous chapter. Unfortunately, as detailed in a subsequent section of the current chapter, such miseries and responses have not disappeared but become routine aspects of life in the new century. To middle-age South Koreans who have unsuccessfully struggled to recover their pre-crisis employment status and young South Koreans who have been denied regular employment opportunities from the beginning of their career, the South Korean state is clearly an anti-proletarian, neoliberal defector.

Ironically, this neoliberal defection of the state in the realm of labor policy is very much an integral element of its reinstated developmentalism focused on export industry and finance. The Kim Dae-Jung government wanted to ensure the survival of most of South Korea's major export firms, which in turn required the survival of the financial institutions with near-defunct or practically defunct loans to these firms. Furthermore, the government realized that the un(der)developed industry of finance was a crucial pitfall of the South Korean economy and decided to aggressively promote its international competitiveness (mainly against would-be foreign rivals in the domestic financial market). Thereby was a new developmental statist project initiated in an industry whose underdevelopment was a paradoxical outcome of decades of developmental statism (Kong, T. 2000; see Chap. 5). The so-called structural adjustments of export firms and banks involved radical changes in labor relations (including, of course, massive and continual layoffs) as well as organizational transitions in ownership and management.

As an ultimate public guarantee for this simultaneously neoliberal and developmental project, the government devised a scheme called *gongjeok-jageum* (public funds).[4] Under this scheme, state funds would be poured into designated banks, firms, and projects alongside pre-targeted processes of structural adjustment, in most cases, entailing massive layoffs under the rubric of "labor market flexibility". (Many may recall South Korea in the 1970s when Park Chung-Hee's developmental state dealt with business and labor in a very similarly discriminatory manner.) In addition, the public funds helped to finance aggressive technological restructuring that enabled industries to radically downsize the current workforce and minimize new demands for labor. Post-crisis industrial restructuring clearly implied "jobless economic development".

Interestingly, but not surprisingly, the IMF and other major representatives of global finance soon agreed on this ostensibly developmental initiative of the South Korean government. It was not surprising because large shares of major South Korean corporations and banks had already been sold off to foreign investors at IMF-set bargain sale terms (in an environment of plummeting nominal prices of stocks, depreciating exchange rates, and shock-therapy high interest rates). As new major stakeholders of numerous South Korean manufacturing firms and banks (see Table 4.2), global financial institutions and investors have been favorably inclined to the reinstated proactive industrial policy of the South Korean state, which is financially buttressed by tax money to be collected from ordinary South Korean citizens. For the same reason, they have not limited praise for the neoliberal side of the government's policy that would ensure sustained increases in corporate profits at the expense of suppressed labor incomes.

As revealed in Table 4.3, the developmental-cum-neoliberal policy of the South Korean government has been remarkably successful to the business community which now consists of both domestic and global capital. It is nothing but startling that the spectacular growth of corporate incomes

Table 4.2   Foreigner shareholding in major South Korean companies (2006 end; unit: %)

Company	Share by the biggest holder (A)	Restriction on foreign ownership (Reason)	Share by foreigner (B)	Difference (B–A)
1 Samsung Electronics	15.94		47.24	31.4
2 POSCO	4.74		59.34	54.6
3 KB	5.46		84.32	78.86
4 KE	53.89	40 (public)	75.48 (30.2)	–23.69
5 Shinhan Financial	9.06		60.96	51.9
6 Woori Financial	77.97		9.95	–68.02
7 SK Telecom	23.10	49 (communication)	100.00 (49)	25.9
8 Hyundai Motors	26.11		41.86	15.75
9 Hynix	9.16		20.19	11.03
10 Hyundai Heavy Machinery	23.27		22.32	–0.95
11 LG Philips	70.78		50.53	N/A
12 KT	7.99	49 (communication)	97.40 (47.7)	39.71
13 SK	15.65		45.27	29.62
14 Hana Financial Holdings	9.62		80.64	71.02
15 Shinsegae	29.61		42.85	13.24
16 Lotte Shopping	68.89		21.83	–47.05
17 Korea Exchange Bank	64.62		80.37	N/A
18 LG Electronics	34.82		35.53	0.71
19 KT&G	10.33		54.08	43.75
20 Samsung Fire Insurance	18.44		53.77	35.33
21 Industrial Bank of Korea	57.69		21.04	–36.65
22 LG Card	22.93		1.39	–21.54
23 S-Oil	35.23		48.66	N/A
24 SK Networks	40.59	49 (communication)	2.09 (0.01)	–40.58
25 Hyundai Mobis	33.49		45.35	11.86
26 Daewoo Shipbuilding	31.26		34.07	2.81
27 Daewoo Construction	32.54		11.78	–20.76

(continued)

Table 4.2 (continued)

Company	Share by the biggest holder (A)	Restriction on foreign ownership (Reason)	Share by foreigner (B)	Difference (B–A)
28 NHN	10.47		56.82	46.35
29 Doosan Heavy Machinery	41.39		20.22	–21.17
30 LG	49.61		30.14	–19.47

Note: Share by foreigners was counted as of 30 March 2007

Source: *Herald Business*, 23 April 2007

Table 4.3 Individual versus corporate disposable income growth (unit: %)

	1980–1989	1990–1996	2000–2003
Economic growth	8.7	7.9	5.6
Individuals	9.9	6.6	0.3
Corporations	6.1	4.3	62.6

Source: Yoon, Jin-Ho (2005, p. 115)

in the first few years of the new millennium had no positive impact whatsoever on worker incomes. According to a latest study based upon the Organisation for Economic Co-operation and Development (OECD) data, the share of labor income in the total income of South Korea's corporate sectors changed from 63.46 percent in 1995 to 60.64 percent in 2000, 59.27 percent in 2005, and 53.97 percent in 2010 (Joo, S. 2018). Among the 20 OECD member countries studied here, as of 2010, South Korea was at the bottom in this indicator of income distribution and remained far below the average of the studied 20 countries at 61.16.[5] In sum, the post-crisis South Korean economy seems to have fundamentally disenfranchised the working population whether they actually work or not. If the rapidly increasing income gap between different classes of wage workers is taken into account, the figures in this table indicate that a majority of the grassroots population have actually experienced income reductions.

4   THE END OF GROWTH-WITH-EQUITY:
BIPOLARIZATION OF SOUTH KOREA

More specifically, the neoliberal policy has fundamentally altered the qualitative nature of labor relations. Along with South Korea's rapid economic
recovery, the magnitude of unemployment did decrease substantially
(except for young people). However, most of the newly offered jobs have
been temporary contractual ones and thus do not assure stable living conditions. The so-called *bijeonggyujik* (non-regular position) has become a
norm in most of the private sectors, as shown in Fig. 4.1. Non-regular
workers emerged as subjects of multifold discrimination in job tenure,
wage level, and various welfare benefits. They have been offered only
about half the wages paid to regular workers and very few of the regular
workers' non-wage benefits, as shown, respectively, in Figs. 4.2 and 4.3.
An entirely new segment of the working class has emerged to be abused in
the process of South Korea's rapid economic recovery.

Under the mounting pressure from and criticism by workers and
would-be workers, the state stepped in to enact a law prohibiting discrimination based on employment status and requiring regularization of

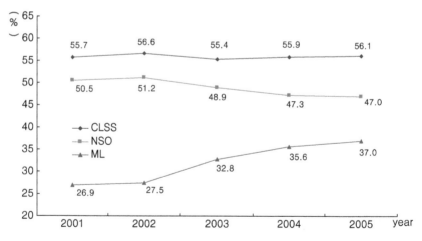

Fig. 4.1 Changes in the percentage of non-regular workers by year as estimated
by different organizations. (Notes: CLSS for the Center for Labor and Social
Studies (NGO); NSO for the National Statistical Office; ML for the Ministry of
Labor. Source: Created from data in Yoon, Jin-Ho, et al. (2005), Fig. 1)

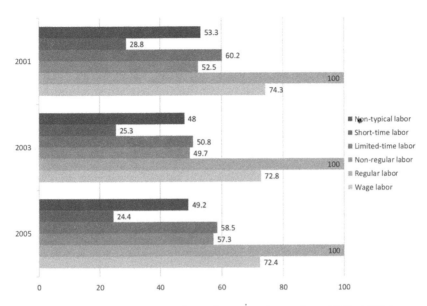

Fig. 4.2 Wage gap between regular and non-regular workers, 2001–2005 (wage of regular labor = 100). (Source: Created from data in *Kukinews* (www.kukinews. com), 22 July 2007)

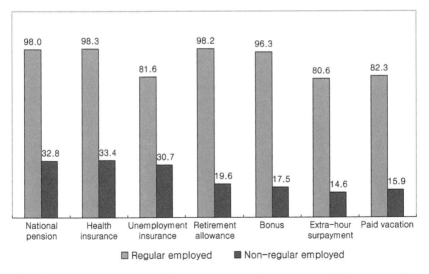

Fig. 4.3 Percentages benefitting from social insurances and fringe benefits. (Source: Created from data in Yoon, Jin-Ho et al. (2005), Fig. 4)

employment after two years of contractual work (Um, E. 2007). Its actual effect has been to immediately generalize under-two-year contractual employment. In 2007, the first year under this law, a majority of non-regular workers who had suffered from discriminatory treatment and been underpaid for about two years were made to leave their jobs (and, if they chose to, accept another two years of exploitation elsewhere).[6]

As temporary and underpaid jobs have become normal, poverty—even in absolute terms—is no more an exclusive outcome of joblessness. That is, rapidly increasing numbers of people have suffered from on-the-job poverty in income. According to a study by a government-affiliated research organization (Lee et al. 2006, p. 132), the proportion of employed people under the official poverty line (in terms of minimum livelihood income) increased from 5.7 percent in 1996 to 9.2 percent in 2000, declined slightly to 7.4 percent in 2003, but rose again to 8.8 percent in (the first two quarters of) 2006. The poverty rate was, of course, much higher among unemployed people (34.3 percent in 2000 and 31.9 percent in 2003) and slightly higher among economically inactive (i.e., dependent) people (19.8 percent in 2000 and 13.7 percent in 2003).

As shown in Table 4.4, the same study documented that the poverty rate (in terms of income below the official poverty line) for the entire population rose from 3.1 percent in 1996 to 8.2 percent in 2000 and further to 10.4 percent in 2003 and 11.6 percent in (the first two quarters of) 2006. One out of ten Koreans had to struggle below a very conservatively estimated level of minimum livelihood. In a related development, the Gini index in income jumped from only 0.2782 in 1996 to 0.3307 in 2000 and

Table 4.4 Gini index, poverty rate, and poverty gap ratio, 1996–2006

	Gini	Poverty rate		Poverty gap ratio	
		Policy poverty line (minimum livelihood income)	Relative poverty line (50% of median income)	Policy poverty line (minimum livelihood income)	Relative poverty line (50% of median income)
1996	0.2782	3.1	9.0	27.3	27.1
2000	0.3307	8.2	13.4	30.4	32.0
2003	0.3449	10.4	16.0	35.4	36.8
2006	0.3364	11.6	16.7	45.0	43.3

Note: 2006 covers the first and second quarters only

Source: Combined from figures in Lee Hyun-Ju et al. (2006, pp. 61–67)

remained at similar levels of 0.3449 in 2003 and 0.3364 in 2006. A return to the "growth-with-equity" model appeared well beyond sight. Even more disturbing were poverty gap ratios which indicated how much of the poverty line on average had to be additionally earned to escape poverty. The sharply accelerated increases in the ratio could not but be disheartening to any concerned observer of development in the country. As of 2006, those who were officially poor earned only 55 percent of the minimum livelihood income on average. It meant not only that the proportion of people under the poverty line arose sharply but also that such officially poor people were so much poorer then than before.

Whereas poor people saw their depth of poverty enlarging, rich people saw their income and wealth continually expanding. Rich households have got richer because of bloating corporate profits, soaring prices of corporate stocks, skyrocketing prices and rents of real estate, sustained interest rates in diversified banking, and so on. Consequently, the gap between rich and poor as measured by the inter-class ratio of household incomes has been widening rampantly. In each year's first quarter, according to the official surveys of the National Statistical Office (2018b), the poorest quintile of households earned on average (in ten thousand won) 79 in 2003, 97 in 2008, 129 in 2013, and 129 in 2018, whereas the richest quintile earned on average 511 (6.47 times more than the poorest quintile) in 2003, 703 (7.25 times) in 2008, 832 (6.45 times) in 2013, and 1015 (7.87 times) in 2018. Income inequality tends to keep worsening rapidly despite occasional minor fluctuations.

5   DIVIDED-AND-RULED: THE DILEMMA OF ORGANIZED LABOR

Amid all these symptoms of a proletarian crisis, how could South Korea's militant labor unions become so dormant? Where has their globally famous social and political activism gone? As earlier explained in Chap. 3, national union leaders sat down with government officials and business representatives in the winter of 1997–1998 in order to discuss emergency measures for overcoming the impending national financial crisis. After stormy debates, two national unions agreed to structural adjustments of corporate management and labor relations in broad terms. The fact that labor leaders publicly spoke of "cooperation" with the government and business under national attention was soon exaggerated as reflecting their consent to liberal layoffs, not to mention "the adjustment of wage and working hours" specified in the tripartite co-declaration. What were verbally offered to labor in return by the government and business turned out to be permanent rain checks as documented in the preceding sections of this chapter. Labor union leaders quite naturally refused further consultations for cooperation in the following years, but the critical moments were already over. Their half-voluntary loss of sociopolitical momentum for organized activism soon became a fatal source of ordinary citizens' indifference to organized labor causes. The election of a handful of labor leaders into the national parliament, for the first time in South Korea's political history, could not change the stalemate because the voters regarded it more as a symbolic political development than as a qualitative political transition.

The economic (and demographic) consequence of labor unions' compromise has been even more devastating to organized labor causes. In a widely publicized labor dispute of 2007, (regular) workers of Hyundai Motors tried to appeal to public sympathy by providing details of their working and living conditions on the web. The majority of public responses, however, were rather extremely hostile. The working and living conditions that Hyundai Motors workers complained about became the object of jealousy for young netizens, most of whom may have been frustrated by underpaid and unstable jobs offered in *flexible* labor markets.[7] Such unsympathetic sentiments of the supposed class allies may not have been unrelated to the immediate compromise of Hyundai Motors workers with their employer. Ordinary members of the organized labor force, most of whom are regular employees of large *chaebol* companies or public corporations, have suddenly joined the rank of the "labor aristocracy" in the judgment of young netizens (and, in fact, the general public).[8]

The neoliberal labor regime has successfully incapacitated organized labor's public legitimacy. In a national economy with structurally segmented labor markets, labor activism is too easily portrayed as egoism. Two decades after the economic crisis now, and two decades after organized labor's inefficacious reaction to it, South Korean labor unions find themselves paradoxically surrounded by critics within the proletarian population. The latter's sentimental defection and/or economic disarticulation implies unions' lack of reproducible social constituencies. That is, the pervasiveness of "non-regular" employment in most industries (as well as the relocation of industrial jobs overseas) has made labor activism even a demographically abortive project. It is not coincidental that national and industrial labor unions are now investing their entire energy and resources to assist non-regular workers' struggle against opportunistic employers and the ambivalent or intentionally conservative state.[9]

Another challenge comes from an abrupt bloating of petty service industry based upon self-employment (*jayeongeop*). Among advanced industrial countries, South Korea shows an exceptionally high proportion of self-employed persons among all working population—namely, 25.4 percent in 2018, as compared to 6.3 percent in the United States, 8.3 percent in Canada, 9.8 percent in Sweden, 10.2 percent in Germany, 10.4 percent in Japan, 11.6 percent in France, 15.4 percent in the United Kingdom, and, for well-known reasons, 23.2 percent in Italy (*Labor Today*, 29 December 2018). The heavy presence of self-employed service traders in the South Korean economy is nothing unprecedented, but their aggregate size in employment grew drastically in the late 1990s and early 2000s amid the massive labor reshuffling accompanying the national financial crisis. No matter how small their business scales remain, these entrepreneurial members of the South Korean economy often converge with large corporate interests in their perception about general socioeconomic conditions and desirable policy directions. In fact, their increasing reliance on temporary, daily, and/or part-time workers—due to the fact that their family sizes are already small, often with their children remaining in school, military, or other jobs—has induced them to become increasingly intolerant of the recent reform of labor market conditions such as legal minimum wage, maximum working hours, and so on (*Hankook Ilbo*, 21 December 2018).[10] This has put not only organized labor but also the currently incumbent Moon Jae-In government in a catch-22 situation, from which no easy exit is foreseen.

CHAPTER 5

Financialization of Poverty: Consumer Credit Instead of Social Wage?

1 INTRODUCTION

Behind the rosy pictures of the South Korean economy as an internationally conspicuous case of prompt recovery from both the Asian financial
crisis in the late 1990s and the latest global financial crisis a decade later,
ordinary South Koreans in rapidly growing numbers are confronted with
their own financial crises, which often force them to react in extreme manners, including suicides and familial killings "for economic reasons".
Among society-shattering incidents,

> A forty-one year-old housewife, who had experienced debt-caused liveli-
> hood suffering (*saenghwalgo*), was found dead together with three daugh-
> ters... Bak told police, "As I returned home at dawn after the night shift,
> there was a memo on the dining table, 'Do not open the room door, and
> report first to 112 (the police number). I am sorry.', and I entered the room
> by unlocking the locked door with a key to find the wife and daughters, all
> four, were dead"... Police is investigating the precise circumstance of the
> case, assuming that Mr. Bak's wife, saddened about the livelihood suffering,
> killed the daughters first and then herself. It is revealed that, although this
> couple divorced due to Mr. Bak's credit card debt of sixty million won
> (about sixty thousand US dollars) and yet lived together in a monthly rental
> apartment, they could not overcome the serious economic difficulty. Police
> noted, "Mr. Bak bought a house but lost his job during the financial crisis
> (*oehwanwigi*), so his debt swelled; although he got another job afterwards,

© The Author(s) 2019
Chang K-S, *Developmental Liberalism in South Korea*,
International Political Economy Series,
https://doi.org/10.1007/978-3-030-14576-7_5

he could not cope with the increasing debt" (*The Hankyoreh*, 17 January 2010).

'The tragedy of father and daughter' – a father killed his college student daughter who worked as hostess at a pleasure bar. It was an atrocious private usurer that drove them to death. Lee (23, female), a college student in Seoul, borrowed three million won (about three thousand dollars) from a financial lending agency run by Kim (30) in March 2007 in order to prepare her tuition. Afterwards, Lee could not repay the debt to which an interest rate of 20 percent for three months was applied, and her debt snowballed to fifteen million won. This was because the lender imposed an unfair loan scheme of *ggeokgi* by which, if the debtor did not repay a certain amount everyday, the sum of the principal and the interest was taken as a new loan. As Lee could not resist Kim's threat, she had to get a job at a pleasure bar from last April. However, Kim colluded with the pleasure bar to extort the eighteen million won Lee earned through prostitution. At the same time, Kim was still urging Lee to repay the debt. At last, Kim visited Lee's father (52) and told that Lee used the private loan and that she was working at a pleasure bar. Lee's father, unable to overcome the anger and shock at his daughter whom he had sent to college despite the destitute livelihood, killed her daughter at his home in Samjeondong, Seoul in November last year, and strangled himself two days later near a reservoir in Pyeongtaek, Gyeonggido. (*Kukmin Daily*, 9 April 2009)

South Koreans' poverty has increasingly been manifested in terms of financial entrapment ensuing from heavy personal indebtedness to banks, family members and friends, and, worst of all, private usurers. That is, post-crisis South Korea has found itself in a constantly worsening process of *financialization of poverty* (Chang, K. 2010c).[1] In a paradoxical development, South Korea's emergency measures for escaping the Asian financial crisis of 1997–1998 have ended up transplanting the financial trouble from banks and industrial enterprises to ordinary households and individuals. This is another, increasingly crucial, component of the so-called financialization trend in the contemporary world political economy.[2]

During the Asian financial crisis, the unprecedented economic calamity even forced South Korea's defiant labor unions to agree to a tripartite pact (with business and the government), under which an across-the-board dismissal of workers would ensue, however, without the fairly shared sacrifices and concessions on the part of the country's economically dominant business conglomerates (*chaebol*) and their politico-administrative allies.[3]

A majority of those who became unemployed and underemployed then have not been rehabilitated into stable regular employment in formal sectors (see Chap. 4). The industrial community immediately and effectively embarked on the next stages of restructuring—massively relocating labor-dependent industrial operations offshore (to China, Vietnam, etc.) for cost reduction and aggressively concentrating in automated high-tech sectors for global competitiveness. While such restructuring has been an enormous success, even enabling many South Korean firms to appear more profitable than their Japanese rivals, it has made the South Korean populace structurally disenfranchised from the mainstream economy in staggering numbers and proportions. On the other hand, the radical international liberalization of the country's capital markets has allowed Western financial capital (not Western industrial capital) to become major—not infrequently, majority—shareholders of lucrative South Korean firms and banks, blurring the national identity of the economy. The rapid thinning of the popular basis of the South Korean economy has been matched with the drastic emergence of global financial capital at its center stage.

In a rather ironic twist of the political economic circumstance, the South Korean government's obsession with a new industrial policy of helping to establish internationally competitive financial enterprises (that would hopefully prevent the country from being abused by global finance again) has made un(der)employed South Koreans and their familial dependents reconceived as patrons for the fledgling yet sizable private financial industries. In particular, the frenzied drive for market expansion by commercial banks, credit card companies, various types of non-bank financial firms, as well as private money lenders, under the tacit endorsement of the government, has easily turned the world's once most earnest savers into some of the world's heaviest debtors within a decade of the new century.

In a sense, the country's working class has been transformed into a new type of social class that is characterized by economic and social subordination to the increasingly financialized ruling class interests through worsening debt services in the process of securing various means of social reproduction. The rich segments of the South Korean economy and society tend to form class relations with their poor counterparts more and more in terms of *financial manipulation and/or monopolization of marketized access to means of social reproduction*—housing being a particularly pertinent issue. Financial indebtedness has become a generic class trait of a rapidly increasing proportion of the economically precarious or surplus population who are frequently or chronically deprived of even very basic means of social reproduction. Un(der)employment, indebtedness, and social reproduction crisis (such as involuntary singlehood, divorce and separation, low or none fertility, and suicide, all at scandalously serious levels) are structurally intermingled class affairs.[4]

Apparently, the South Korean government has lacked any intention to directly rescue financially troubled households and individuals in a comparable manner to its earlier rescue of financially troubled industrial enterprises and banks during the national economic crisis of 1997–1998. Instead, it has been busy inventing various financial schemes for maintaining them responsibly liable for their debts—a posture closely reminiscent of the Washington Consensus by the global creditor nations and banks as to their client debtor nations in the global South. The South Korean state's renewed intervention in finance—mostly in consumer banking this time—attests to its degeneration into what Susanne Soederberg (2014) dubs "the debtfare state", rather than its developmental regeneration with an expanded popular basis or its social democratic evolution into a financially inclusionary welfare state.

2   THE SOCIAL COSTS OF ECONOMIC CRISIS AND RECOVERY: NEOLIBERAL INTERLOCUTION

The Asian (and, for that matter, South Korean) financial crisis of 1997–1998 prompted South Korea to undertake, as an economic rescue measure, a paradigm shift in industrial development focusing on the growth of information and communications technology (ICT) and other new high-tech sectors domestically and the offshoring of assembly lines of existing export sectors. Behind the enviably swift (re)establishment of its global competitiveness in both lines of industrial sectors, two fundamentally risky phenomena have made the South Korean economy structurally vulnerable: first, radical abandonment or overseas relocation of industrial jobs and virtual annulment of stable regular employment in new hiring (under the rubric of "labor market flexibilization", or *nodongsijang yuyeonhwa*), and second, dependence on global finance for corporate financing and stock market sustenance to such a degree as to allow for foreigners' majority or near-majority ownership of many of the most profitable enterprises (see Chap. 4). An apparent delinking between economic growth (and corporate performance) and employment has thereafter manifested, making jobless (and sometimes job-reducing) economic growth a structural feature of the increasingly de-Koreanized national economy. During the period of global crisis between the third quarters of 2008 and 2009, for instance, Samsung Electronics and Hyundai Motors—South Korea's two flagship, but about half foreign-owned, industrial enterprises—recorded net profit increases of 18.9 percent and 67.4 percent, respectively, but their employment increased by only 0.26 percent and 3.09 percent, respectively.[5]

The loss or lack of stable decent jobs among increasing numbers of South Koreans (Kim, Y. 2014) has inevitably led to the stagnation and even decline of wage income across society (in a stark contrast to the phenomenally swelling corporate dividends and financial transaction profits accruing to foreign investors). Ever since the national and corporate financial turbulences settled down on the eve of the new century, the households' average disposable income has remained virtually frozen, while that of the corporations has explosively expanded. During the most conspicuous period of 2000–2003, as shown earlier in Table 4.3, the latter grew at 62.6 percent annually, but the former increased only at 0.3 percent annually (Yoon, J. 2005: 115). During the six years before the financial crisis (i.e., between 1990 and 1996), the corresponding rate was 6.6 percent for the households and 4.3 percent for the corporations. During and after the recent global financial crisis of 2008–2009, South Korea's gross domestic product (GDP) very briefly suffered a sharp dip in the fourth quarter of 2008 but easily recovered its growth vitality. However, the households' income kept stagnating ever since (Bank of Korea: www.bok.or.kr).

The lower strata of the proletariat were hit particularly hard. As shown in Fig. 5.1, even those earning less than the country's legal minimum wage—which itself has remained far below an internationally comparable level vis-à-vis per capita GDP—have constantly grown in number and proportion.[6] Given its relatively low rate of unemployment in (both domestically and internationally controversial) official statistics, the economic hardship mostly concerns the working poor, a high majority of whom are the so-called *bijeonggyujik* (non-regular employees), including temporary, part-time, dispatched, on-call, and home-based workers. As shown in Fig. 5.2, their recent earning on average amounts to a mere half of that of regular workers.

The structural disenfranchisement of an increasing proportion of ordinary citizens from the mainstream economy and their concomitant impoverishment are far from a unique phenomenon limited to South Koreans. Post-industrial societies in various regions have commonly been confronted

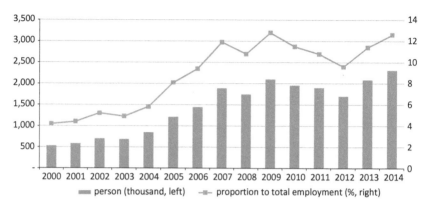

Fig. 5.1 Persons earning less than legal minimum wage. (Source: Created from data in Kim, Yu-seon (2014))

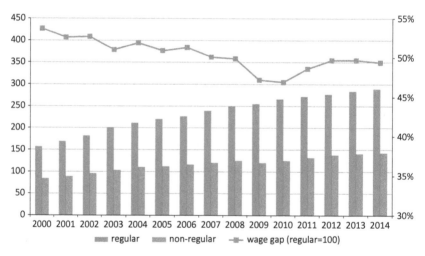

Fig. 5.2 Monthly wage by employment status (in 10,000 won). (Source: Created from data in Kim, Yu-seon (2014))

with similar dilemmas. Nonetheless, the social costs of the South Korean restructuring have been particularly heavy due to, among others, the following reasons.

First, the suddenness, rapidity, and intensity of South Korea's restructuring have been unparalleled even when compared with the recent experiences of other East Asian economies, not to mention the earlier experiences of Latin American economies (Chang, K. 1999b). On the eve of the so-called IMF crisis, both South Korean business and workers were still celebrating an economic boom fueled by sustained trade growth as well as debt-based (over)investment. Politically, the then incumbent president, Kim Young-Sam—a long-time political foe to Park Chung-Hee—wished to outperform Park developmentally by hastily adopting arbitrary measures for instant economic boosting. It took only one winter for the South Korean economy to diametrically turn around for unprecedented structural adjustments and financial austerities dictated by the International Monetary Fund (IMF) on behalf of global finance. The South Korean government would not remain simply dictated by outsiders. It immediately embarked on its own, mostly neoliberal, reforms such as politically coordinated labor reshuffling, administratively commanded industrial sectoral restructuring, unbound liberalization of capital markets, encouragement of overseas relocation or expansion of industrial production, and so forth. It took merely one year or so for the South Korean economy to reassume its vitality, however, of a fundamentally changed socioeconomic nature. Kim Dae-Jung, who had been elected into presidency as a troubleshooter in part thanks to the national financial crisis itself, ended up becoming earnestly praised by Wall Street, but harshly criticized as "the IMF's man in Seoul" by Bruce Cumings (1998). The country's developmental capitalism abruptly shed its socially inclusionary nature, leaving a major proportion of current and future citizens outside the mainstream industrial economy or the regular employment system (see Chaps. 3 and 4 for more details).

Second, as an inevitable trend, poverty has seriously intensified both in absolute and relative terms, but the notoriously ungenerous and underinstitutionalized social security system—even worrying the United Nations repeatedly—has failed to alleviate the inequalities and destitution meaningfully.[7] South Koreans' cherished "developmental citizenship" (Chang 2012a, b; see Chap. 4) based upon sustained full employment implicated a social governance principle diametrically opposite to the "decommodification of labor" in social democracy (Esping-Andersen 1990)—namely, livelihood entirely based upon secure market wage. According to Ku Inhoe's (2006) calculation, as of 2000, the country's Gini index changed, by taxes and pubic transfers, from 3.8 in market income only to 3.4 in disposable income. This indicated the most insignificant public correction to inequalities among all OECD countries. Moreover, as the country's

Continental European-style social security system used to be predicated on stable regular employment, the rapid and massive disappearance of regular jobs has only helped aggravate the hardships of the economically precarious citizens (see Chap. 4).[8] More specifically, the post-crisis structural adjustment lopsidedly focused upon "labor market flexibilization" has produced an additional impoverishment effect by nullifying, rather than strengthening, social security benefits to those workers who have been demoted or stuck to non-regular wage jobs and informal sector work. As shown in Table 5.1, a majority of non-regular employees have been omitted by work-based public social insurances (in pension, health, and unemployment) and excluded from company-level employee benefits (in retirement support, bonus, extra-time surpayment, and paid vacation). Many of them may have been covered by residence-based social insurances in pension and health, but a huge disadvantage has to be accepted by residence-based pensioners. A similar fate has to be shared by most youth as only a tiny minority of them have been admitted to regular permanent jobs. A majority of non-regular employees, whose number has kept bloating ever since the 1997–1998 financial crisis, have not been arranged to fairly participate in the public social insurances. Given these and other institutional problems in social security, the taxation and public transfers have helped very little to reduce income inequalities (as measured by the Gini coefficient) in South Korea. Moreover, the international comparison in this inequality index underestimates the country's adverse situation because the comprehensive and generous in-kind social services in the Western welfare states are not reflected here.

Table 5.1 Benefit rates in social insurances and employment conditions of regular versus non-regular workers (as of August 2014)

	Regular employees	*Non-regular employees*
National pension (work-based)	97.0	32.9
Health insurance (work-based)	98.9	38.3
(Un)employment insurance	85.1	38.0
Retirement support	99.5	30.7
Bonus	96.2	37.1
Extra-time surpayment	71.8	18.6
Paid vacation	90.0	24.4

Source: Adapted and translated from Kim, Yu-seon (2014)

3   Household Debt as Financialized Poverty

Even after struggling to financially survive by minimizing consumption, South Korean households in rapidly growing numbers and proportions have been entrapped into heavy indebtedness to banks, credit card companies, private usurers, family members and friends, and even the state. Within a decade since the Asian financial crisis of 1997–1998, the total debts of South Korean households nearly tripled (Park, C. 2009). In particular, the early 2000s saw South Korean household debt explode. Since the average household income has remained stagnant since the 1997–1998 crisis, the debt servicing capacity of South Korean households has rapidly deteriorated (Kim, S. 2011). The debt-versus-disposable annual income ratio has thereafter kept deteriorating, basically reaching a new historical high every year. Considering that this was also a period of remarkably fast post-crisis economic recovery, such an economic recovery seems to have been in part sustained by South Koreans' borrowing-based consumption.

The extent of South Korea's household indebtedness, vis-à-vis both disposable income and financial assets, now far surpasses those of most of developed countries—including the much troubled United States (Lee, J. 2009). In fact, while the recent global financial crisis forced American households to reduce debts, South Korean households have kept snow-balling debts. Not surprisingly, both domestic and overseas experts in increasing numbers have been warning that this is nothing less than a financial time bomb. It even keeps drawing global media attention (e.g., *The Economist* 2014). In fact, the unprecedentedly heavy indebtedness of South Korean households has already become a focal issue of international public concern both in economic and social dimensions. For instance, the OECD (Organisation for Economic Co-operation and Development) came to publish a special report in 2014 under the title of "Addressing High Household Debt in Korea" (Jones and Kim 2014) besides expressing a similar concern in its annual report on member countries.[9]

Not surprisingly, the poorest group has shown a particularly high debt-service burden. An earlier study of household indebtedness by income quintiles showed that the poorest quintile owed debt equal to nearly twice their annual income, whereas other quintiles managed to keep their debt close to their annual income (Yoo, K. 2009). For the poorest group, moreover, the quality of debt service has been particularly horrendous because they are often denied by regular banks and thus forced to rely on exploitative private usurers (comparable to American "loan sharks").

Shocking incidents in this regard are endlessly reported by the media. Also, according to an earlier survey, seven out of ten college students were indebted in one way or another and thus felt very much stressed about it (Yoo, K. 2009). Since they have been confronted with an extremely bleak future in the job market, such indebtedness would not be terminated easily even after their graduation.

South Koreans used to boast their status as some of the highest savers in the industrialized world until the 1997–1998 crisis.[10] However, it took slightly more than a decade for them to become some of the lowest savers in the world. In South Korea's political economic context where public savings are scanty for social security, the lack of private savings immediately means very little livelihood security. This constitutes a critical difference from the situation of some European societies with high household debt. For instance, many middle class citizens therein have aggressively borrowed for real estate investment.[11] Aside from the core reasons for private indebtedness, most West Europeans remain politically ensured beneficiaries of various social wages (welfare benefits). Moreover, along with more private borrowings, they have also increased private savings and other assets. In a historical context where even households and individuals in welfare states are increasing their savings to cope with recurrent economic uncertainties, South Koreans' severance from their timeworn savings culture (or, more precisely, savings capacity) cannot but be an ominous trend.

In class terms, the country's working class has been transformed into a new type of social class that is characterized by economic and social subordination to the increasingly financialized ruling class interests through worsening debt services in the process of securing basic means of social reproduction. (See Chap. 6 on the recent conditions of social reproduction in South Korea.) While the sustained growth of South Korean industrial enterprises has helped transform rural populations in many neighboring developing countries into industrial proletariat (see Chap. 8), they have domestically taken on increasingly financialized business interests on the basis of rapidly accumulated cash reserves. Likewise, upper-class households have managed their similarly growing private incomes mostly through financial schemes—oftentimes in tight coordination with real estate investment (Son, N. 2008). The rich segments of the South Korean economy and society tend to form class relations with their poor counterparts more and more in terms of *financial manipulation and/or monopolization of marketized access to means of social reproduction.*

Housing, as elsewhere (Soederberg 2014, Chap. 9), is a particularly pertinent matter in this regard. It is widely concurred that poor South Koreans' hardship in housing has not been a matter of insufficient supplies of housing anymore. Thanks to the sustained increases in housing supplies for several decades, if houses and apartments were equally distributed, no one would be without home ownership. However, according to South Korea's national census data (http://www.census.go.kr/mainView.do), the proportion of those living in their own homes had rather declined from 58.6 percent in 1980 to 48.9 percent in 1990, then very gradually increased to 54.2 percent in 2000, and remained unchanged until 2010. The proportion of all home owners, whether living in own homes or renting, has been slightly higher in this period. Rather naturally, housing prices, beyond Seoul and its vicinities, have stagnated recurrently as those without home ownership have turned either reluctant to purchase home at overly inflated prices or simply unable to buy one due to current and prospective financial difficulties. However, renting an apartment or house has become more and more difficult under a virtual collusion among multi-home owners, construction companies, financial firms, and even the government, for arbitrarily sustaining high housing prices against which rent levels are determined in conjunction with general interest rates.[12] Consequently, housing-related borrowings for rental, purchase, and investment (speculation) have accounted for the most significant part of South Korea's household debt. According to a local intellectual critic (Son, N. 2008), South Korea has become a "real estate class society".

It should be noted that the degree of commoditization of the basic means of social reproduction has been particularly high in South Korea due to the *developmental liberal* policy of aggressively mobilizing civilian *entrepreneurial* resources and motivations for social services in a sort of Korean-style welfare pluralism (see Chap. 2). Medicine, education, care, and a host of other essential social services are formally classified as non-profitable concerns, but market principles practically dominate the provision of these services. Among other reasons, the South Korean government's strategy of mobilizing private or civilian resources (and thereby minimizing public spending) in the provision of social services—a practice of the so-called welfare pluralism—has necessitated the de facto commercialization of the thereby delivered services as a sort of incentive to the civilian participants many of whom would otherwise be uninterested (see Chap. 2). In fact, the relationship between the social services providers and the state oftentimes appears very much analogous to that between industrial enterprises/entrepreneurs and the (developmental) state as business-wise considerations are fully taken into account in the entering, operation, and exit in various social services. Besides, the radically abrupt urbanization of South Korean society has almost completely divested South Koreans of traditional resources and relations for communal social services. Even their strong familialism (Chang, K. 2010a, 2018) is practically subordinated to the highly marketized provision of social services and thus involves financial exchanges—including the highly controversial familial debt underwriting—as the main platform for mutual support among family members.

Financial indebtedness has thereby become a generic class trait of a rapidly increasing proportion of the economically precarious or surplus population who are frequently or chronically deprived of even very basic means of social reproduction. Given a relative deficiency of state-provided social services (particularly in comparison to European welfare states), the shortage or lack of personal means of social reproduction has directly implied troubles and crises in various aspects of social reproduction. (Domestic) class relations have increasingly been molded around the means of social production, whereas class relations surrounding the means of economic production have rapidly been globalized amid drastic increases of overseas industrial investment and foreign labor influx. It is no coincidence that widespread un(der)employment and rampant indebtedness have almost instantaneously been accompanied by various symptoms of social reproduction crisis, such as involuntary singlehood, divorce and separation, low or none fertility, and suicide, all at scandalously serious levels (Chang, K. 2015, 2018; see Chap. 6).

It should be indicated that the recent spree of consumer borrowing has not been confined to those poor households whose basic livelihood cannot be met with own income. Given the "asset-based livelihood security system" (Kim, D. 2013) of a large proportion of ordinary households, the widespread employment predicament for middle-aged family breadwinners has induced many of them to explore, often on the basis of aggressive borrowings, alternative sources of income, ranging from self-employed small business to real estate investment (or speculation). This trend is quite ironic in that, during the earlier developmentalist era, the asset-based livelihood security system was responsible for South Korea's incomparably high level of household saving (Kim, D. 2013). About the rapid bloating of debt accruing to self-employed businesses, Kim, D. (2015: 73) offers a very incisive observation:

While the amount of household debt has already gone beyond 100 billion won, the amount of self-employment debt is also estimated to reach 45 billion won... Like the household debt, the self-employment debt has also rapidly increased as a result of the expansion of consumer finance after the Exchange crisis... [T]he increase of self-employment debt is closely linked with the unemployment problem. In other words, the government's active support for the self-employment founding as a sort of the employment policy resulted in the intensification of business competition and subsequently in the increase of business expenses and self-employment debt... [W]hile the support for self-employment had significant effects on overcoming the mass unemployment and delaying the economic crisis, it is now bringing about the new crisis of the increase in self-employment debt.

On the other hand, financial institutions of all sorts have aggressively offered various kinds of real estate mortgage loans to whoever bring basic documents of rights to housing, land, purchase assignment, rental contract, and so on (Kim, M. 2018). Thus, a certain part of South Korea's household indebtedness is correspondent to the recent trend observed even in Western Europe (Denmark in particular) in which many middle class citizens attempt to generate borrowing-based additional income from real estate investment, and so on (Andersen et al. 2012). While it is difficult to locate a clear fault line between financialized poverty and financialized economic activism, they certainly reflect different class situations.

4   A Developmentalist Inertia? Financialization of Poverty as Industrial Policy

Ordinary South Koreans' widespread and heavy indebtedness has been tantamount to financial firms' hugely aggrandized market for domestic consumer financing. As far as most individual borrowers pay interests and principals as scheduled, the financial sector sits on a bonanza-like situation. The South Korean government may have felt paradoxically satisfied, if only partially, with this situation because the tormenting experience of the 1997–1998 financial crisis led it to yearn for a globally competitive and sizable financial industry in the national economy. The swift establishment of globally viable consumer and investment banks began to be discussed as a new industrial policy of the still self-consciously developmental state of South Korea.[13] Remaining keen to overseeing the aggrandizement of the organizational sizes of South Korean banks, the South Korean government radically relaxed regulations over banking practices.[14] Most financial firms, ranging from major banks to specialized credit card companies to corporate usurers, have done everything to capitalize on such a relaxed regulatory environment as they have cunningly approached wage-deprived and socially unprotected South Koreans. The financial industries in South Korea have shown explosive yet unstable expansion since the 1997–1998 crisis.

A lending and borrowing spree began with the credit card industry during the early 2000s, which resulted in a massive number of credit defaulters pushing credit card companies near financial insolvency (Kim, S. 2011). As shown in Table 5.2, the total amount of credit card use (except card loans) kept doubling during the periods of 1999–2000 and 2000–2001. It peaked in 2002 at an amount which was nearly 10-fold that of 1996 and 50-fold that of 1990 (Jeong, C. 2005). South Koreans' frenzied use of credit cards was not always the outcome of their commodity

Table 5.2   Use of credit cards by year

	Total number of credit cards (1000)	Number of credit cards per economically active person	Number of credit card accepting places (1000)	Total amount of credit card use (except card loans) (100 million won)	One payments (100 million won)	Divided payments (100 million won)	Cash advances (100 million won)
1990	10,384	0.6	586	126,046	30,068	23,163	72,815
1991	12,099	0.6	766	133,671	41,331	24,610	67,730
1992	14,705	0.8	948	156,778	51,358	28,610	76,962
1993	19,401	1.0	1400	268,344	69,427	53,219	145,698
1994	25,314	1.2	2055	409,284	109,586	79,164	220,534
1995	33,278	1.6	2760	515,817	150,492	101,025	264,300
1996	41,113	1.9	3461	630,328	203,460	122,783	304,085
1997	45,705	2.1	4257	721,153	243,207	138,593	339,353
1998	42,017	2.0	4649	635,567	206,695	101,613	327,259
1999	38,993	1.8	6192	907,825	302,289	124,050	481,486
2000	57,881	2.6	8611	2,249,082	555,949	239,974	1,453,159
2001	89,330	4.0	12,627	4,433,675	1,283,527	473,554	2,676,594
2002	104,807	4.6	15,612	6,229,084	1,920,044	732,077	3,576,963
2003	95,517	4.1	16,949	4,805,436	1,906,716	504,157	2,374,563

Source: Adapted and translated from Jeong, Chan Woo (2005)

consumption. As the figures on cash advances show, they were relying on credit cards more often as a financial lending agency. As such, the credit card boom (or hidden jeopardy) could not be sustained too long. In 2003, the credit card-based financial bubble finally burst, inducing nearly 2 million people (or slightly more than six out of ten financial defaulters) to default due to their credit card debts. The card issuers were accordingly hit together. As of June 2003, the actual default rate among the specialized credit card companies reached 25.3 percent, accounting for 41.7 percent of their corporate assets! (Jeong, C. 2005). So the government stepped in to bail them out with the painful memory of 1997–1998 still clear.

The next stage was the housing loan scheme, which has involved a staggering proportion of South Korean families and individuals. In the decade of the 2000s, about 60 percent of all household loans were housing-related (Park, C. 2009). Housing prices have hiked in proportion to the increase of housing loans, and the higher housing prices in turn have allowed larger amounts of housing loans. This process has enriched some families and individuals and all banks, but critically damaged the interest of those who have yet to buy new homes (i.e., younger generations without rich parents). The South Korean bubble in the housing market coexisted with the American bubble since the mid-2000s. Thus, the South Korean government did everything to fend off the potential impact of the American subprime crisis on to the South Korean housing market (as well as the South Korean financial market) because it would automatically destabilize the national financial market as well.

A more recent stage involved non-bank financial firms (even including corporate and individual usurers), whose seductive advertisements began to inundate (cable) televisions and city streets.[15] While the bloating of housing loans helped to reduce the share of the so-called second financial sector until 2006, its market stake began abrupt expansion since 2007 to replace that of regular consumer banks which became increasingly weary of the debt servicing capacity of their reckless borrowers (Shyn, Y. 2008). While these are less honored or acceptable partners to the developmentalist government, their function of circulating credits, no matter how exploitatively, through South Korea's disadvantaged and alienated social groups has not been openly rejected.

Through, or despite, this perplexing process, South Korean banks kept reporting record-breaking earnings, mostly through interest-reaping, until the global financial crisis of 2008–2009. During the three years before the global financial crisis, for instance, the estimated total amount of interest payment by households increased by about 50 percent—namely, from 30.4 trillion won in 2005 to 46.7 trillion won in 2008 (Shyn, Y. 2008).[16] However, this was not exactly the kind of financial industrial performance the South Korean developmental state had envisaged in global economic competition. Above all, the capacity building for advanced investment banking has been eagerly anticipated. However, as shown in terms of the extremely low proportion of non-interest-based profits of South Korean banks, the country's financial industry has remained far behind those of Western countries in respect to investment banking capacity (*Hankook Ilbo*, 13 February 2007). Furthermore, even the hitherto existing function of lending to local industries (except for major *chaebol*-affiliated firms) has declined seriously in favor of safer consumer loans.

A more fundamental dilemma has ensued from the radically changed ownership structure of the formal banking sector. During the 1997–1998 crisis, a majority of South Korean banks were either nationalized or practically sold off to foreigners in the absence of any significant civilian group of investors interested in them. More specifically, commercially still viable banks were taken over by foreign investors at bargain sale prices, whereas independently unsustainable banks had to be nationalized by the emergency "public fund" (*gongjeokjageum*; http://www.pbfunds.go.kr/index.jsp). Thereafter, the actual owners of private banks—in particular, foreign shareholders who now constitute an overwhelming majority ownership of many of the supposedly South Korean banks—have felt just fine with the current business directions of their banks, especially because of the windfall dividends they reap (*Edaily*, 14 October 2008). In fact, the foreign financiers eagerly invited by the South Korean developmental state into the local banking industry prefer, for obvious reasons, less developmentally oriented banks. As a political economic consequence of the developmental statist control of finance, South Koreans' well-grounded distrust of local banks' governance and resulting avoidance of bank stocks in their investment portfolios have continued to leave most local banks majority-owned by foreign capital. From a neoliberal perspective, as far as foreign investors have remained comfortable with dividend-reaping, this situation has been alright with the South Korean government. However, from a developmental perspective, its industrial policy motivation sharply diverges from the dominant short-term interest of the actual (foreign) owners of South Korean banks.

5   CONSUMER CREDIT INSTEAD OF SOCIAL WAGE: INCLUSIONARY FINANCIAL CITIZENSHIP OR PERIPATETIC DEBTFARISM

The rampant financialization of the poverty of ordinary South Koreans has been no national secret even among political and technocratic circles. The policy programs presented by the two successive conservative—or supposedly neo-developmental (and neoliberal)—governments of Lee Myung-Bak (2008–2013) and Park Geun-Hye (2013–2017) included various forms of preferential access to finance for poor people and legal-economic rescue of financial defaulters.[17] For instance, individuals with low credit rating could apply for various small emergency livelihood loans arranged by the government; individuals suffering from usury loans could ask for publicly arranged replacement loans at reasonable interest rates; self-employed entrepreneurs without defaulted loans could apply for government-underwritten small business loans, and so forth. Considering their adamant neglect or rejection of workers' rights and social security, such finance-related social protection initiatives appeared quite remarkable. While the engaged banks and other types of lenders have participated in these programs under various forms of governmental underwriting, they still have had to accommodate or endure detailed bureaucratic intervention just like the pre-crisis developmental state period.

The effective programs for financial rescue and support are presented in Table 5.3. *Misogeumyung* (Miso Finance or Smile Microcredit) is the publicly promoted microfinance program designed to help those poor people who have been denied access to regular bank loans. It has been institutionally designed and financially organized by the central government in a manner highly reminiscent of the governmental practices in finance during the high developmental state era under Park Chung-Hee (www.smilemicrobank.or.kr).[18] Major industrial conglomerates (*chaebol*) and banks seem to have been practically ordered to donate huge amounts of seed money and/or operate microfinance programs. *Haetsallon* (Sunshine Loan), the specially allocated government-underwritten loans from *seomingeumyung* (finance for humble or ordinary people) firms such as various cooperatives, mutual funds, and savings banks, specifically assists individuals with low credit ratings and/or low income levels, self-employed persons (without own shops), and casual workers (www.sunshineloan.or.kr). *Huimangholssidaechul* (Hope Seed Loan) and its upgraded version *Saehuimangholssidaechul* (New Hope Seed Loan), offered by regular

Table 5.3 Government support in the four major preferential loan programs (billion KRW and number of participating persons in parentheses; as of November 2013)

Name and beginning of program	2009	2010	2011	2012	2013	Total
Miso Finance (July 2008)	61.2 (15,815)	114.4 (15,192)	310.7 (28,022)	274.6 (29,542)	241.8 (29,191)	1002.7 (117,762)
Sunshine Loan (July 2010)		1385.9 (152,731)	483.5 (56,097)	610.9 (71,130)	1783.0 (198,578)	4263.3 (478,536)
New Hope Seed Loan (November 2010)		267.7 (33,546)	1365.0 (156,550)	1987.4 (215,188)	1727.7 (172,239)	5347.8 (577,523)
Switch-Over Dream Loan (December 2008)	143.1 (14,936)	168.5 (16,569)	475.2 (46,164)	672.7 (62,734)	599.0 (55,125)	2058.5 (195,528)
Total	204.3 (30,751)	1936.5 (218,038)	2634.4 (286,833)	3545.6 (378,594)	4351.5 (455,133)	12672.3 (1,369,349)

Source: Compiled and translated from Financial Services Commission (2010a)

banks initially with governmental underwriting, are similar to *Haetsallon* but reflect the participating banks' substantial discretion. *Baggwodeurimlon* (Switch-Over Dream Loan) is designed to make borrowers of excess-interest loans eligible for transfer to lower-interest loans from public organizations. Also, for college students, *Deundeunhakjageumdaechul* (Feel Secure Study Expenses Loan) is the employment/income-pending repayment loan program for tuitions and living expenses.[19] Aside from these special loan programs, credit defaulters have been offered publicly arranged rescue programs including "pre-workout", "individual work-out", "debts adjustment", and "individual rehabilitation".[20]

While these programs themselves have often alienated poor people by demanding difficult requirements, they nevertheless constitute *a politically framed set of accesses to finance*. No doubt their function has consisted more in popularly legitimating the neoliberal economic order (under which the supposed beneficiaries of these protective financial programs have been sacrificed or alienated) than in seriously reforming the financial system itself. But bringing finance under the political epistemology of citizenship is nevertheless a highly interesting development. This is all the more so in the political economic context where South Koreans' much cherished "developmental citizenship" (that used to be sustained by their universal participation in national industrialization through almost full employment) has been eroding rapidly and irreparably (see Chaps. 3 and 4).

As pointed out above, South Korea's household debt has already become a focal issue of international public concern both in economic and social dimensions. The OECD has offered particularly strong concerns in recent years (Jones and Kim 2014). Its worry is not contained to macroeconomic risks but indicates potential threats to basic social cohesion. Then, do the above financial programs invented or improvised by the South Korean government duly address the international community's social concern? Do they attest to a meaningful transition in South Koreans' social citizenship from developmental to financial basis? That is, do ordinary South Koreans witness the establishment and expansion of a socially inclusionary financial citizenship?

It is still too early to answer these questions definitely, but there is sufficient evidence on the rise of a sort of *debtfare* regime broadly comparable to what Soederberg (2014) has observed in the United States (and Mexico). In both news media and academic research, South Korea's recent socioeconomic difficulties such as worsening inequalities (or bipolarities) in income and asset, widespread poverty, heavy household indebtedness, and family dissolutions are often compared to those of the United States. Likewise, the debtfarism of the United States as a postindustrial or neoliberal governance regime structurally enmeshed with similar social trends may be meaningfully examined for comparison with South Korea. South Korea and the United States do not diverge significantly in the following aspects. On the one hand, the state-driven expansion of consumer debt to industrially disenfranchised and underemployed people is both a macroeconomic measure for sustaining national economic vigor and a quasi-industrial policy for boosting the financial industry with a tacit administrative endorsement of what Soederberg (2014) considers "cannibalistic" business practices (Song, T. 2011). On the other hand, it also serves as a sociopolitical measure for making economically precarious or surplus population remain incorporated in the confines of market capitalism as disciplined *worker-consumer-borrower citizens.*

South Korea's assimilation with debtfare statism, however, has been a "peripatetic" and even accidental process in the wake of the 1997–1998 crisis.[21] In a great paradox, as mentioned above, this process has often been (mis)conceived as a developmental statist agenda, rather than as a (neo)liberal economic necessity. It is difficult to notice any single policy statement of the South Korean government that coherently addresses the rationale and long-term direction of its actually revealed engagement in the financial sectors. Nevertheless, South Korea's apparent convergence with the debtfarist United States can be a serious long-term trend, given the above-indicated similarities in socioeconomic conditions, the sustained global financial and institutional influences of American financial capitalism, and the dependently "reflexive" (Chang 2010b) relationship between the two countries by which South Korean technocrats and experts habitually adopt or follow American standards in economic and social modernization (called now *seonjinhwa*, meaning "becoming advanced" like the United States).

6   Conclusion

The Asian (and South Korean) financial crisis and the neoliberal economic restructuring measures to its rescue have made households replace industrial enterprises as the most indebted subject of the South Korean economy. (Conversely, industrial enterprises have replaced households as the core saving agency in the South Korean economy.) When industrial enterprises aggressively operated on the basis of excessive borrowings from state-controlled banks, their financial default was often prevented or pardoned for statist developmental purposes (Kong, T. 2000; Park, C. 2014). However, when families and individuals now have to survive on the basis of excessive borrowings from privatized (and often foreigner majority-owned) banks, their individual financial default hardly becomes a public concern. However, as the sheer number and proportion of such financial defaulters already account for a crucial part of the national economic population as well as the national political constituency, they collectively constitute a fundamental public concern.

This problem has been well acknowledged even by the ultra-conservative governments of Lee Myung-Bak and Park Geun-Hye, which thus devised and implemented various programs for financial access and rescue designed to promote social and economic integration for those sacrificed and alienated under the neoliberalized economic system. Since no one (even within the governments of Lee and Park) expected that these programs could fundamentally alleviate social and economic devastations ensuing from the labor-abandoning neoliberal system, they would remain, in the short run, mostly an apologetic political gesture in a turbulent economic era for a critical proportion of South Koreans. However, the American debtfare state seems to reveal that there exists a long-term possibility of reforming (or degenerating) the South Korean economy and society into the neoliberal direction that has already been taken even without a corresponding coherent policy paradigm.

Heavy household indebtedness is now a worldwide concern, which may well reflect the systemic nature of today's globally hegemonic financial capitalism. Ordinary South Koreans' hefty household debt does not fundamentally differentiate them from their contemporaries in other societies. But the specific process, speed, and weight by which they have turned from the world's most aggressively saving population to the world's most seriously indebted population are certainly unprecedented and unparalleled. To the extent that this economic calamity originated from the Asian financial crises, as shown in Fig. 5.3, South Koreans' financial dilemma

Fig. 5.3 Household debt, loans and debt securities in selected Asian countries and the United States. (Source: Created on the basis of data selected from International Monetary Fund (2018), "Household Debt, Loans and Debt Securities (Percent of GDP): All Data")

may have been shared with other Asian populations—Thailand in particular. (The Chinese situation differs in that Chinese households, as well as Chinese corporations, are simultaneously borrowing and saving at aggressive scales.) South Korea's industrial recovery from the crisis has dwarfed other Asian economies. Curiously, however, South Korea's household indebtedness has also overwhelmed other Asian societies as well as the United States, the long-time leader nation in this respect. This paradox is not accountable without closely examining South Korea's particular pre-crisis socioeconomic conditions, concrete conditions and measures for financial rescue, and complex adaptations and aspirations for post-crisis developmental regeneration.

Demographic Meltdown: Familial Structural Adjustments to the Post-Developmental Impasse

1   INTRODUCTION

South Koreans' hardship during and after the unprecedented economic crisis of the late 1990s has been manifested in terms of abruptly increased suicides that now put South Korea ahead of most other nations in the suicide rate. According to the World Health Organization (WHO), South Korea was ranked at the world's 10th (after Guyana, Sri Lanka, Mongolia, Kazakhstan, Côte d'Ivoire, Suriname, Equatorial Guinea, Lithuania, and Angola) in 2015 with an age-standardized suicide rate of 24.1 per 100,000 people (http://www.who.int/mental_health/prevention/suicide/estimates/en/).[1] Its crude suicide rate of 32.0 per 100,000 people was the world's third (after Sri Lanka and Lithuania) in 2015. South Koreans used to very curiously observe Japanese people's pervasive suicides but have somehow overtaken them in this unfortunate aspect of (late) modernity. (Japan was ranked at the world's 26th in 2015 with an age-adjusted suicide rate of 15.4.) Both public surveys and in-depth research have consistently revealed that "economic reasons" are the most crucial factor for this unexpected yet understandable sociodemographic trend.[2] Relatedly, suicides among youth and elderly, the two age groups hit particularly hard since the national financial crisis of the late 1990s, have kept increasing most seriously (Table 6.1).

Economic reasons have also been responsible for radical declines in marriage and fertility rates, with marriage reductions serving as the core

© The Author(s) 2019
Chang K-S, *Developmental Liberalism in South Korea*,
International Political Economy Series,
https://doi.org/10.1007/978-3-030-14576-7_6

Table 6.1 Proportion of those who felt suicidal urge and reasons for it

	Felt Suicidal urge (%)	Reasons for suicide urge (%)								
		Economic difficulty	Domestic conflict	Lonely	Illness, disabled	At work problem	Grade school advance	Love trouble	Friend conflict	Other
2014	6.8	37.4	14.0	12.7	11.1	7.8	5.6	5.4	1.6	4.5
2016	6.4	35.5	14.4	14.2	13.5	9.5	4.7	3.1	1.5	3.6
By gender										
Men	5.3	40.0	11.7	12.7	13.8	10.3	3.9	4.3	1.4	2.0
Women	7.5	32.4	16.2	15.3	13.3	9.0	5.3	2.3	1.5	4.7
By age										
13–19	5.7	10.6	11.9	11.1	3.0	1.0	48.1	0.4	9.6	4.3
20–29	7.9	26.6	9.7	14.3	9.5	25.9	4.7	2.4	0.9	6.0
30–39	6.5	32.8	17.6	17.0	4.4	14.3	–	6.0	1.5	6.5
40–49	6.4	45.5	20.1	12.3	10.2	5.4	–	3.5	0.7	2.4
50–59	6.6	46.8	15.2	14.8	14.9	5.0	–	1.8	0.8	0.7
60 and over	5.3	35.7	10.3	14.3	32.8	1.2	–	3.2	–	2.5

Source: National Statistical Office (2016), "The Result of the 2016 Social Survey (Family, Education, Health, Safety, Environment)", 15 November 2016

factor for birth diminutions (Oh and Choi 2012). South Korean society was rocked by the latest revelation of its fertility, practically at the world's lowest level—that is, total fertility rate (TFR) of 1.05 in 2017 (NSO 2018a). In spearheading minimum demographic reproduction, according to TFR figures of 2017 in *The World Factbook*, South Korea (1.26) was only behind Puerto Rico (1.22) and some of East Asia's industrialized neighbors such as Hong Kong (1.19), Taiwan (1.13), Macau (0.95), and Singapore (0.83).[3] Given that most of these ultra-low-fertility rivals have particular political uncertainties and socioecological conditions that discourage domestic childbirths (and encourage overseas childbirths), South Korea now stands virtually as the world's least reproduced non-city-state nation. In fact, South Korea's official final tally on the TFR of 2017 was 1.05, placing the country only behind Macau and Singapore in busted fertility. Demographic analysis has repeatedly shown that the immediate key factor for South Korea's fertility crisis is its young population's caution and hiatus about marriage (Oh and Choi 2012). The rises in men's and women's average ages at first marriage have been accelerated in conjunction with pervasive difficulties in employment and livelihood since the late 1990s.[4] The average age at first marriage has risen particularly precipitous for men from 28.01 (1992) to 29.07 (1999), 30.14 (2003), 31.11 (2007), 32.13 (2012), and 32.94 (2017). For women, it has risen from 25.01 (1993) to 26.02 (1998), 27.01 (2002), 28.09 (2007), 29.14 (2011), and 30.24 (2017). In these years, those who remain unmarried in their 30s and 40s have continued to rapidly increase. At the same time, divorces have also increased quite rapidly. Fast increases in extended or permanent singlehood and divorce also reflect economic difficulties (Chang, K. 2015). Late, foregone, and broken marriages all contribute to radical declines in fertility, whereas even married couples also opt for gradually less fertility despite their continuing rarity in permanent childlessness (Table 6.2).

Broadly speaking, marriage decline, low fertility, and suicide epidemic all point to a pervasive trend of social reproduction hiatus.[5] South Koreans in increasing numbers and with diverse backgrounds seem to have been losing interest in socially reproducing own and familial lives whether through spousal union, parental devotion, or personal resolve. The decisive impact of economic troubles on such avoidances of social reproduction may not be incomprehensible, but the intensity of such sociodemographic reactions cannot be readily clarified within conventional theoretical and empirical accounts. In fact, South Korea's

Table 6.2 Countries with the world's highest and lowest levels of total fertility rate in 2017

Rank	Country	TFR
1	Niger	6.49
2	Angola	6.16
3	Mali	6.01
4	Burundi	5.99
5	Somalia	5.80
219	South Korea	1.26 (1.05)
220	Puerto Rico	1.22
221	Hong Kong	1.19
222	Taiwan	1.13
223	Macau	0.95
224	Singapore	0.83

Note: South Korea's additional figure of 1.05 is its government's official final estimate

Source: *The World Factbook* (24 December 2018), compiled by the US Central Intelligence Agency

macroeconomic recovery from the financial crisis, albeit through massive removal and export of jobs, was as dramatic as its slippage into it.

The social failure of developmental industrial capitalism in the post-crisis era has intensified South Koreans' renowned strategic dependence on familial resources and sacrifices. In this context, family relationships could become and have become a normative conduit for a highly complicated set of social risks that arise in the abrupt neoliberal perversion of the country's developmental liberal system of political economy and social policy. South Koreans have tried to cope with this dilemma by carefully, if not always desperately, managing the effective scope, magnitude, and duration of family relationships. Increases in divorce and separation, delay and avoidance of marriage, and less or no fertility—all at historically unprecedented levels—are manifest symptoms of such familial adjustments to the post-developmental liberal context. Even innumerable instances of suicides, often preceded by deep pities about familial caregivers, or even sympathetic killings of familial dependents, can be understood in the same vein.

The demographic meltdown, as generated by South Koreans' pervasive efforts to pragmatically reshuffle the scope, magnitude, and duration of family relationships, is an ironic testament to the obstinate nature of *familial liberalism* that ordinary citizens have shared with the developmental liberal state, society, and capitalist economy. In a sense, it is the outcome of a sort of *self-imposed structural adjustment in social reproduction of family* by familial liberal individuals and families.

2   Developmental Liberalism, Familial Liberalism

As one of the core sociopolitical attributes of developmental liberalism (explained earlier in Chap. 2), familialization of welfare responsibilities has widely been indicated and documented in previous research (Chang, K. 1997, 2018). To the state's convenience, such practical duty has been rather easily accommodated by most South Koreans. Familialized welfare, however, does not necessarily imply that ordinary South Koreans have personally concentrated on augmenting the stability and quality of private life while entrusting their government with the developmental managerial functions for better material life. To the developmentalist government's joy (or ultimate worry), South Korean families themselves have commonly assumed a strong developmentalist orientation, under which familial resources have been aggressively mobilized and allocated for strategic (developmental) purposes such as education, skill training, own business, investment (particularly in real estate), and so on. The aggregate outcomes of such familial developmental purposes have been rather clearly documented in terms of formal statistics on the biggest share of family spending in formal education in the world, household indebtedness at one of the world's most serious levels, and so forth (Chang, K, 2010a; see Chap. 5).

This is not a widely shared systemic or cultural feature of the industrialized West that are characterized by fundamental cultural and institutional individualism (Beck and Beck-Gernsheim 2002). The institutional primacy of the family in education, housing, finance, work, and care in South Korea critically implies that it may be more *familial liberal* than individual liberal. In pervasively and endlessly manifested instances, it has been the family, rather than the individual, that has functioned as the basic unit of freedom and responsibility in South Koreans' practical world of material and social life. In fact, familial liberalism as practical policy line and popular social practice has been observed in a great number and variety of non-Western capitalist societies. Furthermore, as examined elsewhere (Chang, K. 2014a), most of post-socialist states have turned familial liberal through a series of system transition policies and incidents that have necessitated their citizens to organize work and welfare through familial self-help (Rajkai, ed. 2016).

Most recently, even typical individual liberal societies in the postindustrial era—in particular, the Unites States since the financial crisis of 2008—have increasingly assumed a familial liberal nature as their middle and poor classes have strived to secure work, housing, food, and care through familial support and dependence (Akers 2013).

It should be clarified that familial liberalism is not necessarily buttressed by as a consistent cultural tradition and/or a manifest sociopolitical ideology. More often, it is rather *situationally driven*—that is, necessitated under the imperative historical conditions such as a societal and/or political devastation (e.g., colonialism, invasion, war, etc.), a conservative national development/modernization strategy (as in many East Asian countries), a major national economic/financial crisis (as in South Korea and the United States recently), a wholesale systemic meltdown (as in Russia and Eastern Europe), and so forth. As these situations are characterized by the absence, breakdown, irrelevance, or discriminatory boundary of the public rules and resources for protecting ordinary citizens' material and social life, they are compelled to turn to familial relationships and resources for survival.

In South Korea, as private citizens' familial liberalism is coupled with the state's developmental liberalism—that is, developmentally propelled liberalism in social policy—many macro-developmental outcomes have been conveniently facilitated (Chang, K. 2010a, 2018). Such outcomes include minimized public welfare spending allowing maximum public investment and support for industrialization, heavy familial investment in education enabling effective human capital formation without financially burdening the state, resilient mobilization of familial finance and capital for self-employed business buffering industrial employment instabilities under rapid and recurrent industrial restructuring, and so forth (Chang et al. 2015). It is this developmental alliance between the developmental liberal state and familial liberal citizens that used to make South Koreans' familial liberalism particularly effective and staunch during the pre-crisis period.

These attributes of South Koreans' familial liberalism seem to have kept impressing Barack Obama greatly as he repeatedly mentioned, during his presidency, South Koreans' familial virtues in education, support, and work as worthy of emulation to ordinary Americans.[6] Obama's intention may not have been that Americans' familial efforts would help reduce the state's burden in materially supporting and socially protecting needy citizens, which was the focal position of Anglo-American neoliberal leaders such as Ronald Reagan and Margaret Thatcher in their well-known family value debate (Somerville 1992). Given the grave structural inequalities in income and the extremely conservative (laissez-faire) socioeconomic policy regime of the American state that he could not fundamentally rectify, Obama may have hopefully imagined that Americans' familial self-help efforts would critically help bolster present and future qualities of livelihood. It may have been the developmental nature of South Koreans' familialism that Obama somehow developed a keen interest in as he was not endowed with any convincing systematic theory or policy for pulling underclass Americans out of collective economic depression and despair.

However, South Koreans' familial liberalism has also worked to amplify various social and economic hazards incurring the state's developmental liberalism. Most problematically, South Koreans' propensity to aggressively use up familial resources for private developmental purposes (such as children's education and business) has often induced themselves to experience the risks and costs of macro-developmental crises in a critically aggravated, not mitigated, manner. Both the state and private families have held that the best welfare can be secured from maximum developmental success. Such developmental optimism—often indiscernible from developmental opportunism—has repeatedly been betrayed by the actual process of national development fraught with intense social inequalities (particularly between *chaebol* and laboring class) and chronic structural instabilities (due to recurrent industrial sectoral and technological restructuring, global financial vulnerability, etc.). The national financial crisis and accompanying neoliberal economic restructuring since the late 1990s came to radically amplify such risks of the developmental subscription or subordination of familial liberal South Koreans.

3   DEMOGRAPHIC SQUEEZE AS SELF-IMPOSED STRUCTURAL ADJUSTMENT IN SOCIAL REPRODUCTION

The swift overcoming of the national financial crisis of 1997–1998 spawned two mutually related social problems that have widely been described as crises themselves. They are, namely, "youth unemployment crisis" and "fertility crisis". The first problem is the employment predicament ensuing from the radical reshuffling (*jeongrihaego*) of the urban labor market during the financial crisis and the virtual generalization of "non-regular employment" (*bijeonggyujik*) in the subsequent years (see

Chap. 4 in this book). While not many of those fired or demoted during the financial crisis have been fully reinstated into their original jobs and positions, a majority of new entrants in the labor market (i.e., youth) have been confronted with a distressing prospect that they may have to lead life without ever attaining a regularly employed position in a stable economic sector. The second problem is a sort of national demographic meltdown repeatedly projected on the basis of shockingly radical trends of "ultra-low" fertility, practically normalized delay and avoidance of marriage, widespread divorces, literally epidemic suicides (often involving family killings), and so forth (Chang, K. 2015).

There is an increasing public awareness that the employment crisis is the main cause of the population crisis. The protracted difficulty of youth in attaining stable and reliable employment tends to leave them unmarriageable or marriage-averse, and the plummeting of the marriage rate has been the prime factor for the radically low rate in fertility. In this milieu, South Korean media have described the current generation of youth as *sampo sedae* (a generation of three give-ups—namely, dating, marriage, and procreation). This kind of economically caused fertility decline is all too a familiar phenomenon across the world, but South Korea is one of the particularly complicated and intensified instances.

The above-explained institutional primacy of family in South Korea's familial liberal development has necessitated family formation to become a socially complex and financially costly event. Marriage is a social contract involving, in effect, not only two engaged partners and their parents (usually providing various material and social means for marriage and home) but also the state, economy, and society that operate under the normalized contributions of family in education, housing, finance, work, and, not least importantly, care and protection. Family relationships become the moralized conduit for social and political pressure as to these functions. As spouse, parent, child-in-law, and sometimes grandchild-in-law, married persons should unavoidably carry out multifarious duties and functions that have been *familialized* in the service of the state, economy, and society. In order to deal with such duties and functions, family has become a complex organization that requires a strong material basis and a complicated internal order. It used to ideally consist of a faithful male breadwinner working on a stable long-term basis and a committed housewife fulfilling lifetime services for her husband, children, and parents-in-law (increasingly in addition to her own parents) and sometimes earning complementary income. This organizational composition of family is not particularly unique, but the scope, intensity, and duration of familial(ized) duties and functions have been extraordinary.

The post-crisis structural adjustments in the South Korean economy have widely removed stable long-term jobs and thereby liquidated men's current or prospective status as breadwinning familial patriarchs. However, the familialized duties and functions in education, housing, finance, work, and care have largely remained unreduced. In fact, the rapid reduction of regular employment in main industrial sectors has helped intensify such duties and functions of family by critically sapping both the public and corporate welfare benefits that have been the key components of South Korea's work-linked "conservative" welfare system modeled after Continental Europe (see Chap. 4). On the part of married women, this situation has implied a rapid normalization of their second or replacement income-earning duty. The rapid expansion of married women's "double shifts", however, has not been accompanied by any significant change in their husbands' notoriously prevalent absenteeism from household work (Chang, K. 2018). On the part of an unmarried woman, their marriage could imply an unprecedentedly contradictory combination of an unstably employed husband who nevertheless refuses to (or is unable to) strengthen his contribution to household work, an unreduced set of familial(ized) duties and functions that require her extensive commitment (on behalf of not only her family but also the state, economy, and society), and her own paid work in South Korean intensity.

In post-crisis South Korea, family relationships have become a normative conduit for a highly complicated set of social risks that arise in the abrupt neoliberal perversion of the developmental liberal system of political economy and social policy. Not surprisingly, most South Koreans have tried to cope with this dilemma by carefully managing the effective scope, magnitude, and duration of family relationships. Increases in divorce and separation, delay and avoidance of marriage, and less or no fertility—all at historically unprecedented levels—are manifest symptoms of such familial adjustments to the post-developmental liberal context that are clearly and repeatedly documented in demographic statistics (Chang, K. 2015).[7] Understandably, young women are known to be more proactive in effecting these changes as statistically evinced by trade-offs between their regular economic participation and marriage and fertility (Chung, S. 2010). But men nevertheless follow the trends as well (Chang and Song 2010).

Furthermore, even innumerable instances of suicides—often preceded by deep pities about familial caregivers or even sympathetic killings of familial dependents—can be understood in the same regard.[8] In local news media's coverage of suicides are particularly sensationalized what are often dubbed "family-accompanying suicides" (*gajokdongban jasal*). Numerous South Koreans, before attempting suicide, have taken the lives of their familial dependents. In particular, some of financially troubled parents with very young children seem to have felt that their self-killing would be an unthinkably irresponsible act if their children were left alive but helpless.[9] In another depressing trend, many aged persons, usually under abject poverty and/or chronic illness, have taken own lives in order to relieve their children of the indefinitely elongated filial duties in material support and illness care. At the same time, many other elders' suicides have been due to anger and frustration at their children's alleged betrayal and/or abuse. The rapid extension of South Koreans' life expectancy has been oddly matched with internationally conspicuous levels of old-age morbidity and poverty, which are rarely mitigated, particularly in the post-crisis period, by the deficient and defective social security measures or by pious children's care and support.[10] Under acute and protracted hardship, the supposed Korean virtue of familial solidarity has turned into a decisive factor for moralistic suicides and familial killings. This trend undoubtedly reflects the historically sustained norm of devoted familial support and care, but the state's developmentally propelled liberal policy of inducing various needs for social welfare to be taken up as private familial responsibilities (Chang et al. 2015) is another critical factor.

South Korea's demographic meltdown, as generated by its citizens' pervasive efforts to pragmatically reshuffle the scope, magnitude, and duration of family relationships, is the outcome of a sort of *self-imposed structural adjustment in social reproduction of family* by familial liberal individuals and families in the post-developmental liberal context. Increases in divorce and separation, delay and avoidance of marriage, less or no fertility, and even epidemical spread of suicides all attest to such strategic self-positioning of familial liberal citizens under the radical neoliberal perversion of the country's developmental liberalism. The desperately wished demographic renewal will take a complete systemic overhauling of both the country's dysfunctional familial liberal system of social reproduction and defunct developmental liberal system of political economy and social policy.

4   Pronatal Welfarism and Beyond

South Koreans' cautious reservedness about familial social reproduction is a clearly rational response to a historical situation where various socioeconomic risks of an abruptly neoliberalized developmental capitalism have been familialized. Collectively, however, such popularized timidity about family formation, sustenance, and/or expansion may add up to cause a national demographic meltdown, which is nothing but an unprecedented type of total socioeconomic crisis. The conventional working age population has already begun to taper down in size, and the entire national population is soon to begin to diminish indefinitely (Yeom, et al. 2010). In fact, academic and official predictions about national population shrinkage keep being revised in order to reflect annual fertility declines well beyond hypothesized paces. At the local level, numerous cities and rural counties have already been experiencing the abrupt size diminution and age/gender-compositional distortion of their respective populations (Lee, S. 2018). Both the state and society have turned extremely wary about such prospect of no tomorrow. Since the turn of the century, every new administration, whether conservative or progressive, has promoted a wide range of socioeconomic and cultural policies for promoting marriage, fertility, work-family balance, and so on. In fact, many of basic welfare state agendas—such as child allowance, paid parental leave, maternal health care, and even preferential access to housing—have ended up being finally advocated and fulfilled in consideration of their potential pronatal utilities (Byoun and Hwang 2018). The hitherto dubious effects of these pronatal welfare benefits do not necessarily induce the state and society to withdraw them accordingly.

Crisis-driven welfare promotion is nothing unusual in this "peripatetic" and/or "patchwork" (Goodman and Peng 1996) welfare system. In fact, as another critical instance, the national financial crisis in the late 1990s paradoxically triggered a major bolstering of the South Korean welfare system under the neoliberal rubric of "social safety net". It was neoliberal in that its purpose was to facilitate a hasty economic restructuring by which ordinary workers would almost randomly confront layoffs, demotions, and pay-cuts (see Chap. 3). The cost of the social safety net was to be borne, through taxation, by the public citizenry, whereas its ultimate benefit would be harvested by those corporate and financial elites whose business interests were sheltered and augmented by workers' sacrifice. It was for this reason that even the International Monetary Fund (IMF), on behalf of global finance, urged the South Korean government to promptly revamp the social security system, particularly in respect to unemployment, (re)training, and other labor market matters. By then, as the very core part of the so-called IMF conditionalities for debt renewal and emergency lending, global finance was finally assured their unbridled access to South Korean industries (see Chap. 4). Under both domestic progressive demands and global neoliberal urges, the South Korean welfare system was substantially refurbished with its functionality of social safety net strengthened greatly.

However, South Korea's impending demographic meltdown as caused by familialized risks of neoliberal restructuring apparently attests to the limited effect of such social safety net. Likewise, it seems unlikely that the state's pronatal welfare policy will effectively reverse the persistent trends of marriage hiatus and fertility decline by overriding all such familialized risks with positive incentives for familial social reproduction. Nevertheless, it is undeniable that both post-crisis social safety net measures and recent pronatal welfare benefits have somewhat helped ease the immediate socio-economic difficulties of those workers and families inflicted by abrupt job crises and unreduced familial duties. After all, almost all of social security measures and benefits included in the social safety net mechanism and the pronatal policy may have been necessitated even without the economic and demographic crises. In this respect, the South Korean government recently announced a "paradigm shift" in its policy on "low fertility and aging society" by acknowledging "a majority of citizens (93%) strongly support the policy direction change from fertility goal-based pronatal policy to 'policy for improving the quality of life for citizens'" (Presidential Committee on Ageing Society and Population Policy, 7 Dec 2018). This was rather a candid confession on the impossibility of significant fertility reversal.

PART III

Dual Transitions

CHAPTER 7

From Developmental Liberalism to Neoliberalism

1 Introduction

The world before global neoliberalization was a complex of disparate ideologies, political economies, and social structures. Despite the seemingly all-encompassing forces of global neoliberalism, the wide diversities in the pre-neoliberal systems of politics, economy, and society have critically shaped the motives, conditions, processes, and consequences of neoliberal reforms. Capitalist East Asia, where the nature of economic, political, and social orders used to be decisively molded by the nationalist economic initiatives of the so-called developmental states, has confronted global neoliberalism in its own distinct historical context.

In capitalist East Asia, the active political pursuit of industrial catching-up and export promotion was backed up, as explained in detail in the earlier chapters, by what can be characterized as developmental liberalism in social policy. State policies involving, among others, labor and welfare were generally regarded conservative and/or liberal in terms of both spending levels and institutional configurations, but the developmental proactivism of each state frequently effected a systematic harnessing and/or sacrificing of social policies and grassroots interests for the sake of maximum economic development. That is, these East Asian states were developmentally liberal in social policy. However, the dual sacrifices of grassroots due to repressed labor rights and minimalized welfare protection became untenable as democratic transitions significantly empowered industrial

Chang K-S, *Developmental Liberalism in South Korea*,
International Political Economy Series,
https://doi.org/10.1007/978-3-030-14576-7_7

workers and other grassroots citizens in their confrontation with the authoritarian developmental bureaucracy and its business allies. It was during this crisis of developmental liberalism that Western neoliberalism in social policy (as well as in economic policy) was politically embraced, now by the supposedly democratic political regimes, in order to fend off the political challenges from below to developmental liberal policies. The nature, processes, and consequences of neoliberal reforms in social policy have been critically enmeshed with developmental liberalism and its political economic supporters.

In the case of South Korea—and, to a lesser extent, in neighboring capitalist countries—global neoliberalism was also actively incorporated in the financial sector, however, only to fatally destabilize the entire national economy. Ironically, as explained in detail in Chap. 3, the unprecedented national economic meltdown of 1997–1998 resulting from hasty financial (neo)liberalization, in turn, necessitated intensification of neoliberal social policies and economic practices. Ramified thereby were indiscriminate layoffs and pay-cuts, generalization of casual contractual jobs, practical annulment of social security benefits through employment casualization, as well as unrestrained overseas relocation of industrial jobs to China, Vietnam, and so on.

As these tormenting troubles were not effectively relieved but rather implicitly endorsed, under the pretext of reviving the national economy, by the democratic and even pretentiously progressive governments (under Kim Dae-Jung and Roh Moo-Hyun), South Koreans had to find themselves in a serious political epistemological obfuscation. Political progressivism became an almost irrelevant issue when South Korean voters began to search for an alternative leadership for remedying their utmost troubles ensuing from economic and social neoliberalization in the post-developmental liberal context. A man mimicking Park Chung-Hee was elected into the next presidency, which he would manage in a developmentally disguised neoliberal way. Lee's successor was Park Geun-Hye, a daughter of Park Chung-Hee, who rekindled popular illusion about the nation's developmental revival (in spite of her pledge for a Korean-style welfare state). In fact, such developmental nostalgia as an outcome of the intricate interaction between ambiguous democratic politics and neoliberal social pulverization decisively shaped the political landscapes across Asia—for example, from South Korea to Taiwan, Malaysia, Thailand, and so on.[1]

This chapter summarizes the sociopolitical challenges and repercussions in the treacherous trajectory of South Korea's developmental liberalism since the late 1980s. Specifically, the country's simultaneous democratization and neoliberalization since the late 1980s, its national financial meltdown of 1997–1998 and accompanying neoliberal restructuring thereafter, and its neo-developmental populist turn are, respectively, examined with an analytical focus on the specific conditions and impacts engendered by developmental liberalism in each of these drastic and fundamental transitions.

2   NEOLIBERALISM AND COUNTER-DEMOCRATIC RENEWAL OF DEVELOPMENTAL POLITICS

In international scholarship on comparative democratization, insufficient attention has been paid to the post-democratic impacts of the specific nature of each authoritarian rule. Authoritarian or dictatorial rule officially became something to be abolished in the political institutional sense, but many nondemocratic political orders had shaped and/or had been shaped by the structural political economic interests, relations, and ideologies that could not be reshuffled or eradicated by political institutional changes alone. In particular, the "successful" developmental political economies in East Asia orchestrated by the authoritarian developmental states had nurtured and had been nurtured by the structurally aligned interests of industrial entrepreneurs, economic technocrats and other state functionaries, media, as well as intellectual collaborators.[2] Regardless of democratization (i.e., the replacement of an autocratic regime by a democratically elected government), the core members of these coalitions would continue to identify themselves as the main basis of the developmental political economy and social system. They would do their best to preserve the currently prevalent economic and social orders and extend the economic and social policies of the state that had buttressed such orders. As a cold reality, the democratically elected state leaders and grassroots citizens committed to democratization had to confront these firmly entrenched elite groups without comparable material, institutional, or even techno-intellectual resources. Furthermore, the ambiguous ideological origin of the democratically elected governments—for sure, not being socialist or even social democratic—would easily result in political compromise with such entrenched interests under the pretext of pragmatic or realistic governance.

In this context, the political life span of developmental liberalism (and that of developmental statism in the economy) was not anywhere near the end. These core members of the conservative developmental political economy managed to realign themselves into a neo-developmental coalition pivoting around the pecuniary power of business (*chaebol*) and attempted to capitalize on the global spread of neoliberalism in order to resuscitate developmental liberalism.[3] A neoliberal rebirth of developmental liberalism would take place, causing an extreme confusion about the politico-ideological nature of South Korea's political economy and social policy in the democratic era.[4]

As everywhere else on earth, neoliberalism has been an extremely controversial subject for political debate and scholarly discussion in South Korea. To begin with, even liberalism in South Korea's economic and political history has remained a highly ambiguous issue. The international scholarship on South Korea's developmental state (vis-à-vis a supposed market-centered liberal paradigm) has reinforced such vague epistemological and ideological status of liberalism in the country. Nonetheless, there seem to have been four major trends or components of neoliberalism that have critically influenced the South Korean political economy and social policy—namely, global free trade and investment, financialization, institutional deregulation, and social policy liberalization.[5] The first two components are generally considered direct economic policy concerns, whereas the latter two are seen as noneconomic conditions for economic progress or rationalization. However, as explained below, all of them have had fundamental social policy ramifications.

Social policy liberalization was nosily heralded by frequent references to Western discourses on the supposed economic pitfalls of the welfare state. Interestingly, European welfare states became a major topic for public policy debate in two mutually contradictory directions. That is, no sooner had the (West European-style) welfare state become a national political objective in democratized South Korea than its supposed economic limits and moral risks began to be widely publicized.[6] Such conflict seemed to be resolved in terms of "productive welfare" (*saengsanjeok bokji*), but it by and large remained an empty slogan without systematic policy substances.[7] In effect, productive welfare functioned to contain social voices and political moves for welfare expansion. The most crucial social policy area in which actual liberalization was seriously pursued was labor relations. Under the neoliberal rubric of labor market flexibilization, the basic conditions of wage labor were subjected to radical proposals for liberalization, including easy layoffs, labor dispatching and outsourcing, transitory employment, and so on.[8] The Kim Young-Sam regime tried to enact a new labor law full of aggressive neoliberal substances, without seriously seeking political cooperation or compromise from opposition parties and labor unions, but a societal upheaval awaited Kim, requiring a long process of social and political negotiations.

Institutional deregulation (*gyuje gaehyeok*) took on an almost sacred political status since the late 1980s.[9] This trend occurred under a strong developmentalist ideology of national economic competitiveness. Broadly speaking, labor market flexibilization was one of such deregulation projects in the area of social policy. But a much wider range of policy domains—health and safety protection, social security, environmental control, agricultural preservation, geographic management, industrial licensing, corporate financing, foreign currency transaction, and so forth—were subjected to the deregulation spree. When social policy domains were brought under deregulation, it usually implied reduction in governmental, corporate, and/or social commitment to the social protection of workers, farmers, small business, handicapped/dependent/deprived individuals, environments, communities, and so on. Thus, deregulation often constituted an indirect way of sapping various social rights of citizens.

South Korea's aggressive pursuit of global free trade has basically reflected the national and corporate interest in rapid economic expansion. But the concomitant radical economic restructuring has ramified serious economic and social sacrifices on the part of various consequently weak links of the South Korean economy—including, above all, farmers, labor-intensive producers, and unskilled workers, all of whom began to rapidly lose international economic competitiveness in the face of their counterparts in much more populous and much less expensively livable societies. The socially exclusionary nature of the South Korean developmental state got even more intensified under the supposedly democratic leader Kim Young-Sam, who in fact tried to outperform Park Chung-Hee in economic development. Furthermore, more and more South Korean industrial firms began to relocate part or all of their production bases overseas in order to tap much cheaper and more easily exploitable labor and/or acquire secure bigger markets for their products. In particular, South Korea's geographic location as China's next door began to engender radical outcomes in the new international division of labor. Even when their employers somehow decided to stay in the country, South Korean workers now had to sell their labor under China-level working conditions. Not having sufficient supplies of such willingly exploitable domestic workers, South Korean companies also asked for the opening of the domestic labor market to "unlimited" supplies of poor Asian workers (cf. W. Arthur Lewis 1954). Having become one of Asia's most open labor markets, South Korea is now busy dealing with social and cultural ramifications of its accidental ethnic plurality.[10] All these tendencies have coalesced to bring to a near end the most fundamental condition of South Korea's timeworn developmental politics, namely, stable employment.

Financialization is a highly complex theoretical as well as practical issue (Fine 2012). If most broadly interpreted in respect to the economic life of grassroots South Koreans, they have been induced and/or urged to financialize the economic troubles attending on the widespread employment crisis by relying on various old and new products of the financial industries. Since such reliance does not fundamentally solve any financial problem for desperate South Koreans, the cumulative effect of ultimate individual bankruptcies has been manifested in terms of the financial crisis of the financial industries—for instance, the near insolvency of many South Korean credit card companies during the first several years of the twenty-first century (Chung, U. 2004). Such experience has made the South Korean government become much more cautious in the monitoring and regulation of the financial industries. Ironically, this has resulted in a further jeopardy of the widespread reliance of poor people on often illegally existing or behaving private usurers—a dangerous trend which often coerces helpless borrowers into complete insolvency, physical abuse, mental disorder, suicide, prostitution, and even human organ transaction (Song, T. 2011). Financialization at the other pole of the economy has involved indiscreet corporate borrowings from overseas, aggressive portfolio investment (as opposed to industrial investment) by global financial speculators, and so forth (Kong, T. 2000). The extreme velocity of such international financial incorporation of the South Korean economy became directly responsible for runaway inflationary pressure and, consequently, aggravated the above-mentioned financial troubles of grassroots people. However, it was not grassroots alone that had to confront the perilous outcome of the injudicious financialization. An alarming number of major South Korean enterprises and then the entire national economy had to instantly skid into financial insolvency during the so-called Asian financial crisis of the late 1990s.

While neoliberalism was initially adopted as a countermeasure to the democratic social and political challenges to developmental liberalism, neoliberal policies and practices, in effect, functioned to critically undermine various conditions and components of developmental liberalism. First, labor market flexibilization in combination with the unrestrained relocation of industrial jobs to China and elsewhere came to gradually demolish the full and stable employment regime as the most essential political basis of the developmental state's economic enfranchisement of citizenry (Chang, K. 2012a; see Chap. 4). Second, the neoliberal ideological propensity to liquidate social and political concerns away from economic activities—often under the rubric of deregulation—was directly antithetical to developmental liberalism as an economically integrative social policy regime. Third, the industrial restructuring for strengthening the global competitiveness of major export firms in technology/capital-intensive sectors, accompanied by the trade policy of securing wider markets for such firms at the sacrifice of domestic labor-intensive sectors, made the close state-business relationship devoid of developmental justification for ever-increasing proportions of population. Fourth and relatedly, the massive dismissal of family breadwinners in urban industries and the structural decline of family-based petty producers in agriculture and urban tertiary sectors came to crucially damage the essential material basis of their families as the key provider of welfare and protection. Finally, the globalization of corporate business operations, individual job careers, and even citizenship arrangements as combined with the intrusive engagement of foreign capital and international regulatory forces in the South Korean economy could not but deplete communitarian nationalism as the key ideological basis of pluralist welfare provision. These tendencies, in combine, effected an irreversible weakening of the developmental liberal regime of social policy.

3   ECONOMIC CRISIS, NEOLIBERAL DEMOCRATIC GOVERNANCE, AND POLITICAL OBFUSCATION

The decisive cause of the economic crisis of 1997–1998 in South Korea (and Asia) is still debatable. The US-originated global financial crisis of 2008–2009 reaffirms the fundamentally problematic nature of globalized financial capitalism with deleterious impacts on anyone on earth. But the fact that South Korea incurred national financial calamities in both instances with supposed "sound economic fundamentals"—that is, balanced state budget, manageable inflation, internationally competitive industries, and so forth—seems to require a particular explanation for tackling the structural vulnerability of the South Korean political economy directly. While seeking such answer remains beyond the purpose of this study, it is sufficiently safe to point out that the haphazard combination of developmental and neoliberal elements of political economy was destined to engender structural instabilities in the national economy. (This is equivalent to what happened in the social policy area under the similarly haphazard combination of developmental liberal and neoliberal elements.) While neoliberalism was occasionally presented by domestic and international experts as a reform platform for state-led developmental political economy, both state economic bureaucracy and *chaebol* thought and behaved otherwise. That is, they tried to incorporate (or reinvent) neoliberalism as a convenient mechanism for expansively renewing the timeworn developmental political economy in the increasingly globalizing economic environment. Without rectifying *chaebol*'s inherent tendencies of debt-financed corporate expansion, aggressive yet opaque management, and reliance on the politico-administrative underwriting of their operations, the developmentally promoted policies of corporate deregulation and (domestic and international) financial liberalization— what may be called developmental neoliberalism—instantly coalesced to engender a financial runaway situation. All this process took place under Kim Young-Sam's government, noisily inaugurated under the developmentalist slogan of New Economy (Singyeongje) which, according to Kim's propagandists, would finally place South Korea to a status of *seonjinguk* (advanced nation).

A political paradox of the 1997–1998 economic crisis was the political defeat of the rightwing developmentalist party after ruling South Korea nearly three and a half decades under various different names. In December 1997, South Korean democracy came to be headed by a political leadership symbolizing national democratic struggle, but its economic and social policy line did not necessarily represent anything seriously progressive—be social democratic or socialist. Under the staunch (and opportunistic) urge of the Wall Street-dispatched international financial regulators, the new South Korean administration led by Kim Dae-Jung basically agreed that neoliberal principles would be respected and adopted in order to thoroughly reform the state-business collusive economy.[11] The so-called structural adjustment program indeed ramified a serious alteration of the state-business economic relationship, *chaebol*'s corporate structure and management, and even the national industrial structure.[12]

Rescuing the national economy through neoliberal policy measures was not tantamount to rescuing people from sudden material destitute. To the contrary, the structural adjustment of the national economy as well as individual industries and firms involved intensification of neoliberal social policies such as labor market flexibilization and exhortation of economic self-reliance (Ji, J. 2011). Although the Kim Dae-Jung government remained quite ambiguous in the official social policy paradigm, its subscription to neoliberal economic reform by consequence implied the sustenance of neoliberal social policy.[13] In fact, as detailed in Chap. 3, Kim successfully forged the historical "labor-business-government tripartite agreement" for a collaborative rescue of the national economy by emphatically persuading organized labor to accept neoliberal programs for labor reshuffling.[14] However, the sheer scale of the all-encompassing national economic restructuring did not allow the Kim administration to sit on a passive social policy line indefinitely. As millions of South Korean breadwinners and their family dependents suddenly found themselves on the verge of permanent poverty, an instant provision of nationwide relief programs—again in neoliberal forms such as temporary public employment, job skills development, job placement assistance, corporate employment subsidy, and so on—was carried out. This was encouraged even by the International Monetary Fund and other international predatory forces under the rubric of "social safety net".[15] Despite its neoliberal implication, the prompt establishment of the social safety net seemed to afford the Kim government a political excuse, though very briefly, for self-consolation.

On the other hand, many South Korean exporters managed to rehabilitate themselves instantly and helped to accelerate national economic recovery. This induced the Kim government to concentrate its energy in the boosting of corporate competitiveness and the expansion of export markets—not in the establishment of a serious welfare state regime. The economic crisis kept the supposedly progressive Kim Dae-Jung government from seriously attempting to alter the socially exclusionary nature of the South Korean developmental state. Furthermore, to the extent that the successful recovery of major South Korean exporters was due to sustained concentration in technology/capital-intensive sectors, their contribution to national economic recovery fell short of rescuing grassroots South Koreans—in particular, middle-agers who had been dismissed from work during or after the 1997–1998 crisis and youth who began to confront unprecedented difficulties in job finding. While unemployment did decrease, most of the new or renewed jobs offered under the flexible labor market regime were *bijeonggyujik* (non-regular position). South Korea thereby became the only advanced industrial economy with more non-regular employees than regular ones. Most non-regular jobs come with unstable and unpredictable tenure, lower pay, and practically nullified social security benefits.[16] As even the modicum of social security programs had been devised in accordance with people's regular employment (following the conservative welfare state model initiated by Bismarck's Germany), joblessness or non-regular employment came to imply a practical disenfranchisement from the national social security system.

Despite such complicated economic and social conditions, Kim Dae-Jung managed to see Roh Moo-Hyun, a candidate from the same political party, succeed his presidency. Roh, having quite recently built up his career as a democracy fighter, was much more concerned with political issues (in particular, interregional confrontation and disparities), so that no serious departure was made from the economic and social policies of his predecessor.[17] Consequently, the above-mentioned structural problems in industrial change, employment, and social security remained unchanged in their nature but got worsened in their extents. Without the same excuse of "rescuing the national economy" as his predecessor, Roh's passiveness in social (and economic) policy was subjected to harsh political criticism from his own political supporters as well as organized labor and progressive intellectuals and media.[18] Roh began to react quite sensitively, however, not through socioeconomic policy changes but through apologetic political propaganda. While continuously relying on conservative technocrats in neoliberal(ized) economic and social management, Roh began to launch colorful verbal attacks on neoliberalism and conservative domestic forces feeding on it besides developmental (liberal) legacies from the past. His final and proudly pragmatic project was, ironically but not surprisingly, the South Korea-United States Free Trade Agreement.

Roh's "right turn with the left-turn signal" resulted in an unprecedented political epistemological mayhem. For those South Koreans who had been systematically disenfranchised from stable work and social security, pretentiously progressive Roh seemed to suggest that social democratic, socialist, or other progressive political lines would offer no fundamental relief or alternative. Without any apparent policy debacles (at least on his mind), Roh's political approval rate remained extremely low throughout his term. However, even more serious political injury would be experienced by those genuinely progressive politicians formally representing labor rights, social democratic policies, and so on. For instance, the Democratic Labor Party had to suffer devastating losses in the presidential and parliamentary elections at a time its theoretical policy constituencies appeared larger than ever before (Chang 2012a).

The materially troubled and politically puzzled South Koreans instead turned nostalgic as manifested in terms of the so-called Park Chung-Hee nostalgia. The conservative opposition party successfully capitalized on such public sentiment by launching a noisy and colorful presidential election campaign focused on national economic revival and actually winning the election by a wide margin in late 2007. Lee Myung-Bak, the lucky winner, had proudly introduced himself as one of the most successful CEOs during the Park era and implicitly suggested himself as another Park of the twenty-first century.[19] However, he and his political staff lacked any serious theories or programs for systematically implementing another round of developmental statist governance—particularly in respect to those developmentally disenfranchised South Koreans. Concerning social policy, wide neglect seemed to constitute a policy line itself (except occasional repetitions of the neoliberal allegation on the economically negative side effect of redistributive welfare).[20]

After bungling on the very first move for supposedly developmental intervention in the economy—that is, arbitrary boosting of high exchange rates on the eve of the global financial crisis that would cause a near collapse of the South Korean currency anyway—Lee's administration became an empty-shell developmental regime. Under the pressure of entrenched economic and political supporters, Lee simultaneously pursued a variety of neoliberal policies and projects.[21] As such neoliberal turn was carried out still under the developmental statist propaganda, it was as if a developmental neoliberal regime had come into existence. However, even this characterization of the Lee regime was not sustainable in the long run. On the one hand, his technocratic staffs seemed to realize that there was nothing much left to be neoliberalized further; on the other hand, his obsession with the mammoth infrastructural developmental projects led him to sound as if he were a neo-Keynesian. Furthermore, as some of his political and intellectual staffs were firmly convinced that the regime's political survival necessitated more conciliatory treatment of *seomin* (grassroots people), Lee was suddenly posing himself as an apparently populist leader with a supposed willingness to implement any social or economic policies useful for less privileged categories of people.[22]

4   SOUTH KOREA'S POST-DEVELOPMENTAL LIBERAL
     TRANSITION TO THE WELFARE STATE?

Lee Myung-Bak's apparent failure in national developmental regeneration, with all showy developmentalist propaganda, instantly induced progressive intellectuals, civil activists, and critical media to collectively explore alternative paradigms for national socioeconomic advances. The nation's transition to a welfare state was most prominently discussed, echoing the late 1980s and early 1990s when South Koreans were converging on social democracy as a sort of third way in their optimistic imagining about national future on the basis of proudly achieved democracy and economic development.[23] In the early 2010s, however, their call for a welfare state was quite desperate under a broad realization that both democracy and advanced capitalism would not automatically guarantee fairly and stably shared happiness in life.[24]

Interestingly, it was Park Geun-Hye, Park Chung-Hee's daughter, who most promptly and actively accommodated civil society's yearning for a welfare state (Kang, B. 2016; Kim, T. 2012). Park lost the main conservative party's candidacy for presidential election to Lee Myung-Bak in 2007 but somehow managed to fight her way into the same party's presidential candidacy in the next election of 2012. Despite her political capital as a daughter of the nation's developmental hero Park Chung-Hee, Park Geun-Hye could not replicate Lee's developmentalist campaign especially after his notorious failure. As a key election pledge, she proposed "the construction of Korean-style welfare state" (Kim, T. 2012).[25] The main opposition party's would-be candidate, Moon Jae-In, could not but trail Park's lead in welfare state pledges. To most of those who eagerly favored her, however, Park's main political appeal derived not from her progressive pledges for social welfare but from her political cultural status as an essential signifier of the high developmental era under her father's leadership (Kim, S. 2013). Nonetheless, Park's practical political profit from her welfare state propaganda consisted in Moon's loss of a critical opportunity of establishing himself firstly as a potential national leader for social democratic transition. (Park may not have to feel sorry for Moon about this political effect because he would not adopt the welfare state as a key political pledge anyway in the next election in which he finally won presidency.)

Park's presidency did not have much to do with the welfare state. In fact, she ended up being impeached by the Constitutional Court after shocking revelations about her corruption scandals involving secret cronies. To South Korean citizens' utmost embarrassment, there was not much room for political critique or praise on her socioeconomic policy and actual administrative performance because she virtually idled on her job until her departure from the Blue House. If she did anything comparable to her father's role, it was the practical annulment of the welfare state promises politically presented and/or legally stipulated.

Constitutionally speaking, South Korea was already a serious welfare state during her father's lengthy rule. But this legal feature of the Republic of Korea was not devised for the sake of political deception but reflected the particular mode of reflexive institutional modernization in which the so-called West was syncretistically copied for the best institutional makeup of the state (Chang, K. 2019, Chap. 3). Park Chung-Hee's neglect of citizens' welfare rights—and, in fact, even his suppression of citizens' civil and political rights—did not entirely enrage them because his developmental performance was unprecedentedly strong to most South Koreans' eyes. Park's actual regime of social policy, developmental liberalism, was effectively applied to South Koreans amid the country's explosive industrialization and economic growth during most of his presidency. If his daughter had differed by actualizing serious welfare state programs, Park Chung-Hee's (developmental liberal) slogan, or strategy, of "growth first, distribution later" would have been upheld by South Koreans as a truly clever political move. Unfortunately, Park Geun-Hye did nothing much except reminding herself of being her great father's daughter.[26]

As another historical sin, she suddenly transferred presidency to Moon Jae-In virtually as a political gift and thereby helped usher in another period of socioeconomic instabilities. Curiously, in the presidential election of 2017, Moon abandoned his previous election pledge on the welfare state and instead presented an ambiguous package of selective social benefits and political and economic reforms.[27] His moderate yet vague policy line in socioeconomic affairs was characterizable more as selectively populist than as social democratic. Although his administration's initial drives for "regularizing" (*jeonggyujikhwa*) non-regular employees in public sectors, raising legal minimum wage consecutively, and legally restraining weekly labor hours reflected a serious effort at rectifying various labor market irregularities accumulated during the developmental and neoliberal eras (*Maeil Labor News*, 6 November 2017), these measures have failed to address the most fundamental predicament of ordinary South Koreans' massive disenfranchisement from the mainstream capitalist economy.[28] In all logical accounts and actual appearances, the Moon administration is not likely to effectively lead South Korea's perplexed and troubled post-developmental citizens into a new systemic terrain of socio-economic governance. This is particularly problematic to young people who have to agonize about their current and prospective difficulties without any optimistic clue to a viable alternative system of economic order and social policy in so many years to live.[29]

5   Conclusion and Comparative Implications

The dramatic twists and turns in the South Korean social policy regime have reflected the complex historical circumstances and transformations in polity, economy, and social structure. In particular, the seemingly paramount hegemony of the liberal order in this world's last bastion of the Cold War against communism has been in fact a clutter of historical interactions among its political, economic, and social forces. In this complicated context, developmentalism has served not merely as a provisional and partial adjustment to the liberal order but as a forceful melting pot for dissolving endless internal contradictions of the liberal order in South Korea. The developmental state has as much harnessed as revised the liberal order, particularly in the economy. Its social policy regime of developmental liberalism has been an indispensable instrument for that function.

As South Korea entered the global neoliberal era and its own democratic era simultaneously, developmental political economy and social policy, democratic forces, and neoliberal ideology and policy began to interact with one another in quite complex manners. Democratic forces representing labor, women, poor, handicapped, or civil society in general did seriously challenge the basic conditions and components of the developmental liberal social policy regime. The neo-developmental forces tried to utilize neoliberal ideology and policy as a countermeasure to the democratic challenges to developmental liberalism but ended up further undermining its conditions and components. The 1997–1998 national financial crisis required neoliberalism to be used, this time by a supposedly progressive political leadership, more as an economic reform platform than as a developmental renewal strategy, but the social policy dimension of neoliberalism remained virtually unchanged. Even the social safety net was sought after as a complementary social policy component of the neoliberal structural adjustment of the South Korean economy (rather than as a social democratic initiative). The developmentally and socially disenfranchised groups of voters opted to elect Lee Myung-Bak, a Park Chung-Hee mimicking president, but neither renewed developmental statist economic governance nor developmental reincorporation of unemployed and underemployed South Koreans successfully took place under the new leadership. Lee's successor Park Geun-Hye, a daughter of Park Chung-Hee, only helped tó reinforce popular disillusionment about the nation's developmental revival and ended up chauffeuring Moon Jae-In into sudden presidency. Developmental liberalism as a social policy regime has been critically emasculated through the complicated processes of democratization, neoliberalization, and economic crisis, but a sustainable alternative regime has not even been envisioned yet. Ironically, the impressive economic recoveries from the two externally caused economic crises (of 1997–1998 and 2008) do not seem to have functioned as material bases for social policy renewal but rather have intensified the socially adverse nature of South Korea's neoliberalized economy.

Although developmental liberalism and its neoliberal degeneration have been presented here on the basis of South Korean experiences, a majority of national political economies governed by effective or ineffective developmental states may have confronted similar trends. Outside the Western families of social democratic and liberal welfare states (in Europe, North America, and Oceania), the conventional categories of social policy regimes such as those of Esping-Andersen (1990) are hardly useful. By contrast, the developmental orientation of the ruling governments and their political constituencies, whether successful or not, is an almost universal phenomenon. Accordingly, developmental liberalism in social policy, with variant forms and contents, may have been quite a widespread phenomenon. The social, political, as well as economic predicaments of neoliberal transitions in such societies have to be appraised precisely in this post-developmental liberal context.

The Rise of Developmental Liberal Asia: South Korean Parameters of *Asianized* Industrial Capitalism

1 INTRODUCTION: ASIA AS DEVELOPMENTAL COMMUNITY AND *ASIANIZED* INDUSTRIAL CAPITALISM

Asia has been the fulcrum of global capitalism's sustained growth in the recent few decades. The twenty-first century has hence been called "the Asian century" in varieties of media, institutional, and scholarly descriptions. Asian Development Bank (ADB), for instance, observed in its special report of 2011, *Asia 2050: Realizing the Asian Century*:

> Asia is in the middle of a historic transformation. If it continues to follow its recent trajectory, by 2050 its per capita income could rise sixfold in purchasing power parity (PPP) terms to reach Europe's levels today. It would make some 3 billion additional Asians affluent by current standards. By nearly doubling its share of global gross domestic product (GDP) to 52 percent by 2050, Asia would regain the dominant economic position it held some 300 years ago, before the industrial revolution (Asian Development Bank 2011: 3).

> Asia's march to prosperity will be led by seven economies, …: PRC, India, Indonesia, Japan, Republic of Korea, Thailand and Malaysia (Asian Development Bank 2011: 5).

The Asian century is celebratively predicted as a historical period of Asia's collective developmental surge. Asia is hereby *imagined as a developmental community* composed of a variety of (political) economies with wide

© The Author(s) 2019   153
Chang K-S, *Developmental Liberalism in South Korea*,
International Political Economy Series,
https://doi.org/10.1007/978-3-030-14576-7_8

differences in affluence, industrialization, institutional setup, demographics, as well as sociocultural tradition. Even without a strong institutional framework for collective governance like the European Union—not to mention such an authoritative developmental state as has been responsible for "miraculous" national industrialization and economic growth in Japan, South Korea, and Taiwan—Asian countries have rapidly been developing with quite active and usually peaceful integration with each other in economic and sociocultural terms (Funabashi 1993; Chang, K. 2014b).

During most of the twentieth century, Asia remained a physical aggregate of nations whose mutual relationships were often characterized by protracted socioeconomic segmentation and even frequent politico-military hostility. Each country yearned for national economic development, but such common developmental desire did not induce them to keenly engage in mutual collaboration and utilization—except for exceptionally early-developed Japan's industrial integration with a few Southeast Asian capitalist economies. In fact, some countries' early-stage industrialization and trade growth were closely linked to Western economies, often fused with neocolonial political influences. Now in the twenty-first century, virtually every Asian country, with some exceptions and particularities involving West Asian countries, is energetically gearing up its economic and other relationships with the other Asian countries. The latest participants are the so-called transition economies undergoing post-socialist system reform and external economic opening—China being by far the most critical participant, even taking up a collective financial initiative of the Asian Infrastructure Investment Bank (AIIB), potentially rivaling West-led/monitored international financial institutions (i.e., the International Monetary Fund (IMF), the World Bank, etc.).[1]

In a sense, Asia as a developmental community is an organic sum of bilateral and multilateral alliances of developmentally governed economies and peoples. The most critical collective effect of such alliances is a *transnational capitalist industrialization of which Asia a whole has become a basic unit.* By nature, this transnational industrialization is a decentralized process in which even the role of already industrialized economies has to be situationally tailored to suit various local conditions and interests in their destination economies and in which most of involved transnational economic relationships and transactions are not centrally regulated (Asian Development Bank 2016).[2] Nevertheless, Asia's wholistic capitalist industrialization has, on the one hand, necessitated various politico-administrative and social conditions for its initiation and sustenance and, on the other hand, generated diverse political, social, cultural, and ecological problems beyond simple economic solutions. Consciously and unconsciously, the governments, firms, workers, farmers, and traders engaged directly or indirectly in Asianized industrial capitalism have entered a delimited structure of sociopolitical as well as economic relationships that can and should be identified as a meaningful unit of latently coordinated governance.

This chapter argues that Asia has been transforming into a developmental liberal community—that is, a developmentally driven liberal entity in political economic and social policy characteristics. As explained in Chap. 2, developmental liberalism used to characterize the national political economic and social policy features of many Asian countries before their series participation in Asianized industrial capitalism. Particularly in East Asian nations' active developmental pursuit of catch-up industrialization and condensed economic growth, state policies regarding, among others, labor, welfare, and education were generally considered conservative and/or liberal in terms of both spending levels and institutional configurations. But each state's developmental proactivism frequently effected a systematic harnessing and/or sacrificing of social policies and grassroots interests for the sake of maximum economic growth. In this milieu, these Asian countries were *developmentally liberal*, rather than simply liberally liberal, in various domains of social governance.[3] Among the core characteristics of developmental liberalism are depoliticization/technocratization/developmental obfuscation of social policy, developmental cooptation of social policy constituencies, state-business entrepreneurial merge and direct state engagement in labor relations, familial reconstitution of social citizenship, and welfare pluralism and demobilization of civil society. The main concern of each developmental state was no doubt rapid capitalist industrialization and economic growth, but social governance was not delegated to a different political body. Both economic developmental goals and liberal social policies were essential attributes of the developmental state. The current chapter will show that the aggressive promotion of transnationalized industrial capitalism across Asia, a sort of neoliberal globalization project, has induced Asian societies, peoples, and industries to be enmeshed with each other in developmental liberal manners. We will also examine, as a highly critical and illustrative incidence of the rise of a developmental liberal Asia, South Korean capitalism's transnational industrial expansion and its developmental liberal effects on host societies and peoples.

2   THE RISE OF DEVELOPMENTAL LIBERAL ASIA

The developmental community as which Asia is imagined or approached takes on various liberal attributes. The above-mentioned ADB report of 2011 argues:

> Given its diversity, Asia will need to develop its own model that builds on the positive experience of East Asia: a market-driven and pragmatic approach supported by an evolving institutional framework that facilitates free regional trade and investment flows throughout Asia, as well as some labor mobility. An Asian economic community must be based on two general principles— openness and transparency. Openness will be a continuation of Asia's long-standing policy of open regionalism, a key factor in East Asia's past success (Asian Development Bank 2011: 8).

Asian countries are undergoing developmentally motivated market-economic integration with one another. A developmentally driven liberal Asia, or developmental liberal Asia, is on the horizon.

The most critical effect of Asia's developmental liberal order of mutual association is Asianization of industrial capitalism, that is, Asia's formation as a collective unit of transnational capitalist industrialization. Above all, East Asia's nation-based experience of labor-intensive industrialization in the twentieth century has been extrapolated into the entire Asia's region-based project of collaborative industrialization in which the so-called *demographic dividends of mega-population societies are transnationally tapped by East Asian and other industrial investors* in conjunction with their local allies and competitors (Kinugasa 2013; Gubhaju 2013; Thomas 2017). This process has not necessarily been exclusionary to non-Asian interests, but the utility of such transnational economic alliances has been most pertinent to within-Asia interests in technological, geographic, and cultural terms.[4]

Asia's developmental liberal order of mutual association in the making of Asianized industrial capitalism has direct implications for various social policy dimensions and components of Asia as an evolving community of developmental and social governance. In fact, various features of developmental liberalism as the national social governance regime of East Asian developmental states are correspondingly found at the regional level of Asia. That is, the following features of developmental liberalism are now detectable, albeit usually in intangible forms and dispersed effects, as developmental liberal Asia's regional features:

Developmental Cooptation of Social Policy Constituencies The ultimate common purpose of developmentally interrelated Asian states is to enhance the material affluence and security of their populations as broadly as possible. It is this purpose of a social policy that in principle legitimates various Asian states' often authoritarian practices of developmental governance both in domestic and international affairs.[5] In their promotion of Asianized industrialization, accompanying economic opportunities in employment, management, and trade are assumed to be automatic facilitators for local citizens' popular welfare. For this reason, foreign investors are welcomed as a de facto policy instrument for developmentally (re)framed social governance by the local and central governments of the host countries (Morrissey and Udomkerdmongkol 2011; ADB 2016). In fact, such local and central governments often offer suspension or annulment of social security requirements and labor protection regulations as an incentive for luring foreign industrial investors.[6] This practice is particularly appreciated by investors from other Asian countries who have long benefitted from a similar national practice in their home countries. Promoting industrialization by actively inviting transnational investment from industrialized neighbors is considered to be a developmental platform for in-effect social policy.

Depoliticization and Developmental Substitution of Social Policy Like domestic capitalist industrialization, transnationally promoted capitalist industrialization inevitably generates a wide range of social problems unresolvable by immediate stakeholders' private measures. For instance, there have been innumerable incidents in which abusive labor practices and environmental damages by foreigner industries have ignited collective rages and riots by local workers and neighbors (Global Investment & Business Center 2017). Resolving these social problems, however, rarely constitutes a systematic social policy agenda of the hosting central or local state because of local institutional unpreparedness and political hiatus in social policy, besides frequent official corruption that, in fact, may have helped cause the concerned social problems (Rock 2017). Needless to say, such defectiveness in social policy is extant even concerning social problems caused by domestic industrial investors. A sort of default solution thereby adopted is to accelerate or expand industrialization with a hope that accompanying improvements in employment, business, and income would ultimately solve the concerned social problems by strengthening local citizens' self-help capacity.

In this sense, foreign industrial investors have been expected to fulfill a sort of *corporate developmental responsibility* no less significantly than corporate social responsibilities (ADB 2016).

State-Business Entrepreneurial Merge and Direct State Engagement in Labor Relations Those local and central governments of late industrializing Asian countries which aspire to attract foreign industrial investors by nature tend to show business-friendly posture, but the managerial relationship between them is not likely to display such systematic entrepreneurial nurturing as has been documented in respect to the developmental state-local business relationship in industrialized East Asian countries. Nonetheless, foreign industrial investors often expect the local and central authorities of the host countries to serve as business-supportive guardians in labor relations under the assumption that their industrial investment is developmentally essential to local economic conditions (Blanton and Blanton 2012; ADB 2016). Furthermore, when foreign investment is accepted in certain strategic industrial sectors, the central or local governments of the host countries often directly participate as joint owners of the invested industrial ventures.[7] In such cases of direct legal merge between foreign industrial capital and the host state, labor relations are inevitably complicated due to both the developmental and sociopolitical interest of the host state in containing labor disputes.

Familial Reconstitution of Social Citizenship When corporate decisions are made to transnationally relocate industrial production sites to those countries abundantly endowed with supposedly cheap labor, the low price of labor is not determined merely as an outcome of large supplies of docile workers. Historically speaking, capitalist industrialization, whether initiated domestically or promoted transnationally, is generally a human social process in which labor from familial subsistence sectors (mostly farming) are reallocated to capitalist industrial sectors mainly as adaptive responses of local population to new economic opportunities. This process was analytically explained by W. Arthur Lewis (1954) who fundamentally changed the direction of economic thinking on the relationship between (surplus) population and capitalist industrialization. The willingness of those workers shifting from their parents' family farms to capitalist urban factories for laboring even for subsistence-level wages is made possible because their parents would not claim the long-term sunk cost for raising them into able adult bodies. Furthermore, these parents are often willing to sacrifice their own economic sectoral interests by intensifying parental support for urban-based children's education, job training, and urban livelihood under a strategic judgment on the long-term structural primacy of urban economic development.[8] Within each industrialized country, capitalist industrial firms cannot expect such long-term familial shouldering of human capital formation and proletarian livelihood as they are demanded by the state and labor unions to help socialize the concerned costs through social security taxation, "family wage", and so forth (Ochiai 2011). In fact, they are recently required to thoroughly change work conditions to help assist governmental efforts at promoting fertility of women workers as well as men workers' spouses under the ominous prospect of demographic meltdown (Straughan et al. 2009). The corporate evasion of such social cost-sharing by transnational relocation cannot be permanently achieved within a certain destination because any country is ultimately ordained to socialize such costs. However, Asia's abundance in candidate destinations for labor cost-wise corporate relocation implies that the local familial shouldering of labor expenses will remain a fairly long-term feature of Asianized industrial capitalism.

Welfare Pluralism and Demobilization of Civil Society Asia's transnational industrial integration has been accompanied by a remarkable expansion of transnational social services and advocacies mostly in the same directions as transnational industrial investment (Chapple and Moon 2005; Taylor et al. 2001). Some of these transnational welfare contributions are openly intended to lubricate the local sociopolitical conditions for effective and stable industrial investment, while some other social contributions conversely take industrially promoted transnational relationships as a useful platform for landing their operations locally (Koli et al. 1999). Some social contributions take on a developmentalist nature of helping spread local economic self-help and grassroots entrepreneurship (Amberg and McGaughey 2017). The involved transnational donators include pure civilian NGOs, specially motivated individuals and groups, evangelical religions, as well as public agencies. All these contributors consciously and unconsciously reflect the industrially promoted expansion of transnational relationships as their operational reason, background, and/ or basis. Asia has thereby become a social terrain of transnational welfare pluralism. In fact, such transnational facilitation of welfare pluralism was significantly extant in the current donor countries' past under European and American influences.[9] The transnational dealings in social services and advocacies have an inherent effect of depoliticizing the concerned social groups and problems in the destination countries because they are strictly prohibited from injecting political opinions and organizing political activities as measures for promoting their causes.

Asia's above-explained developmental liberal features correspondent to those of developmental liberal nations in East Asia present us a fundamental theoretical question as to the systemic unit or basis of the social policy regime for developmental governance. In the South Korean experience, for instance, various elements of developmental liberalism were sustainable only under an authoritarian developmentalist government, so democratization since 1987 has critically weakened the sociopolitical conditions for developmental liberal governance and then induced *chaebol* and its technocratic allies to devise surrogate mechanisms for reviving it. Transnational Asia's developmental liberalism has no political framework corresponding to the state behind national developmental liberalism, whereas the economic character of transnational industrial relationships (practically underwritten by mutually separate sovereign states) by nature prevents any directly political authoritarianism as a routine condition. It is market-driven mutual developmental necessities among industrially interdependent Asian countries that serve as the critical basis for Asia's historical transition to a developmental liberal community. That is, *mutual developmental necessities espoused through transnational market forces tend to function as an in-effect governance platform for Asianized developmental liberalism.* Broadly speaking, this trend seems to constitute a key aspect of Asia's neoliberal developmental globalization.

3   SOUTH KOREAN PARAMETERS

The unrivaled pioneer in transnationally reorganizing Asia as an integrated capitalist industrial entity has been Japan (Encarnation 1999; Shujiro 2008), a country with an aged ambition to become the hegemonic center of "co-prosperous" Asia. Despite its devastating defeat to the United States in a war staged to establish monopolistic politico-military and economic influence across Asia, it stunned the world by swiftly rebuilding its economy and aggressively expanding its industrial influence over Southeast Asia. Japan's regional influence, however, would be critically confined under the rapid rise of China as a new economic as well as politico-military superpower. China has prepared its own blueprint for restructuring Asia (or Eurasia) according to its strategic economic as well as politico-military needs (Yeh, E. 2017). In most Asian countries, Japanese and Chinese industrial firms have operated as critically influential elements to local economic development. In many such countries, to one's surprise, South Korean industrial firms also have exercised no less strong—and, sometimes, dominant—influences (Ahn et al. 2008).

According to the *2016 Directory of Overseas-Advanced South Korean Firms*, compiled and published biennially by the Korea Trade-Investment Promotion Agency (KOTRA 2016: 3–4), there were 3639 South Korean firms in China and 5493 South Korean firms in other Asia-Pacific countries, excluding West Asia (or Middle East), respectively, accounting for 30.4 percent and 46.0 percent of all reported firms in the Directory (11,937 firms). (The latter area is denoted as "Asia rest & Pacific" hereafter.) If South Korean firms in Middle East and CIS (respectively 374 firms and 333 firms, or 3.1 percent and 2.7 percent of all reported firms) are added, 82.2 percent of all reported overseas operations of South Korean firms were concentrated in the greater Asia region. Between 2014 and 2016, there were particularly drastic increases in South Korean corporate operations in the rest of Asia and Pacific—from 4190 firms to 5493 firms, an increase by 31.0 percent. Such increase was mostly observed in Vietnam, in which the number of South Korean firms kept growing explosively, from 1340 in 2014 to 2723 in 2016. Other notable host countries of South Korean firms were, as of 2016, the United States (783 firms), Indonesia (522 firms), Japan (395 firms), Thailand (372 firms), India (294 firms), the Philippines (228 firms), Myanmar (198 firms), Mexico (183 firms), and so forth. Among China-based South Korean firms, 2604 of them were established since 2000, 688 between 1990 and 1999, and only 39 before 1990 (KOTRA 2016: 7). Among Asia rest and Pacific-based South Koreans firms (except those in China, CIS, and Middle East), 3910 of them were established since 2000, 895 between 1990 and 1999, and 226 before 1990. In short, while South Korean industries' corporate transnationalization, mostly within the greater Asian region, was already noticeable in the 1990s, this transition became literally explosive in the twenty-first century.

The industrial sectoral distribution of Asia rest & Pacific-based South Korean firms was heavily concentrated in manufacturing (i.e., 2855 firms in 2016), followed by wholesale and retail (721 firms), services (712 firms), construction (464 firms), and transportation (358 firms) (KOTRA 2016: 5). China-based South Korean firms were similarly distributed—2095 firms in manufacturing, 581 firms in wholesale and retail, 538 firms in services, 222 firms in transportation, and so forth. South Korean firms' focus on manufacturing was also found in Central and Latin America, Europe, and Middle East, but their preponderance of manufacturing was unrivaled in China and Asia rest & Pacific. Relatedly, the predominant organizational-legal form of South Korean firms in China (1861 firms in 2016) and Asia rest & Pacific (2583 firms in 2016) was a legal corporation for production (as opposed to a legal corporation for sales or service, liaison office, or a branch) (KOTRA 2016: 6). South Korean firms' overseas operations, mostly as production establishments, maintained sizable volumes of local employees. Among those established in Asia rest & Pacific, as of 2016, 699 firms employed more than 500 local workers; 975 firms 101–500 local workers, 537 firms 51–100 local workers, 1394 firms 11–50 local workers, and 1888 firms 10 or less local workers (KOTRA 2016: 8).[10] Among those established in China, as of 2016, 213 firms employed more than 500 local workers, 661 firms 101–500 local workers, 381 firms 51–100 local workers, 832 firms 11–50 local workers, and 1552 firms 10 or less local workers. By contrast, most of these South Korean firms were staffed very little by employees from their mother firms in South Korea. Among those established in Asia rest & Pacific, 4782 firms had five or less employees from their South Korea-based mother firms, 441 firms 6–10 such employees, and 275 firms more than 10 such employees (KOTRA 2016: 8). Among those established in China, 3185 firms had 5 or less employees from their South Korea-based mother firms, 303 firms 6–10 such employees, and 151 firms more than 10 such employees.

The above-presented figures on South Korean firms' aggressive transnationalization, mostly into other Asian countries, reveal several characteristic features of South Korea's capitalist economic globalization: (1) corporate transnationalization attained full velocity as a strategic industrial reaction to the national economic crisis of 1997–1998; (2) it has mainly reflected the overseas relocation or expansion of South Korean manufacturers' industrial production bases; (3) it has generated large numbers of industrial jobs overseas with a critical effect of transnationally replacing domestic industrial employment within South Korea; and (4) it has been geoeconomically concentrated in the Asian region, with two countries under post-socialist reform, China and Vietnam, accounting for staggering proportions. With all its superb performance in global industrial trade, the South Korean economy before the crisis used to be characterized by fairly limited degrees of both inbound and outbound corporate globaliza-

tion—inbound in terms of foreign capital's industrial and financial influences within South Korea and outbound in terms of South Korean capital's
overseas direct investment. South Korea's domestic economic impervious-
ness had long been criticized by Western investors and their governments,
and the national economic crisis coerced South Korea to accept Western
demands for wholesale corporate and financial liberalization (see Chaps. 4
and 5 in this book). At the same time, South Korean manufactures, often
under tacit encouragements of their government, began to aggressively
search for and approach foreign, mostly Asian, platforms for industrial
production with those conditions unavailable in South Korea anymore—
namely, abundant supplies of cheap and docile labor, loose social and environmental regulations over corporate activities, and, sometimes, flexibly
favorable politico-administrative authorities (Ahn et al. 2008).[11] South
Korea's overseas industrial investors have found (and sometime developed) such conditions in numerous Asian countries, including China and
Vietnam as their most coveted destinations. South Korea's such dramatic
industrial integration with China and Vietnam requires some special systematic explanation.

The post-socialist economic reform of China and Vietnam has placed the
two countries in a common path of transnationally dependent industrialization "with unlimited supplies of labour" mostly from rural areas (Huang, Y.
2002; Masina, 2006).[12] Among former state-socialist countries, China and
Vietnam were two of the most underindustrialized economies with most of
their respective populations remaining as huge "surplus" labor in rural areas.
When the two countries' pragmatist state leaderships formally declared fundamental reforms to the stagnant socialist economic systems, their historical
mission consisted as much in *initiating industrialization* for the hitherto
segregated rural populations as in systemically transforming the existing
socialist economies. Such initiation of a new path of industrialization—
above all, labor-intensive as opposed to capital-intensive as in Stalinist heavy
industrialization—necessitated conditions that were not immediately met
domestically. In both countries, state industries in urban areas, despite their
relative limitedness vis-à-vis those in Russia, Eastern European countries,
and North Korea, remained chronic financial burdens and systemic managerial impediments with no hope for functioning as a meaningful industrial
catalyst for their rurally arrested comrades in huge numbers. Thus, the two
countries peripatetically embarked on externally dependent industrialization according to domestic and global market conditions.[13] A sort of
industrialization-cum-marketization-cum-globalization process has been set

in full motion so that Chinese and Vietnamese villagers' labor has been systemically integrated with those foreign industrial investors with quite recent experiences in utilizing their compatriotic villagers' labor for labor-intensive and export-oriented industrialization.[14] East Asia, encompassing South Korea, Taiwan, and so forth, is a world region much more abundant in such kind of investors than any other world regions. In a great historical paradox, the successful experience and laudable outcome of some formerly hard-line anti-communist countries' capitalist industrialization have been utilized by China and Vietnam as convenient resources for industrially jumpstarting their backward economies.

The externally dependent industrialization as the post-socialist development strategy of China and Vietnam seems to have generated a unique regime, in effect, of social governance with various transnational elements and characteristics. Broadly interpreted, this tends to constitute another line of developmental liberalism, encompassing developmental mobilization and cooptation of citizenry, developmental reframing of public governance, state-business nexus in labor relations, familialization of livelihood and welfare, and pluralist social services. Let us very briefly examine these aspects.

Above all, the strategic departure of China and Vietnam from socialist farming in the early 1980s and accompanying decollectivization of social services required Chinese and Vietnamese rural populations to socioeconomically reestablish themselves as mostly family-based entrepreneurial-cum-welfare entities (Chang, K. 1992; Pingali and Xuan 1992). Such socioeconomic transition implied their political rebirth into developmental citizens whose increasingly market-based interests and rights are promoted as the post-socialist states' primary purpose, even at the costs of substantial economic disequalization and social displacement. Concomitantly, "getting rich" autonomously, instead of relying on the state for income and welfare, has been encouraged and legitimated as (formerly) socialist citizens' sociopolitical virtue in the market-economic era. The supposedly traditional virtue of familial support and protection based upon gender- and generation-based moral responsibilities has been formally reinterpreted and redeclared as a highly desirable public attribute under the post-socialist dilemma of collective welfare liquidation.[15] All such institutional reframing of rural livelihood and welfare has been predicated upon each family's individualized establishment and sustenance of sufficient income sources, for which private farming alone would offer no long-term solution under the extremely adverse man-land ratios in China and, though to a less extent, in Vietnam.

As the practically defunct state industries in urban areas offered no assistance for rural people's employment and livelihood, the interests and resources of industrialized capitalist neighbors have been quite eagerly accommodated in initiating a new path of labor-intensive industrialization. A sort of *dependent Lewisan industrialization with unlimited supplies of decollectivized rural labor* has been pursued, with South Korea serving as one of the most aggressive yet useful partners. Therefore, foreigner-invested industrial firms utilizing abundant supplies of Chinese and Vietnamese rural labor have usually been conceived by the central and local governments as convenient instruments for developmental governance. Such position of public authorities, in turn, has been conceived by foreign industrial investors as an essential sociopolitical platform for managing labor relations and handling local social environments under administrative auspices (KOTRA 2015; Koo, Y. 2017). In a sense, for foreign industrial investors in the two post-socialist political economies, a sort of *corporate developmental responsibility* has been no less important than the so-called corporate social responsibilities. Even the legally required labor unions—de facto state arms for controlling both labor and business—often function as an indirect tool for arbitration between foreign industrial capital and local state authority in dealing with labor affairs (Lee, G. 2005; *Labor Today* 2005). In return, foreign industrial firms have often been demanded or expected to offer a wide range of employee welfare benefits and communal social services to make up for the increasing defects in collective and governmental social security programs, thereby becoming a significant constituent of post-socialist welfare pluralism in the countries.[16] All such strategic sociopolitical relationships and corporate managerial practices have been particularly well-accommodated by South Korean firms due to their very recent experiences in similar affairs within their home country.

In short, under the aggressive participation of South Korean and other countries' industrial firms in China's and Vietnam's market-based industrialization, a transnational form of developmental liberalism has been forged as a critical part of the two countries' post-socialist regime of social governance. This trend may appear highly unique in its political economic backgrounds and social conditions, but it should be emphasized that China and Vietnam have undergone a new stage of elementary industrialization which is systemically separated from their earlier Stalinist heavy industrialization and, instead, akin to their advanced capitalist neighbors' labor-intensive industrialization in earlier decades and less-developed capitalist neighbors' similar industrialization nowadays. When South Korean firms enter these less-developed capitalist countries with abundant "demographic dividends", they seek to establish themselves basically in similar ways to their recent approaches in China and Vietnam (and their earlier approaches within South Korea). What nevertheless appears extremely interesting in South Korea's corporate globalization into China and Vietnam is that the two nations' particular systemic dilemmas generated from defunct state socialism have ironically facilitated their pragmatic integration with South Korea's boldly approaching industrial capital. Such industrial integration has been not only economically rewarding (by significantly generating employment and improving labor income and public revenue) but also sociopolitically instrumental (by helping forge a social governance regime of developmental liberalism). In comparison, and as a paradox, South Korean firms in Asia's less-developed capitalist countries seem to have been much less effectively integrated with local authorities, workers, and communities as evidenced by frequent conflicts, disputes, riots, and reprimands involving them.

4   In Perspective: Twofold Developmental Liberalism and Post-National Democracy

In Asian countries' national development, beginning with Japan and now generalized across Asia, capitalism has been conceived as a fundamentally collective venture—as opposed to private individual(ist) venture as in European and American history—necessitated for imminent national survival and prosperity. In this historical context, the state has often assumed the status and authority of bourgeoisie-in-chief. In particular, the capitalist developmental states in Japanese, South Korean, and Taiwanese development used to conceive themselves as collective public bourgeoisie orchestrating capitalist development as a national political goal.[17] Developmental liberalism was formed and consolidated as a common mode of developmental social governance under such sociopolitical characteristics of the East Asian developmental states.

Now in the new century, almost all of the other Asian states, on the one hand, aspire to emulate the East Asian developmental states and, on the other hand, seek to build and strengthen economic and other relationships with other Asian countries. In a sense, Asia as a developmental community is an organic sum of bilateral and multilateral alliances of national collective bourgeoisies. This fact is most vividly illustrated by state heads' frequent official visits among Asian countries, often accompanied by large groups of business leaders posing like a sort of lieutenant bourgeoisies. As Asia is (re)constituted by various bilateral and multilateral alliances of both effective and aspirant developmental states as the region's national collective bourgeoisies, developmental liberalism has recently arisen as a regionalized regime of developmental social governance.

The double-layer structure of developmental liberalism has critical implications for East Asia's national democracies—for South Korean democracy in particular. Developmental liberalism has been much inhibitive to South Korea's political evolution from procedural to substantive democratization along the historical course of West European social democracy. South Korea's democratization in 1987 accompanying two decades of swift capitalist industrialization immediately generated structural strains to developmental liberal governance and intensified sociopolitical aspirations and pressures for social democratic reformation. Unfortunately, the neoliberal counteroffensive—or, more precisely, the neoliberally reframed developmentalist campaign—by *chaebol* and their bureaucratic and professional allies led the country to a national financial meltdown, not to a welfare state. The domestic futility of developmental liberal governance in the post-crisis period prompted South Korean industries to rapidly and widely relocate their production bases to other Asian countries under the tacit encouragement of their patron bourgeois state, thereby helping to form and benefiting from transnationalized developmental liberalism that is sponsored by host-country governments with dependent developmental aspirations. Domestically, South Korea's welfare state transition may now be less frontally resisted by *chaebol* and their technocratic and political patrons thanks to their overseas industrial relocation and expansion, but a social democratic transition devoid of inclusive and stable industrial employment is a sort of catch-22 project, especially because of the Continental Europe-style institutional setup of the South Korean social security system predicated upon the beneficiaries' stable regular employment.

Such systemic dilemma faced by South Korea and other former developmental states in an era of Asianized industrial capitalism may be seen as an East Asian expression of what Colin Crouch (2004) analyzes as "post-democracy". According to Crouch, national democracies under postindustrial and neoliberal conditions have been subjected to structural discrepancies of political institutions in democratic social representation. While citizens as sovereign constituencies of the national polity are structurally alienated due to the increasing ambiguity and irrelevance of conventional formal politics as to diversely volatile everyday realities of social classes, globalized corporate interests exercise insuperable influences over not only their immediate employees and consumers but also nominally (post-)democratic governments whose socioeconomic performance is sensitively affected by global firms' opportunistic positions and policies. National governments and political parties may endeavor to make only adaptive efforts to adhere to the structural trends of industrial and financial globalization, leaving national social interests, agendas, and opinions progressively more displaced. Such subordination of national democracy to neoliberal economic globalism tends to reinforce the prerogatives of entrenched political and technocratic oligarchies, whose public identities and functions grow increasingly ambiguous amid their frequent occupational shift to (domestic and global) private corporate sectors.

In South Korea's twenty-first century, neoliberal economic globalism has been manifest both inbound (global financial capital's appropriation of South Korean industries) and outbound (South Korean industries' overseas relocation, particularly across Asia), exposing the country to all such factors for post-democracy as explained by Crouch (2004). However, the historical sociopolitical nature of the South Korean state, the industrial capitalist system it has led as a national collective bourgeoisie, its developmental liberal regime of social governance, and its contribution to Asianized industrial capitalism and developmental liberal governance all add to critical complexities and particularities in the country's post-democratic transition (or degeneration). Most critically, a sort of *public bourgeois consciousness* of the South Korean state (and other Asian states) is blended with the logic of neoliberal economic globalism, so the neoliberal prioritization of corporate interests and prerogatives is even more intensified while social democratic demands of the working population are more and more disregarded (Chang, K. 2019). All such social detriments and political predicament accompanying the country's post-developmental and post-democratic transition are widely shared among those other Asian countries similarly industrialized under the respective developmental states. The transnationalized regime of developmental liberal social governance consciously and unconsciously constructed on the basis of capitalist industrial integration between these industrialized countries and those other Asian countries which aspire to dependently industrialize by hosting foreign industrial capital from them is quite likely to help assimilate the latter countries with the former countries in respect to the long-term difficulty in politically evolving into genuine social democratic polities.

NOTES

1 INTRODUCTION: DEVELOPMENTAL SOCIAL GOVERNANCE IN TRANSITION

1. *Chaebol* is a term (in Korean) for South Korean business conglomerate(s) that operates multiple corporations in diverse industries with tight ownership and management control by a family (Kang, M. 1996). *Chaebol's* indiscreet borrowings from international lenders in the 1990s were mainly held responsible for the national financial crisis of 1997–1998 (Kong, T. 2000).
2. Social policy was for the first time formalized into the organizational structure of the government during the Roh Moo-Hyun presidency as Roh had been harshly criticized for neglecting social policy concerns during the early phase of his term. He set up a new post of "the chief secretary of social policy" in the presidential office in 2004.

2 DEVELOPMENTAL LIBERALISM: THE DEVELOPMENTAL STATE AND SOCIAL POLICY

1. By then, it needs to be pointed out, the ownership of many competitive industries had rapidly been transferred into the hands of Western financial players to varying degrees. The survival of these Asian industries having become a shared stake to Western financial

© The Author(s) 2019
Chang K-S, *Developmental Liberalism in South Korea*,
International Political Economy Series,
https://doi.org/10.1007/978-3-030-14576-7

capital, their posture suddenly turned so lenient on governmental support for business.

2. Kim Dokyun's (2013) thesis on the "asset-based livelihood security system" touches on an interesting aspect of this entrepreneurial pact between the developmental state and its opportunistic citizenry.

3. In *Pressian* (9 November 2004), No Hoechan, a congressman from Democratic Labor Party, was quoted as saying "Ten million citizens poised to demonstrate, [do you] wish to be beaten to death?" after hearing from a minister of the Roh Moo-Hyun government that about ten million people were in serious poverty already or immediately (http://www.pressian.com/news/article.html?no=28461). No was criticizing Roh for refusing political discussion and negotiation for solving such problems in the parliamentary sessions.

4. Lee adopted an explicitly neo-developmentalist election campaign in 2007 which successfully ushered him into presidency. However, Lee's developmental failure in his actual presidency led Park to camouflage herself through election pledges in 2012 for welfare state and economic democratization. Once elected, she did not bother to pursue these goals (or, in fact, any serious national agendas) and instead ended up being impeached in 2017 for scandalous abuses of her office and authority for civil rights violation, coerced bribery, and so forth. Given the political propagandic contamination of welfare state and economic democratization by Park, the next president, Moon Jae-In, has avoided formally referring to these catchwords either during his presidential election race or in his presidency even though his socioeconomic policy has apparently been focused upon them.

5. Moon's approval rate began to stagnate from roughly one year after his inauguration. This was mostly due to sluggish socioeconomic conditions that, according to his opposition critics, were aggravated by the Moon government policy line in economic affairs (*JoongAng Ilbo*; https://news.joins.com/article/23131387)

6. This reflects an ironic liberal bias of developmental state research unconsciously reflecting bourgeois hegemony. Such bias is even liable for the deficiency in research on internal organizational and social characteristics of developmental bureaucracy.

7. For instance, Esping-Andersen 1990 categorized social policy regimes (welfare states) as liberal, conservative, and social democratic. But none of these categories are sufficiently suitable to depict those Asian states whose social policies are neither wholly negligible in practical importance nor indistinguishable in fashion. On the other hand, many scholars have attempted to identify distinct cultural and/or religious traits in Asian social policy regimes—a practice called by White and Goodman (1998) "welfare orientalism". However, as Goodman and White appraised, such cultural categorization of Asian social policy regimes has failed to receive wide agreement.

8. Social democracy began to be chosen as the most favored system in many social surveys of ordinary citizens as well as opinion leaders. Such preference, however, did not translate into the electoral support for progressive political parties and politicians. See Yang, J. (2017) for a succinct explanation of political, social, and ideological factors underlying the failure of labor-led social democratic politics.

9. See Song, H. (1997), Shin, K. (2015), Kim, Y. (1998), etc.

10. This does not deviate from Esping-Andersen's (1999) own brief appraisal of East Asia. He noticed a mixture of conservative and liberal elements in East Asian social policies but predicted that the conservative nature would be strengthened along the maturation of various social insurances.

11. So far, the most serious criticism in this line was presented in the collective study led by Gordon White and Roger Goodman. On the basis of comparative examination of Japan, South Korea, Taiwan, Singapore, Hong Kong, and mainland China, they arrived at the following unreserved conclusion (White and Goodman 1998: 15):

> We found 'cultural' explanations in terms of Confucianism and the like, whether indigenous or foreign, unhelpful in our attempt to understand the evolution of East Asian welfare systems. When measured against the strategic impact of basic political, economic and demographic factors, 'culture', as presently portrayed at least, proved to be of residual explanatory value. While it is truism that welfare systems may reflect deep-seated elements of social structure and values, it is hard to establish this empirically and take analysis beyond mere assertion or analogy.

Such conclusion, however, should not contradict the importance of Confucian orders and values in private arrangements of care and protection for most of ordinary citizens in the region (Chang, K. 2018).

12. Besides the German social situation associated with classic developmental statism, there is a substantial body of influential literature on interventionist social policies for facilitating capitalist industrialization in more liberal settings (e.g., Donzelot 1979).

13. In a series of studies adopting or elaborating the "resource curse" thesis (Auty 1993), many scholars argue that natural resource richness can present a political trap for underdevelopment because it induces state elite to cajole populace with immediate material gifts drawn from natural endowment and idle on long-term national economic development. This possibility is much higher under an undemocratic regime, which naturally feels less pressure for being pushed out for a poor economic performance. This is one way of explaining the different developmental outcomes of political authoritarianism between some East Asian and Southeast Asian countries. Most recently, however, such differential appraisals of the two regions have been subjected to empirical refutations (e.g., Sovacool 2010).

14. Developmentally promulgated liberal policy was applied to the economic sphere as well. When certain industries were judged to be lacking international competitiveness and thus did not merit strategic policy support, the developmental state turned ruthlessly liberal, leaving them vulnerable to hostile market conditions. In fact, urging them to practically dissolve as soon as possible was another critical component of developmental statism as evinced by a serious of strategic laws for facilitating industrial restructuring through swift reallocation of public resources from declining to emerging industries under the rubric of *saneopgujo godohwa* (industrial structural upscaling). The state needed to turn liberal to declining industries in order to become developmental to emerging industries. Incidentally, industrial policy transition necessitated a social policy expansion for population in declining industries.

15. This may relate to Huntington's (1968) thesis on the relationship between political authoritarianism and economic development in developing societies. However, at least in South Korea, the economic functional utility of political authoritarianism did not prevent forcefully organized social resistances and, ultimately, democratization from below. Such social counter-movements, in

turn, seem to have pressured state elite to perform hard and earnestly for economic development as a political counter-strategy.

16. See Kim Yeon-Myeong (1993) for a comprehensive analysis of the impacts of South-North Korean Cold War on social welfare in the two states.

17. As recently as in 2013, a social democratic party, named Tong-hapjinbodang (Unified Progressive Party), was disbanded by a Constitutional Court ruling. During the presidential election in 2012, this party expressed extreme antagonism to Park Geun-Hye as a supposed political heir of her dictatorial father, Park Chung-Hee. Once elected, Park did not hesitate to exercise her political executive power in removing this party through one of the most controversial political cases in the Constitutional Court's history.

18. It is undeniable that North Korea's prior success in land reform and industrialization generated a formidable pressure for South Korea's catch-up. But these two tasks were not ideology-specific, that is, exclusively socialist or capitalist. Of course, the ways in which these tasks were promoted differed between socialist and capitalist regimes (Kihl, Y. 1984).

19. Besides this ideological taboo on redistributive justice, the Cold War led to an enormous burden of defense expenditure, and thereby put a critical constraint on social expenditure. Furthermore, the slogan of *bugukgangbyeong* (rich nation, strong army) served a forceful ideological basis of developmentalist rule.

20. It was introduced to the constitution under Park Chung-Hee, but its largely cosmetic political purpose was never substantiated in terms of actual administrative policy line. In the 1990s, civil activists successfully launched a constitutional suit against the government neglect of supposedly constitutional rights to basic livelihood and forced the enactment of the National Basic Livelihood Protection Law under which needy households and individuals are entitled to the public support of certain minimum living conditions (Park, Y. 2002).

21. Huntington's (1968) argument on the functional utility of political authoritarianism for economic development was warmly embraced in South Korea.

22. For instance, Americans did not have a national health insurance scheme (except elementary programs for extremely poor and elderly groups) until Obama's presidency. Nor did exist free or subsidized public medical services. Kim Young-Sam, a betrayer to heightened social expectations for progressive social policy in the

post-military era, seemed delighted to point it out before the Social Welfare Policy Appraisal Committee convened in 1994 (of which I was a member) that South Koreans had what Americans did not have in general health protection. However, the national health insurance scheme had been promulgated in the Park Chung-Hee era, whereas Kim's government only refused to the reformist demand for integrating work-based and residence-based programs of public health insurance.

23. On the academic front, research and debate on social policy have been led by social welfare studies and economics which, like most other academic disciplines, have been dominated by PhDs from American universities. The prevalent influence of neoclassical economics and apolitical studies of social work is not unrelated to the extremely conservative ideological and political environment of social policy.

24. This is one of the crucial factors for which the South Korean developmental state would remain much more reserved in (re)distributive social policy and repressive in social control than other development states such as Germany, Japan, and Taiwan at times of similar economic development. The social policy regimes of Japan and Taiwan, at least as compared to that of South Korea, appear more conservative than liberal according to Esping-Andersen's typology. This political situation even induced South Korean capital (represented by *chaebol*) to remain extremely conservative and repressive in labor relations, always expecting a lopsided support from the developmental state in terms of relentless suppression of labor resistance. A paradox of the political and industrial elites' protracted authoritarian conservatism would be revealed in 1987 when neither the state nor capital turned out capable of coping with the sudden outburst of strong labor movements organized through incessant struggles against the state-capital developmental alliance (No, J. 2012). The historically given political boon for the developmental state and its client entrepreneurs turned into a critical political entrapment in their management of grassroots interest and power.

25. The episode of Chung Ju-Yung, the deceased founder of Hyundai Group, who fled to Seoul with the money stolen from his father—the price for a cow sold the day before—is symbolically talked about in this regard.

26. The distribution of (Japan's) *jeoksan* (enemy-left assets) in the 1950s to those cliquey figures connected with state elites served a historical precursor to the later developmental creation and transformation of strategic industries and firms. See Kang, M. (1996).

27. As a lucid critique of fundamental sociopolitical limits of the developmental state in South Korea, see Chang, D. (2009), *Capitalist Development in Korea: Labour, Capital and the Myth of the Developmental State.*

28. Police often worked together with privately organized or purchased forces of *gusadae* (company-saving corps) in cracking down on workers. See Koo, H. (2001).

29. An interesting type of labor resistance has been *junbeoptujaeng* (law-abiding struggle), in which workers challenge the labor-abusive industrial system by keeping regulations and/or laws strictly. See Chang, K. (1998).

30. In this sense, the liberal state of early industrial capitalism was *pro-industrial liberal*, if not developmental liberal. This trait would be revitalized in the neoliberal era in terms of family value debate (Somerville 1992).

31. See Kim, K. (2017) for a broad account of the importance of Confucian culture in South Korean development.

32. A related social practice is what Kim Dokyun (2013) explains as "the asset-based livelihood security system" involving most of ordinary households. Under the radical neoliberal restructuring of the South Korean economy since the national financial crisis, the widespread employment predicament for middle-aged family breadwinners has further intensified this practice—in particular, real estate investment (Kim, M. 2018). Because real estate investment in recent years is pervasively debt-based, this practice, in turn, has helped cause South Korea's household indebtedness at one of the world's highest levels.

33. For a lucid historical institutional account of voluntary sector elements of the South Korean welfare system, see Kim, T. (2008).

34. On European countries' difference in this regard, see Baldwin (1990), *The Politics of Social Solidarity: Class Bases of the European Welfare State, 1875–1975.* For a latest concise comparison of European welfare regimes in all subregions, see Abrahamson (2012).

35. It needs to be pointed out that corporate welfare as well as lifetime employment has been characteristic much more of Japanese firms than of South Korean firms.

36. Individual medical practice has been a profit sector assuming the nature of self-employment.

37. In fact, endless instances of embezzling school budgets and assets by founder/owner figures and their family members have frustrated South Korean society. For the case of Sangji University—perhaps one of the most notorious cases in modern Korean history—see Chung, D. (2017), *Sangji University Democratization Struggle 40 Years*.

38. One of the most notorious examples was Hyeongjebokjiwon (the name meaning "brotherly welfare institution"), an ad hoc institution for accommodating *burangja* (floating persons) during the *Singunbu* (New Military) era of the 1980s (Kim, J. 2015). All kinds of human rights violations—arrestment-like institutionalizations, physical attacks, uncompensated forced labor, thefts of personal belongings, embezzlements of public allowances, malnourishments, denied health treatment, and even summary burials of deceased inmates—have been revealed by external investigations and victims' testaments.

39. In a latest incident, numerous privately founded kindergartens (operating with public funds allocated in proportion to the size of accommodated children) have been found to have used public funds for private needs and purposes of the "owners", including brand bags, karaoke bars, and so on. While such deviances had widely been known to regulatory government organs, they used to share with kindergarten operators an interpretation that privately founded kindergartens are private properties whose public use (for children) should be directly compensated by government funds. That is, publicly allocated operating funds used to be virtually seen as private income from a sort of small business.

40. Most of *chaebol* run various types of *gongikbeopin* (public interest foundations), often with mammoth sizes. Many of them have been utilized as critical components of the familial control structure of the corporate conglomerates and thus criticized as camouflaging entities for illicit private interests (People's Solidarity for Participatory Democracy 1998). See Korea Fair Trade Commission (2018) on the latest official appraisal on this affair.

41. For a classic functionalist interpretation of political authoritarianism in the Third World context, see Huntington (1968), *Political Order in Changing Societies*. On the South Korean case, see Im, H. (1987), "The Rise of Bureaucratic Authoritarianism in South Korea".

42. This policy transition was not yet framed through the government's formal conception of social policy, which would take place only during the Roh Moo-Hyun administration.

43. See Chang, K. (2010a), "Chapter 7. *Chaebol*: The Logic of Familial Capitalism".

44. See Nam, J. (2000) for a more positive assessment of women's role in South Korean democratization.

45. South Korea ultimately launched a separate ministerial government unit under the name of "The Ministry of Gender Equality", which not coincidentally would expand into "The Ministry of Gender Equality and Family".

46. The most successful example is, no doubt, People's Solidarity for Participatory Democracy (http://www.peoplepower21.org). See Cho, D. (2006), "Korean Citizens' Movement Organizations".

3   Coping with the "IMF Crisis" in the Developmental Liberal Context

1. According to frequent surveys in South Korea, Kim Dae-Jung's early performance was rated as superb in the areas of financial crisis management and foreign policy. But Kim was considered disappointing in the areas of political and administrative reform, unemployment relief, *chaebol* reform, labor relations reform, and so on. In these areas, only tiny minorities saw Kim's performance as satisfactory. See *Sisa Journal* (11 June 1998) and so on.

2. I conceptualize these economic, social, and political achievements and changes of South Korea as *compressed modernity* (Chang, K. 1999a).

3. This does not imply that Krugman attributes all responsibility for the financial fiasco to Asia alone. At least since the International Monetary Fund (IMF) rescue programs in the region caused economic aggravation and social confusion, he has been a vocal critic of international financial manipulators, including both the IMF and transnational financial speculators.

4. Moreover, in the 1960s and the 1970s, South Korea was by nature a transition economy (from family farming to capitalist industry), in which the combination of abundant village-provided migrant labor and new industrial technology led to economic growth, both input-driven and efficiency-driven. Without this condition, the Lewisian development could not have occurred (cf. Lewis 1954). Krugman's

view on the efficiency-driven nature of Western economic growth takes for granted a stable, already industrialized economic system—a condition that cannot be taken for granted in non-Western, mostly transitional economies.

5. See Palat (1999) for his emphasis on this overproduction problem.

6. In addition, the owner management of *chaebol* (i.e., the direct control of corporate management by *chaebol* owners) precludes the Dahrendorfian conciliation between employee managers and workers (cf. Dahrendorf 1959). The target for workers' class struggle has always been clear—*chaebol* head and other owner-managers from his family.

7. It is this feature of the South Korean economy that IMF officials ignored in devising their supposed rescue programs based upon high interest rates, thereby aggravating the situation critically.

8. The official unemployment rate in South Korea is calculated by assuming one hour of work per week constitutes the employed status and thus excludes severely underemployed workers (who are usually considered "unemployed" in advanced industrial economies).

9. Relatedly, a survey of 15,900 people in nine Asian countries in 1998 (conducted by the South Korean branch office of FSA Sofres) revealed that, among South Koreans, 90 percent experienced income reductions, 89 percent experienced reductions in purchasing power, and 78 percent experienced reductions in asset values (quoted in *The Hankyoreh*, 16 October 1998). These were the highest figures for the nine countries surveyed.

10. It should also be noted that the economic crisis already broke out in the fourth quarter of 1997, so that the comparison between the fourth quarters of 1997 and 1998 did not fully represent the effect of crisis. For instance, the third quarter of 1997 showed a 7 percent increase in the urban worker household income over the previous year, whereas the fourth quarter of 1997 showed only a 0.6 percent corresponding increase (National Statistical Office 1999).

11. As explained in the previous note, since the economic crisis had already broken out in the fourth quarter of 1997, the comparison between the fourth quarters of 1997 and 1998 did not fully represent the effect of crisis manifested in consumption.

12. Media have presented many mutually contradictory reports about lavish consumption by rich people under the economic crisis. The rich have been portrayed as unconscionable conspicuous consumers enraging unemployed workers and other troubled ordinary citi-

zens. Their expanded consumption, however, has been called for in order to stimulate the national economy. For instance, see *Sisa Journal* (11 June 1998).

13. Cheil Communications, 1998, "IMF Half Year, Self-Portrait of South Koreans" (in Korean; an unpublished survey report), p. 7.

14. There are floods of related media reports, personal records, and research findings. For instance, see "Twenty Years after the Applying for the IMF Rescue Financing... Non-Regular Employees in the Sixties Missing the Hope Forty Years Ago" (*JoongAng Ilbo*, 21 November 2017).

15. A similar situation is observed even in China, a much poorer but relentlessly growing economy, where a majority classify themselves as middle class in various social surveys (e.g., Korea Broadcasting System and Yonsei University 1996).

16. The figure for South Korea was around 80 percent, and the second highest was Japan's 50–60 percent (*The Hankyoreh*, 25 November 1998).

17. As Ravi Palat (1998) points out, the term "crony capitalism" should be qualified in regard to its different developmental consequences for different countries. Even grassroots South Koreans would not deny that some positive economic outcomes were produced by the state-business collusion. It was ironic that, confronting the boomerang effect of the Asian and Russian economic crises, even the US government had to reveal its crony capitalist position by rescuing Long-Term Capital Management, a notoriously speculative hedge fund, from bankruptcy with astronomical amounts of public financial resources. Inevitably, this self-contradictory act caused wide criticism both within and outside the United States (*The Hankyoreh*, 21 October 1998).

18. In this context, it is quite understandable that, in late 1998, the South Korean government was busy publicizing optimistic predictions for the economic situation of the coming year. Its research organs began to present predictions for economic growth in 1999 which were much more optimistic than predictions by international agencies and domestic *chaebol*-run research institutions (*Kukmin Daily*, 9 November 1998). Government officials reportedly pressured *chaebol*-run research institutions to cooperate with the government by presenting similarly rosy predictions (*Chosun Ilbo*, 6 November 1998).

19. According to Korea Institute for Health and Social Affairs, only about ten percent of the unemployed people in 1998 received unemployment allowances, and most of them received benefits for no more than four months (*The Hankyoreh*, 18 November 1998).

20. Simultaneously, the Confucian family ethic for mutual support was emphasized repeatedly as a fulcrum for social stability (Chang, K. 1997; Kim, D. 2002). It has been an important task for the Ministry of Health and Welfare to find out, and award special prizes to, individuals whose self-sacrificing effort for supporting aged parents, handicapped children, and other needy persons under extremely destitute situations could be considered exemplary to other people.

21. Even under the Kim Young-Sam administration, ministers in charge of welfare, health, labor, and environment used to attend the "Meetings of Economic Policy Ministers" in order to adjust their public work according to the guidelines set by the ministers in charge of economic affairs. There were no separate meetings of ministers of social policy matters. The notion of "social policy" was first adopted only during the Roh Moo-Hyun administration, under the mounting social criticism on its indifference and inexperience about social security issues.

22. Rapid economic growth, as the core condition for supposedly full employment in South Korea, was somewhat comparable to Amartya Sen's (1981) social entitlement system.

23. In fact, once they are laid off, they cannot maintain labor union membership of any kind. Against the urgings of the ILO (International Labour Organization) and the labor-business-government agreement in early 1998, the right of unemployed workers to maintain or seek union membership at an industrial or regional level still remains legally prohibited under the strong resistance of prosecutors and other conservative bureaucrats (*The Hankyoreh*, 19 November 1998). Thus, unemployment automatically leads to detachment from organized social power.

24. Owning a large restaurant was a distant second, preferred by 11.3 percent of the respondents. The preference for large restaurant ownership is interesting but quite understandable in that the restaurant business—a self-employed activity without worry for getting fired—has become fashionable among those with certain amounts of capital.

25. It is paradoxical that Kim Dae-Jung had to rely on business initiatives from *chaebol* in his most praised political work, the "Sunshine

Policy Toward North Korea". In particular, the Hyundai Group's North Korea tour programs and other business deals with North Korea constituted the crux of Kim's "politics-business separation" policy (*Sisa Journal*, 19 November 1998).

26. According to a 1998 survey by the Korea Development Institute (1998), of 1000 ordinary South Koreans, 40.9 percent of the respondents thought that business owners and managers had no remorse whatsoever for corporate mismanagement. Another 46.4 percent replied that the remorse of these businessmen was insufficient. Such negative perceptions were even stronger among 305 economic affairs specialists surveyed separately. According to 42 percent of them, South Korean businessmen had no remorse for corporate mismanagement; according to 51.1 percent of them, South Korean businessmen had only insufficient remorse.

27. According to an estimate of government-affiliated researchers in June 1998, only 6.6 percent of the unemployed population received unemployment allowances from the national employment insurance (*The Hankyoreh*, 29 July 1998). It was suspected that a large majority of the currently unemployed population were formerly underemployed people.

28. According to figures from the Ministry of Agriculture, 4141 urban households moved back to villages for the first six months in 1998 (*Sisa Journal*, 19 November 1998). This is more than double the figure for the entire year of 1997, that is, 1823 households.

29. In promoting their own material interests in this dire situation, college students were not able to show the same effectively organized power as they used to command in their political struggle against military dictatorship in earlier decades.

30. It was paradoxical that recent legal changes and decisions encouraged children to support for elderly parents by allowing those providing for parents to receive larger portions of parental inheritance (*JoongAng Ilbo*, 28 July 1998; *Chosun Ilbo*, 30 September 1998). Although not many ordinary citizens would oppose such legal arrangements, provider children may ask for functioning public welfare programs to share their burden.

31. Incidents of human right abuse such as slave labor, physical violence, and sexual abuse had been revealed in numerous welfare institutions across the country (*The Hankyoreh*, 11 April 1998). But officials of the central and the local governments in supervisory positions had never taken serious measures to improve the situation fundamentally.

Part of the reason, of course, lies in the rampant corruption of these officials. The most recent case was in Yangjimaeul, where accommodated homeless people were found out to have suffered from beating, sexual assault, lockup, unpaid forced labor, and death (*The Hankyoreh*, 6 August 1998). Responsible officials, not to mention managers of this institution, denied any such incident even after media made a comprehensive report about the shocking reality. Civil organizations and activists called for the breakup of the collusion between *bokjijok-beol* (welfare mafia family) and the welfare bureaucracy as the most crucial condition for solving the problem. Incidentally, the South Korean government was then discussing the urgent need to establish numerous welfare institutions to accommodate the rapidly increasing population of homeless, runaway, and deserted persons amid the economic crisis.

32. This problem was particularly serious among female-headed families. Women were the first to be laid off, and many of these newly unemployed women had families whose sheer survival depended on their income. For a description of the desperate situation of unemployed women and their dependent families, see Kim, Lee, and Yang (1998).

33. See Stepan (1978) on inclusionary versus exclusionary modes of labor politics.

34. In 1998, a high-ranking official in Ministry of Labor circulated into various government offices and newspapers a statement which directly criticized the conciliatory posture of the current political leadership toward labor and called for harsh measures for compelling workers' and unions' compliance with labor reform programs. He was considered to reflect the widespread reservation of bureaucrats to the corporatist treatment of labor (*The Hankyoreh*, 31 July 1998). On the other hand, many bureaucrats attempted to sabotage the current political leadership's attempts at a thorough overhaul of *chaebol* conglomerates, among other practices, by withholding crucial information on corporate financial structures (*The Hankyoreh*, 16 October 1998).

35. The two national unions, Minjunochong and Hanguknochong, claimed that only two of the fifteen reform items business leaders agreed to implement as their responsibility in February 1998 had actually been fulfilled (*The Hankyoreh*, 21 October 1998).

36. For instance, see "IMF *Satae?*" (in Korean) by SaKong Il (*JoongAng Ilbo*, 21 April 1998).

37. Even Bill Clinton personally remarked the need for thorough *chaebol* reform during his meeting with Kim Dae-Jung in Seoul, late November 1998 (*The Hankyoreh*, 22 November 1998).

38. In its comprehensive report on the South Korean economy in 2018, two decades after the national financial crisis, the OECD voiced a basically unchanged concern about the continuing economic dominance of *chaebol* and concomitant social detriments (OECD 2018).

39. According to its list of requirements for the social safety net, the World Bank suggested 17 social policy goals for South Korea, including a decent standard of living for the elderly, welfare benefits for the unemployed, the medical coverage for the sick, and so on (*The Hankyoreh*, 21 September 1998).

40. In fact, the IMF had in earlier years urged South Korea to liberalize and open financial markets, with essentially the same mistake of ignoring the local context, that is, the unrestrained propensity of South Korean companies for borrowing and the poor governmental capacity for monitoring and regulating international financial transactions. No sooner had the financial markets been liberalized and opened externally than national and corporate debts began to snowball. The ratio of the total national debt to GDP remained around the 10 percent level in the early 1990s and then swelled to 32.5 percent in 1996 and 34.9 percent in 1997 (Samsung Economic Research Institute 1998). Thanks to the near collapse of the South Korean won since late 1997, the ratio reached 50.2 percent as of August 1998. In this respect, South Korea could not be said to have overcome its financial crisis. Instead, the financial malady was only anesthetized with a much enlarged locus.

41. Mahathir's apparent success in protecting the Malaysian economy from the harassment of international financial speculators on the basis of strict foreign currency control presented an even stronger case for the necessity of active state intervention (*Sisa Journal*, 17 September 1998). His strategy drew supporters from many regions and lines of thought. Paul Krugman's recent prescription for controlling the so-called hot money presents a serious sympathy with Mahathir.

42. Most of the new budget for social relief programs was to be secured by the drastic increase in indirect taxes. Among the 3393.9 billion won increase in taxation for 1999, indirect taxes would account for

66.4 percent (*The Hankyoreh*, 21 October 1998). This would reverse the relative weights of direct and indirect taxes in the total budget in favor of the latter, that is, 49.3 percent versus 50.7 percent. As a consequence, according to a report by the Korea Institute of Public Finance, the tax burden increased far disproportionately for the poorer classes. For those urban households earning 850, 000 won (roughly 700 US dollars) or less a month, the combined tax burden (i.e., direct income taxes and indirect consumption taxes) literally skyrocketed from 7.1 percent in 1997 to 14.1 percent in 1998. For those earning 3,610,000 won (roughly 2970 US dollars) or more a month, it remained unchanged at 10.3 percent in this period (*Chosun Ilbo*, 15 March 1999).

43. For instance, see various proposals for civil social relief efforts submitted to the Office of the National Movement for Overcoming Unemployment (*The Hankyoreh*, 19 October 1998, 16 November 1998, 18 March 1999).

44. PSPD (People's Solidarity for Participatory Democracy) was particularly active and effective in this regard. Its success later led to a practical incubation of many politicians who would aggressively promote the legalization of basic social rights. For instance, see Cho, H. (1995), "The Necessity of the Campaign for National Livelihood Minimum and Its Action Measures".

45. On this aspect of democratic politics, see Rueschemeyer, Stephens, and Stephens (1992: 274).

46. A popular news magazine recently branded Kim Dae-Jung as "neoliberal statist" (*Sisa Journal*, 26 November 1998).

47. The visit of Anthony Giddens—Tony Blair's mentor for his "third way politics"—to Seoul in October 1998 had left an interesting repercussion. While it is not certain if his speeches on contemporary politics gave the South Korean audience any coherent idea about the supposedly new line of politics in Tony Blair's United Kingdom, many South Korean politicians and scholars aired quite congenial expressions during their meetings with Giddens. Part of the reason may be due to the fact that Tony Blair's third way politics itself was a similarly complex mixture of various mutually contradictory goals and policies. See Anthony Giddens' *The Third Way: The Renewal of Social Democracy* (1998).

48. Bryan S. Turner (2016: 679) emphatically points to the contemporary global trend of "erosion of citizenship" by declaring that

"we are all denizens now". In South Korea, the national financial crisis and accompanying neoliberal restructuring have made rapidly increasing numbers of its citizens to turn into a sort of post-developmental denizens.

49. When Bill Clinton visited South Korea in late November 1988, he offered his highest praise for Kim Dae-Jung's compliance with American economic and political policies. He was explicitly thankful for Kim's defense during the Asia-Pacific Economic Cooperation (APEC) summit in Malaysia of the open and free economic relationship (i.e., the American doctrine to deal with Asia). *Los Angeles Times*, on 23 November 1988, explained that Kim's congenial stance toward the United States amid the rapidly spreading anti-American sentiment in Asia provided a critical support for the American influence in the region. It was no coincidence that Clinton avoided, without giving any convincing excuse, participation in the APEC summit only a week before where an unfavorable and even hostile feeling against the United States was expected concerning the Asian financial crisis.

4   DEVELOPMENTAL CITIZENRY STRANDED: JOBLESS ECONOMIC RECOVERY

1. See Chang, K. (2012a), "Economic Development, Democracy, and Citizenship Politics in South Korea" for details on this political occasion.

2. According to Loïc Wacquant (2008: 26–27),

[E]conomic restructuring has brought not simply loss of income or erratic employment: it has meant outright denial of access to wage-earning activities, that is, *deproletarianization*. Thus most West European countries have witnessed a steady rise not only in unemployment... but also, more significantly, in the number of the *long-term* unemployed who come overwhelmingly from the lower class.

In recent years, deproletarianization reflects not only neoliberal labor reforms but also radical scientific-technological innovations that help to replace human labor with automated and digitalized mechanisms of production, often under the rubric of "the fourth industrial revolution". It should be indicated that the direction of scientific-technological innovations centered on human labor replacement, in turn, constitutes a neoliberal impetus.

3. I elsewhere conceptualized this developmental attitude of private families with respect to education as *the social investment family* (Chang, K. 2010a).

4. The first issue of the *Whitebook of Public Fund Administration* in 2002 revealed that 156.7 trillion won had been mobilized and used under this scheme by June 2002. Interests to this fund amounted to 24.3 trillion won (Ministry of Finance and Economy, 12 Sept 2002).

5. The 20 member countries of the OECD studied here are Austria, Belgium, Czech, Denmark, Finland, France, Germany, Greece, Hungary, Italy, Japan, the Netherlands, Portugal, Slovakia, Slovenia, Sweden, Swiss, the United Kingdom, the United States, and South Korea. Among other countries, as of 2010, Japan (55.13%), Italy (57.30%), and Sweden (58.79%) showed relatively low levels of labor income share (Joo, S. 2018, Table 1).

6. The current Moon Jae-In government was ushered in with a strong commitment to promote the "regularization" (*jeonggyujikhwa*) of non-regular workers in public sectors and encourage the same in private sectors (Lee, J. 2018).

7. Conservative media love to make a critical issue of such cold responses of netizens to organized labor actions. See "'Hyundai Motors Union Violence'... Hot Internet: Netizens, Anti-Union On-Line Protest" (*Korea Economic Daily*, 5 January 2007).

8. See Kim Won's (2007) "The Social Isolation of South Korea's Big Factory Unions: With a Focus on Hyundai Motors in Ulsan".

9. On 30 June 2017, for instance, the Korean Confederation of Trade Unions (KCTU)—the progressive national umbrella organization for a large number of industrial and corporate unions—helped launch a "societal general strike" (*sahoejeok chongpaeop*) centered on non-regular workers. The KCTU claimed that more than 30 percent of 180,000 non-regular worker members participated in the strike (*Labor Today*, 3 July 2017).

10. SBS (Seoul Broadcasting Service) aired a special report on "Tears of the Republic of Self-Employment" on 9 September 2018 (www.sbs.co.kr)

5   FINANCIALIZATION OF POVERTY: CONSUMER CREDIT
     INSTEAD OF SOCIAL WAGE?

1. See Philip Mader's (2015) *The Political Economy of Microfinance: Financializing Poverty*, as a latest study on financialization of poverty in conjunction with microfinance.
2. See Fine (2012) for a succinct account of various components and trends of financialization in the global neoliberal era.
3. See Chang, K. (1999b) for detailed social and political circumstances during the financial crisis in South Korea.
4. See Chang, K. (2015), "From developmental to post-developmental demographic changes: A perspectival recount on South Korea", for a comprehensive account of such demographic changes.
5. Based upon data directly accessible from the electronic public disclosure (DART) by the Financial Services Commission, Republic of Korea (http://darf.fss.or.kr).
6. The original data for Figs. 5.1 and 5.2 are electronically accessible on the website of the Ministry of Labor (www.molab.go.kr).
7. The United Nations has kept warning against South Korea's adamant neglect of social welfare. See the Committee on Economic, Social and Cultural Rights, the UN Economic and Social Council (2001).
8. See Esping-Andersen (1990) for an authoritative classification of different welfare state regimes. While Esping-Andersen did not include South Korea in his early classification, local South Korean scholars have applied his categories in order to classify South Korea.
9. Broadly speaking, household debt has recently become Asia's region-wide problem, especially since the 2008 global financial crisis (see *Financial Times*, 5 February 2016). According to HSBC data quoted by this newspaper, Thailand, Malaysia, and Singapore have experienced particularly rapid increases in household debt in this period, ultimately overtaking South Korea in household debt-to-GDP ratio, whereas Taiwan has surpassed South Korea throughout. In this respect, it appears that industrializing and industrialized countries in East and Southeast Asia are converging in the trends of financialization of livelihood (or poverty). But this does not necessarily indicate that the same political economic forces and processes are observable behind such financial outcomes.

10. According to OECD data on national economic outlook, as of 1998, South Korea's rate of household savings in disposable income was 24.9 percent, distantly followed by Belgium at 15.6 percent, Spain at 14.0 percent, France at 12.5 percent, and so on (www.oecd.org/eco/outlook/). As of 2008, it was 2.8 percent for South Korea, whereas Denmark, the United States, and a few other European countries showed lower rates. It should be indicated that South Korea's fairly low level of social welfare savings (i.e., public pensions, etc.) makes decreasing household savings particularly problematic because it often implies a total absence of any type of social safety net during economic hardship or personal disaster.

11. Danish households are particularly noticeable in this regard (Andersen et al. 2012).

12. College education, under the remarkable conditions of "the world's second most expensive tuitions", the world's highest rate of college entrance among high school graduates and the far dominant share of private colleges and universities, presents another cause of wide indebtedness to youth and their parents (Korea High Education Institute 2011; Park and Cha 2008). This phenomenon appears analogous to the situation of the United States (Soederberg 2014, Ch. 5) in which college education is the world's most expensive.

13. In early February 2010, the South Korean government organized an international seminar on "Future Vision for Korea's Financial Industry: Takeoff in the Post-Crisis Era". The general spirit during the seminar was still quite *developmental* in respect to the financial industry. See Presidential Council for Future and Vision, Ministry of Strategy and Finance, and Financial Services Commission (2010). Also, see Ha J. (2007), "Nurture big investment banks".

14. Such deregulation of finance, as a supposed policy measure for helping develop private financial industries, has not necessarily led to the abolition of state-ruled developmental finance. See Thurbon (2016), *Developmental Mindset: The Revival of Financial Activism in South Korea.*

15. Appearing in commercial advertisements of these usury financial firms offers a highly lucrative opportunity for entertainment stars. However, many of their fans and ordinary citizens often consider it an unethical act, so their popularity and respectability have sometimes been crucially damaged (*Sagunin*, 12 October 2015).

Sometimes this criticism is conflated by the anti-Japanese nationalist sentiment because Japanese capital, allegedly including that of Japanese mafia (*yakuza*), has aggressively entered various types of South Korea's usury businesses.

16. One trillion won was equivalent to about 0.9 billion dollars in 2010.

17. Lee Myung-Bak, under a showy slogan of neo-developmentalism ("Korea 747"), stepped into presidency by aggressively capitalizing on South Korean grassroots' frustration with un(der)employment and poverty (Lee, M. 2007). But his actual policy was immediately dictated by the neoliberal interests of *chaebol* and the financialized upper-middle class, exasperating the deprived classes (Chang, K. 2012a). After confronting a society-wide condemnation of his neo-liberal policy, some pragmatists among his staff persuaded Lee to veer toward more inclusive economic and social policies. Park Geun-Hye learned a lesson from Lee's failure, so she adopted reformist pledges, such as "welfare state" and "economic democra-tization", during her presidential election campaign. This political strategy successfully inducted her into presidency, but she immedi-ately turned her administration to another neo-developmental direction, including deregulation and labor market flexibilization (Seoul Institute of Economic and Social Studies 2014).

18. See Financial Services Commission and Smile Microcredit Bank (2010b), "The implementation plan of Smile Microcredit in 2010".

19. Even this program has been harshly criticized due to the ostensibly ungenerous terms of financing. *The Korea Herald* (29 March 2010) noted: "Korea's interest rate on its 'study-now-pay-later' loan is the highest among countries that have the same program, … higher than the country's base mortgage rate of 5.2 percent and more than double the average level of the five OECD member countries during the 2004–2005 period".

20. See Financial Services Commission and Smile Microcredit Bank (2010a) for "Special financial service/rehabilitation programs for poor people (*seomin*)". See Kim, S. (2011) for a comprehensive explanation of the ultimate risks and disadvantages to end users accruing to these programs.

21. See Goodman and Peng (1996) on the peripatetic nature of Asian social policy regimes.

6   DEMOGRAPHIC MELTDOWN: FAMILIAL STRUCTURAL
    ADJUSTMENTS TO THE POST-DEVELOPMENTAL IMPASSE

1. To proportion and compare the *prevalence* of suicide for different
   countries, the WHO adjusts for age (*age standardization*) every
   country's crude mortality rate based on other relevant statistical
   data such as median population ages, sex ratios, and age distribution
   (i.e., age groups), enhancing cross-national comparability. Another
   way to think of it is that since populations' age structures are often
   very different, but the likelihood of dying by suicide is generally
   increased with age, in order to avoid masking the sensible differences given by each country's age distributions, countries' rates are
   reciprocally *weighted* into the overall trend to globally frame
   national suicide rates, and the *epidemiological* prevalence (or likelihood) of suicide.
2. For instance, National Statistical Office (2016), "The Result of the
   2016 Social Survey (Family, Education, Health, Safety, Environment)",
   15 November 2016; Lee, Noh, and Lee (2012), "Policy Issues and
   Directions for a Rapid Increase in Suicides in Korea", KIHASA
   Research Report 2012–64
3. *The World Factbook*, 24 December 2018 (https://www.cia.gov/
   library/publications/the-world-factbook/rankorder/2127rank.
   html)
4. Korean Statistical Information Service (2018b), "Average Age at First
   Marriage by Cities and Provinces, 1990–2017" (http://kosis.kr/sta-
   tisticsList/statisticsListIndex.do?menuId=M_01_01&vwcd=MT_
   ZTITLE&parmTabId=M_01_01#SelectStatsBoxDiv)
5. See Chang, K. (2018), *The End of Tomorrow? Familial Liberalism
   and Social Reproduction Crisis.*
6. For instance, see Chai, J. (2014), *Obama Praises the "Korean
   Education Fervor": Should We Emulate It?*
7. In this respect, the world's lowest levels of fertility found among
   South Korea and its industrialized neighbors reflect a fundamentally different social trend from Europe's fertility declines (cf.
   Billari and Kohler 2004).
8. The rapid increase in suicides does not reflect any cultural trait of
   Koreans inherited from their ancestors. To the contrary, Koreans
   used to consider harming themselves physically a highly impious
   act because they were normatively reminded that their physical

bodies are precious "parental gifts". In numerous troubled families, ironically, such parental gifts haven been taken away from little children by parents themselves. Needless to say, this parental killing is not any cultural trait, either.

9. Lee, H. (2012) compared South Korea, Japan, and China in this trend and found that Chinese people are more likely to see it as killing of human life than South Korean and Japanese people.

10. OECD (2017), *Preventing Ageing Unequally*. See "Chapter 5. Aged People's Individualization without Individualism" in Chang, K. (2018), *The End of Tomorrow? Familial Liberalism and Social Reproduction Crisis* (in Korean), Seoul: Jipmundang.

7   FROM DEVELOPMENTAL LIBERALISM TO NEOLIBERALISM

1. See "The Politics of Practical Nostalgia", *Newsweek*, 7 April 2008.

2. Part of these coalitions constituted what Peter Evans (1995) calls the "embedded autonomy" of the state.

3. This trend is described by the pejorative phrase of "*chaebol* republic". As Samsung has been incomparably aggressive in this regard (Kim, S. 2007; Song, B. 2007; Choi, H. 2005; Ha, S. 2011; Cho, Lee, and Song 2008), the country is even phrased as "Samsung republic".

4. Lim and Jang (2006) offer a lucid broad account of various factors and contexts for the rapid neoliberal transition of the South Korean developmental system.

5. Privatization (of public enterprises and services) was another component, however, with relatively limited social policy implications. But the new government of Lee Myung-Bak allegedly purported to pursue privatization of various essential social services, including even public utilities.

6. I personally noticed this tendency as a member of the Social Welfare Policy Appraisal Committee during 1994–1995.

7. On productive welfare in South Korea, see Mishra, et al. eds. (2004).

8. Labor market flexibilization is a direct translation of the Korean phrase, *nodongsijang yuyeonhwa*.

9. The South Korean government even set up in 1998 a special administrative organ for deregulation, named "Regulatory Reform

Committee", which is currently co-chaired by a prime minister and a civilian expert (www.rrc.go.kr).

10. Another factor for such ethnic pluralization is the massive arrival of foreign brides, mostly, to rural areas.

11. He also agreed to freely offer South Korean industries and public assets to international investors.

12. In an interesting development, many reform-minded South Korean economists and civil activists came to accidentally align with international neoliberal regulators in respect to the reform of *chaebol*'s corporate governance. To these reformers, the national economic crisis was no less an outcome of the legally and financially problematic nature of *chaebol*'s corporate governance than that of the volatile and irresponsible structure of the global financial industry and the poor reaction of the South Korean government to its influences. The mounting social (and international) pressure for *chaebol*'s managerial transparency and accountability was once so daunting that they even tried to arouse a nationalist sentiment from public, hinting at a supposed possibility of corporate takeover by foreign investors amid their financial difficulties. Such manipulative strategy was not entirely unsuccessful, but the reform of *chaebol*'s corporate governance remained as a national priority on the public mind. In another interesting development, because major *chaebol*, such as Samsung and Hyundai, continued to confront social and legal challenges as well as administrative pressures, they suddenly began to make pledges for phenomenal amounts of public donations. While such pledges fell short of constituting an integrated trend of corporate social responsibility, they at least attested to the acknowledgment that they share the responsibility for social protection of underprivileged and/or deprived groups even in the global neoliberal era.

13. Such neoliberal betrayal of a supposedly progress state leadership has not been limited to Kim Dae-Jung but widely observed in contemporary world politics. Tony Blair's Third Way politics was a showy example, followed by Bill Clinton and so on. The common politico-historical background to these neoliberalized progressive leaders is that they all got elected into power thanks to the national economic and/or government budgetary crises caused by the conservative governments and thus were obliged to immediately tackle with such economic and budgetary crises. Rescuing urgently the defunct national economy and/or the bankrupt state seems to

have required these seemingly progressive leaders to turn to conservative or neoliberal measures in their economic and social policies. Barack Obama's presidency may be interpreted in the same vein in spite of his strong will to execute serious reforms in health care and so on.

14. See "Labor-Business-Government Committee Co-Declaration" (in Korean), 20 January 1998 (in Chap. 3).

15. Provision of the social safety net, as a condition for radical economic restructuring and labor reshuffling, was part of the so-called Washington Consensus.

16. The Bismarckian social security system in South Korea is predicated upon permanent regular employment. Thus, the denial of regular employment consequently implies annulment of social security benefits (or denial of social citizenship rights). See Chap. 4.

17. If any, special policy attention was paid to the issues of extremely low fertility and hyper population aging. While these issues reflected typical (neo)liberal concerns, some progresses were made in the areas of child care and elderly protection.

18. It was only in the latter half of his term that he placed an explicit separate attention to social policy in general, for instance, by setting up the position of "social policy advisor".

19. See Lee's "Korea 747" pledges (http://english.mbplaza.net/default/korea/?type=html/ 747_01&wgrp=42&m=2).

20. "Active welfare" (*neungdongjeok bokji*) was initially discussed as its social policy paradigm, but even this would be bluntly ignored by the regime itself.

21. Broadly seen, the "Candlelight Protests" that lasted a few months in 2008 were an expression of the civil resistance to the Lee Myung-Bak government's neoliberalization, ranging from the completion of the FTA with the United States to aggressive privatization of public enterprises and concerns.

22. As the political approval rate recovered immediately after such populist turn, this political line was sustained quite a while.

23. For instance, *Kyunghyang Daily*, a center-left newspaper, ran a special series on "Saying the Welfare State" for nearly two months, between 8 May and 6 July 2011 (http://welfarekorea.khan.kr/). *The Hankyoreh*, another progressive newspaper, also covered welfare state issues through extensive special reports, conferences, interviews, and so on. These media coverages functioned as public

venues for the public debates on the welfare state as South Korea's future among prominent academics, experts, activists, and so on.

24. For a useful critical account of the welfare state's limit in South Korea's post-crisis transition, see Kuk, M. (2012), *Developmental State, Welfare State, and Neoliberalism*.

25. As early as 2009, she alluded to this political course by remarking, in her eulogy at the 30th year memorial service for Park Chung-Hee (on 26 October 2009), my "father's ultimate dream was to construct the welfare state... Although he endeavored so much for economic growth, economic growth itself was not his end" (*OhmynewsTV*, 11 October 2017; https://www.youtube.com/watch?v=4V9Ylnb5ZWA).

26. It was during the Roh Tae-Woo administration (1987–1992) that social welfare was upheld as a core policy agenda, in order to materially fend off social challenges to the military's succession of state leadership even after democratization. The expansion of welfare expenditure during this period was greater than any previous years and even most of the following years (Seo, B. 1997).

27. His ten major pledges included "job creation, reform of political and institutional state powers, anti-corruption and *chaebol* reform, strengthening of the ROK-US alliance and securing of self-reliant national defense, youth-empowering nation, abolition of gender discrimination, nation of happy elderly, state responsibility for education and childrearing, rescuing of self-employed and small business people, safe and healthy nation" (*The Hankyoreh*, 14 April 2017).

28. For instance, self-employed service traders whose number has increased explosively since the national financial crisis have been extremely unhappy about their business conditions being rather worsened under these labor market reforms, whereas yet-to-be-employed youth have been frustrated at the very sluggish pace of corporate job expansion (*Hankookilbo*, 21 December 2018).

29. In a latest poll by *Realmeter*, President Moon's approval rate was the lowest (29.4 percent) among those men in their twenties, which was worse than the approval rate among those in their sixties and above. Thanks to a series of gender equity campaigns, those women in their twenties showed the highest approval rate of 63.5 percent (*Realmeter*, 17 December 2018; www.realmeter.net).

8   THE RISE OF DEVELOPMENTAL LIBERAL ASIA:
SOUTH KOREAN PARAMETERS OF *ASIANIZED* INDUSTRIAL
CAPITALISM

1. See Callaghan and Hubbard (2016), "The Asian Infrastructure Investment Bank: Multilateralism on the Silk Road" and Yu, H. (2016), "Motivation behind China's 'One Belt, One Road': Initiatives and Establishment of the Asian Infrastructure Investment Bank" for lucid analysis of the global context and Chinese intent for the AIIB.

2. Asia's industrial integration has facilitated and has been facilitated by Asia's financial integration. See Asian Development Bank (2017), *The Era of Financial Interconnectedness: How Can Asia Strengthen Financial Resilience?*

3. For instance, these two systems of political economy can be simplistically compared as follows: in a *liberally liberal* society, bourgeoisie as the dominant class will insist on minimal social spending in order to minimize its financial burden of taxation, whereas in a *developmentally liberal* society, the developmental state will try to minimize social spending in order to maximize economic developmental investment within a given budget.

4. See The Economist Intelligence Unit (2015), *integrAsian: How Asia's Economic Ties Are Changing the Business Landscape.*

5. For a recent lucid analysis in this regard, see Rock (2017), *Dictators, Democrats, and Development in Southeast Asia.*

6. Special economic zones mushrooming across Asia's late industrializing countries and regions often function as an ad hoc institutional framework for nullifying labor protection and welfare measures for local workers. This is particularly serious in India (Parwez 2015) and so on.

7. In China's post-socialist reform of the urban state sector, similar arrangements have been strategically promoted as a convenient way of repositioning the state's share in the marketized economic system (Lin, Y. 2014).

8. In this respect, rural families bear various "social transition costs of industrialization" (Chang, K. 2010a, Chapter 6) in the Lewisian dual-sector model of industrialization. This has been particularly pertinent in Asia's late industrialization at both the national and the transnational levels.

9. Welfare pluralism is an essential historical characteristic of the welfare systems of various East Asian and Southeast Asian countries (Desai 2013). The thereby induced complexity of Asian social welfare has been further strengthened in recent years due to intra-Asian governmental, corporate, and civilian inputs. For instance, the Hong Kong-based Centre for Asian Philanthropy and Society (http://caps.org/who-we-are/mission-and-goals/) is a distinct regional initiative for "private" philanthropy initiative with heavy corporate financial support.

10. KOTRA is mistaken in stating 7394 firms hired 11–50 local workers; 1394 firms were in this category.

11. Simultaneously, the South Korean government gradually opened up the domestic labor market in such a way as to allow local sweatshop industries, under an increasing shortage of eager Korean workers, to utilize guest workers from populous Asian countries at affordable costs and under convenient conditions (Seol, D. 2002). Without any intention to accept them permanently, except those with high levels of strategic human capital, the government has devised and implemented various schemes for maintaining the circulatory nature of these guest workers (Seol, D. 2014). As of early 2019, they work in South Korea under the status of "industrial trainee" with a three-year term, which is renewable after a departure from South Korea.

12. See Chang, K. (1993), "The Peasant Family in the Transition from Maoist to Lewisian Rural Industrialization" for a systematic account of post-socialist industrialization tapping Chinese rural labor as a variant of Lewisian industrialization (cf. Lewis 1954).

13. The degree of external dependence in industrialization has been lower in China, thanks to the unexpected booming of rural industries since the mid-1980s (Chang 1993), which, in turn, was triggered by the drastic improvement in rural income due to the interactive effect between agricultural managerial privatization and procurement price raising for crops.

14. In this respect, there has been some substitutive relationship between China and Vietnam as prime destinations for labor cost-sensitive foreign industrial investment. South Korean firms have most evidently responded to this consideration. See POSCO Research Institute (2014), "No Eggs in One Basket: Foreign Companies Leave China and Head Towards Vietnam".

15. In various localities of China, an official campaign of *funuhuijia* (women returning home) was launched in order to facilitate familialization of social care and protection in the post-collective context (Zhang and Ma 2014).

16. In conjunction with transnational industrial investment, South Korea's NPOs and public agencies also concentrate their social assistances and services to those countries hosting South Korean enterprises. Vietnam has occupied a lion's share in various domains of South Korea's social as well as developmental assistance (Pham 2017; The Government of the Republic of Korea 2016).

17. This orientation led to a highly interesting equivalence to the commander position of the socialist states in constructing and managing the socialist economies on behalf of all people (cf. Riskin 1987).

References

Abrahamson, Peter. 2012. European Welfare States: Neoliberal Retrenchment, Developmental Reinforcement, or Plural Evolutions. In *Developmental Politics in Transition: The Neoliberal Era and Beyond*, ed. Chang Kyung-Sup, Ben Fine, and Linda Weiss, 92–115. Basingstoke/New York: Palgrave Macmillan.

Ahn, Sanghoon, Siwook Lee, and Cheonsik Woo. 2008. The Internationalisation of Firm Activities and Its Economic Impacts: The Case of South Korea. In *Multinational Corporations and the Emerging Network Economy in Asia and the Pacific*, ed. Juan J. Palacios, 139–162. London: Routledge.

Akers, Beth. 2013. Assessing the Plight of Recent College Grads. *Brookings Report*, October 30.

Amberg, Joe J., and Sara L. McGaughey. 2017. *Fostering Local Entrepreneurship in a Multinational Enterprise*. London: Routledge.

Amsden, Alice. 1989. *Asia's Next Giant: South Korea and Late Industrialization*. New York: Oxford University Press.

Andersen, Asger Lau, et al. 2012. The Wealth and Debt of Danish Families. *Monetary Review*, 2nd Quarter 2012, Part 2, 1–40.

Asian Development Bank (ADB). 2011. *Asia 2050: Realizing the Asian Century*. Manila: ADB.

———. 2016. *What Drives Foreign Direct Investment in Asia and the Pacific (Asian Economic Integration Report 2016)*. Manila: ADB.

———. 2017. *The Era of Financial Interconnectedness: How Can Asia Strengthen Financial Resilience? (Asian Economic Integration Report 2017)*. Manila: ADB.

Auty, Richard. 1993. *Sustaining Development in Mineral Economies: The Resource Curse Thesis*. London: Routledge.

© The Author(s) 2019
Chang K-S, *Developmental Liberalism in South Korea*,
International Political Economy Series,
https://doi.org/10.1007/978-3-030-14576-7

Bae, Jun-Ho. 1998. Life Changes of Low Income Strata Under Employment Uncertainty (in Korean). Paper presented at the National Statistical Office Seminar on "The Changes and Trends in the Living Conditions of South Korean Households", 1 Sept 1998.

Baldwin, Peter. 1990. *The Politics of Social Solidarity: Class Bases of the European Welfare State, 1875–1975.* Cambridge: Cambridge University Press.

Bank of Korea. 1998. The Analysis of Corporate Management in the First Half of 1998 (in Korean). Unpublished survey report.

Beck, Ulrich, and Elisabeth Beck-Gernsheim. 2002. *Individualization: Institutionalized Individualism and Its Social and Political Consequences.* London: Sage.

Billari, Francesco, and Hans-Peter Kohler. 2004. Patterns of Low and Lowest-Low Fertility in Europe. *Population Studies* 58 (2): 161–176.

Blanton, Robert G., and Shannon L. Blanton. 2012. Labor Rights and Foreign Direct Investment: Is There a Race to the Bottom? *International Interactions* 38 (3): 267–294.

Byoun, Soo-Jung, and Hwang Nam-Hui. 2018. Plan for Ageing Society and Population: Issues and Challenges (in Korean). *Health and Welfare Forum* 258 (April 2018): 41–61.

Callaghan, Mike, and Paul Hubbard. 2016. The Asian Infrastructure Investment Bank: Multilateralism on the Silk Road. *China Economic Journal* 9 (2): 116–139.

Central Intelligence Agency (CIA), the United States. 2018. *The World Factbook*, 24 Dec 2018. https://www.cia.gov/library/publications/the-world-factbook/rankorder/2127rank.html

Centre for Asian Philanthropy and Society. http://caps.org/who-we-are/mission-and-goals/

Chae, Oh. Byung. 2014. The Social Policy of the Rhee Syngman Regime from a Viewpoint of Constitution Making and Revision, 1948–1958 (in Korean). *Social Theory* 46: 417–448.

Chai, Ju-Chun. 2014. *Obama Praises the "Korean Education Fervor": Should We Emulate It?* Platform: CreateSpace Independent Publishing.

Chang, Dae-oup. 2009. *Capitalist Development in Korea: Labour, Capital and the Myth of the Developmental State.* London: Routledge.

Chang, Hong Geun. 1999. The Transformation of the 'Labor Regime' in Korea, 1987–1997 (in Korean). PhD dissertation in Department of Sociology, Seoul National University.

Chang, Hye Kyung, and Kim Yeong-Ran. 1999. *A Study of the Changes in Family Life and the Role of Women Under Unemployment* (in Korean). Seoul: Korea Women's Development Institute.

Chang, Jin-Ho. 2014. The *Chaebol* and the Economy of Irresponsibility in South Korea (in Korean). *Critical Review of History* 108: 91–119.

Chang, Kyung-Sup. 1992. China's Rural Reform: The State and Peasantry in Constructing a Macro-Rationality. *Economy and Society* 21 (4): 430–452.

―――. 1993. The Peasant Family in Transition from Maoist to Lewisian Rural Industrialisation. *Journal of Development Studies* 29 (2): 220–244.

―――. 1997. The Neo-Confucian Right and Family Politics in South Korea: The Nuclear Family as an Ideological Construct. *Economy and Society* 26 (1): 22–42.

―――. 1998. Risk Components of Compressed Modernity: South Korea as Complex Risk Society. *Korea Journal* 38 (4): 207–228.

―――. 1999a. Compressed Modernity and Its Discontents: South Korean Society in Transition. *Economy and Society* 28 (1): 30–55.

―――. 1999b. Social Ramifications of South Korea's Economic Fall: Neo-Liberal Antidote to Compressed Capitalist Industrialization? *Development and Society* 28 (1): 49–91.

―――. 2010a. *South Korea under Compressed Modernity: Familial Political Economy in Transition*. London/New York: Routledge.

―――. 2010b. The Second Modern Condition? Compressed Modernity as Internalized Reflexive Cosmopolitisation. *British Journal of Sociology* 61 (3): 444–464.

―――. 2010c. Proletarianizing the Financial Crisis: Jobless Industrial Restructuring and Financialized Poverty in Post-Crisis South Korea. Paper Presented at the First International Conference in Political Economy of the International Initiative for the Promotion of Political Economy (IIPPE) on "Beyond the Crisis", 10–12 September 2010, Rethymno, Crete, Greece.

―――. 2012a. Economic Development, Democracy, and Citizenship Politics in South Korea: The Predicament of Developmental Citizenship. *Citizenship Studies* 16 (1): 29–47.

―――. 2012b. Developmental Citizenship in Perspective: The South Korean Case and Beyond. In *Contested Citizenship in East Asia: Developmental Politics, National Unity, and Globalization*, ed. Chang Kyung-Sup and Bryan S. Turner, 182–202. London/New York: Routledge.

―――. 2014a. A Theoretical Account of the Individual-Family-Population Nexus in Post-Socialist Transitions. In *Family and Social Change in Socialist and Post-Socialist Societies*, ed. Zsombor Rajkai, 19–35. Leiden and Boston: Brill.

―――. 2014b. Asianization of Asia: Asia's Integrative Ascendance Through a European Aperture. *European Societies* 16 (3): 1–6.

―――. 2015. From Developmental to Post-Developmental Demographic Changes: A Perspectival Recount on South Korea. *Korean Journal of Sociology* 49 (6): 21–45.

―――. 2018. *The End of Tomorrow? Familial Liberalism and Social Reproduction Crisis* (in Korean), Seoul: Jipmundang.

―――. 2019. *The Logic of Compressed Modernity: The Transformative Structure of Korean Society*. Under revision for University of California Press.

Chang, Kyung-Sup, Chin Meejung, Sung Miai, and Jaerim Lee. 2015. Institutionalized Familialism in South Korean Society: Focusing on Income

Security, Education, and Care (in Korean). *Journal of the Korean Family Studies Association* 27 (3): 1–38.

Chang, Kyung-Sup, and Song Min-Young. 2010. The Stranded Individualizer Under Compressed Modernity: South Korean Women in Individualization without Individualism. *British Journal of Sociology* 61 (3): 540–565.

Chapple, Wendy, and Jeremy Moon. 2005. Corporate Social Responsibility (CSR) in Asia: A Seven-Country Study of CSR Web Site Reporting. *Business and Society* 44 (4): 415–441.

Cheil Communications. 1998. IMF Half Year, Self-Portrait of South Koreans (in Korean). Unpublished survey report.

Cho, Dae-Yop. 2006. Korean Citizens' Movement Organizations: Their Ideologies, Resources, and Action Repertoires. *Korea Journal* 46 (2): 68–98.

Cho, Donmoon, Lee Byung Cheon, and Song Won-Geun, eds. 2008. *South Korean Society, Questioning Samsung* (in Korean). Seoul: Humanitas.

Cho, Heungsik. 1995. The Necessity of the Campaign for National Livelihood Minimum and Its Action Measures (in Korean). *PSPD Magazine*, May 1995.

Cho, Oak La. 1998. Modernity and Conservatism in Rural Families (in Korean). *Korean Cultural Anthropology* 31 (2): 377–405.

Cho, Seok-Gon. 2015. The Trends of Land Productivity Growth during Colonial Period and during Land Reform at Hojeo-Myeon, Wonju-City (in Korean). *Trend and Prospect* 94: 204–250.

Choi, Han-Su. 2005. Unchecked Power, Samsung in Anatomy (in Korean). *Culture Science* 43: 239–256.

Choi, Jang-Jip. 1998. Speak of the Fundamental Nature of D.J. Reform (in Korean). *Shin Dong-A* 41 (11): 88–98.

———. 2002. *Democracy After Democratization: Crisis and Conservative Origin of Korea's Democracy* (in Korean). Seoul: Humanitas.

Choi, Sun-Young, and Chang Kyung-Sup. 2016. The Material Contradictions of Proletarian Patriarchy in South Korea's Condensed Capitalist Industrialization: The Instability in the Working Life Course of Male Breadwinners and Its Familial Ramifications. In *New Life Courses, Social Risks and Social Policy in East Asia*, ed. Raymond Chan, Jens Zinn, and Lih-Rong Wang, 149–166. London: Routledge.

Chosun Ilbo. www.chosun.com

Chung, Chung Kil. 1988. Meetings of Economic Ministers and Policy Decision (in Korean). *Korean Journal of Public Administration* 26 (2): 370–380.

Chung, Dae-Hwa. 2017. *Sangji University Democratization Struggle 40 Years: Lively Records of the Struggle and Experimentation for the Future of South Korean Private Schools* (in Korean). Seoul: Hanul.

Chung, Sung-ho. 2010. Causal Model of Low Fertility Determinants in Korea (in Korean). *Journal of Social Sciences* 49 (1): 69–91.

Chung, Un-Chan. 2004. An Evaluation of the Financial Policy and Policy Agenda. Paper prepared for Korea Institute of Finance.

Cotton, James. 1992. Understanding the State in South Korea: Bureaucratic-Authoritarian or State Autonomy Theory? *Comparative Political Studies* 24 (4): 512–531.

Crouch, Colin. 2004. *Post-Democracy*. Cambridge: Polity Press.

Cumings, Bruce. 1981. *The Origins of the Korean War: Liberation and Emergence of Separate Regimes, 1945–1947*. Princeton: Princeton University Press.

———. 1998. The Korean Crisis and the End of 'Late' Development. *New Left Review* 231: 43–72.

Daewoo Economic Research Institute. 1998. The Phenomenon of Pain Transfer from Advanced Countries to Asian Countries and Its Implication for the South Korean Economy (in Korean). Unpublished report.

Dahrendorf, Ralf. 1959. *Class and Class Conflict in Industrial Society*. Stanford: Stanford University Press.

DART. Data Analysis, Retrieval and Transfer System, Financial Supervisory Service, Republic of Korea. http://darf.fss.or.kr

Desai, Murli. 2013. Social Policy Approaches, Human Rights, and Social Development in Asia. *Social Development Issues* 2: 1–17.

Dong-A Ilbo. www.donga.com

Donzelot, Jacques. 1979. *The Policing of Families*. New York: Pantheon.

Edaily. www.edaily.co.kr

Encarnation, Dennis J., ed. 1999. *Japanese Multinationals in Asia: Regional Operations in Comparative Perspective*. New York: Oxford University Press.

Esping-Andersen, Gøsta. 1990. *The Three Worlds of Welfare Capitalism*. Princeton: Princeton University Press.

———. 1999. *Social Foundations of Postindustrial Economies*. New York: Oxford University Press.

Evans, Peter. 1995. *Embedded Autonomy: States and Industrial Transformation*. Princeton: Princeton University Press.

Financial Services Commission (Republic of Korea), and Smile Microcredit Bank. 2010a. The Current Situation of Establishment and Management of Smile Microcredit for One Month, etc. (in Korean). Press brief, 18 Jan 2010.

Financial Services Commission (Republic of Korea), and Smile Microcredit Bank. 2010b. The Implementation Plan of Smile Microcredit in 2010 (in Korean). Press brief, 20 Jan 2010.

Financial Times.

Fine, Ben. 2012. Neo-Liberalism in Retrospect? – It's Financialization, Stupid. In *Developmental Politics in Transition: The Neoliberal Era and Beyond*, ed. Chang Kyung-Sup, Ben Fine, and Linda Weiss, 51–69. Basingstoke/New York: Palgrave Macmillan.

Funabashi, Yoichi. 1993. The Asianization of Asia. *Foreign Affairs* 72 (5): 75–85.

Gerschenkron, Alexander. 1962. *Economic Development in Historical Perspective*. Belknap: Cambridge.

Giddens, Anthony. 1998. *The Third Way: The Renewal of Social Democracy.* Cambridge: Polity Press.

Global Investment & Business Center. 2017. *South-East Asia – Investment Resources and Capital for South-East Asian Countries Handbook: Strategic Information, Opportunities, Contacts.* Alexandria: International Business Publications.

Golub, Philip S. 1998. Bitter Fruits of a Miracle: When East Asia Falters. *Le Monde Diplomatique,* July.

Goodman, Roger, and Ito Peng. 1996. The East Asian Welfare States: Peripatetic Learning, Adaptive Change, and Nation-Building. In *Welfare States in Transition: National Adaptations in Global Economies,* ed. Gøsta Esping-Andersen, 192–224. London: Sage.

Gubhaju, Bhakta B. 2013. Demographic Dividends in South Asia: A Window of Opportunity. *East Asia Forum Quarterly* 5 (1). https://www.eastasiaforum. org/2013/04/06/demographic-dividends-in-south-asia-a-window-of-opportunity/

Ha, Joonkyung. 2007. Nurture Big Investment Banks (in Korean). *National Economy* 2007 (9): 12–13.

Ha, Seung-Wu. 2011. Samsung Republic, Are We Citizens? (in Korean). *Silcheon Munhak* 103: 163–172.

Hankookilbo. http://www.hankookilbo.com

Herald Business. www.heraldbiz.com

Hong, Duck-Ryul. 2006. Jaebeol's Power, Past, Present and Future (in Korean). *Critical Review of History* 77: 95–117.

Hong, Yong-Pyo. 2007. An Analysis of Syngman Rhee's Anti-Communist Line from Realist Perspective (in Korean). *Journal of World Politics* 28 (2): 51–80.

Huang, Yasheng. 2002. *Selling China: Foreign Direct Investment during the Reform Era.* Cambridge: Cambridge University Press.

Huntington, Samuel. 1968. *Political Order in Changing Societies.* New Haven: Yale University Press.

Im, Hyug Baeg. 1987. The Rise of Bureaucratic Authoritarianism in South Korea. *World Politics* 39 (2): 231–257.

International Monetary Fund. 2018. Household Debt, Loans and Debt Securities (Percent of GDP): All Data. https://www.imf.org/external/datamapper/ HH_LS@GDD/CAN/GBR/USA/DEU/ITA/FRA/JPN

Jeong, Chan Woo. 2005. Current Issues of Credit Card Industry (in Korean). Special Report at Korea Institute of Finance, March 2005.

Ji, Joo Hyoung. 2011. *The Origin and Formation of Neoliberalism in South Korea* (in Korean). Seoul: Book World.

Jones, Randall S., and Myungkyoo Kim. 2014. Addressing High Household Debt in Korea. OECD Economics Department Working Papers No. 1164.

Joo, Sang Yeong. 2018. A Macro Analysis of Causes of the Changes in Income Inequality Indices (in Korean). *Monthly Labor Review* 161: 75–83.

JoongAng Ilbo. www.joins.com

Kang, Byung Ik. 2016. The Conservative Parties' Reform of Welfare State: The Case of South Korea and UK (in Korean). *Korean Politics Studies* 25 (2): 145–174.

Kang, Myung Hun. 1996. *The Korean Business Conglomerate: Chaebol Then and Now*. Berkeley: University of California Press.

Kihl, Young Whan. 1984. *Politics and Policies in Divided Korea: Regimes in Contest*. Boulder: Westview Press.

Kim, Dokyun. 2013. The Formation and Transformation of the Asset-Based Livelihood Security System in Korea: Savings Mobilization and Tax Politics in a Developmental State (in Korean). PhD dissertation in Department of Sociology, Seoul National University.

———. 2015. The Duality of Self-Employment Debt and Its Increase After the Exchange Crisis (in Korean). *Economy and Society* 108: 73–107.

Kim, Dong-Choon. 1995. *A Study of Labor in South Korean Society: Focusing on the Post-1987 Period* (in Korean). Seoul: Yukbi.

———. 2002. Confucianism and Korean Familialism: Is Familialism a Product of Confucian Values? (in Korean). *Economy and Society* 55: 93–118.

Kim, Jae Wan. 2015. Liability, Memory and the Future of Human Rights Violation: The Case of Hyoungje Welfare Institution (in Korean). *Democratic Legal Studies* 57: 13–53.

Kim, Keunsei. 2012. The Nature and Historical Origin of Park Chung-Hee's Developmental Bureaucracy (in Korean). Presented at the 2012 Summer Meeting of the Korean Association of Public Administration.

Kim, Kyong-Dong. 2017. *Korean Modernization and Uneven Development: Alternative Sociological Accounts*. Basingstoke: Palgrave Macmillan.

Kim, Myeong-Yeon. 2006. Results and Questions for the Human Rights of Inhabitants in Social Welfare Facilities (in Korean). *Journal of the Korean Public Law Association* 35 (2): 109–134.

Kim, Myoungsoo. 2018. Housing Politics and Stratification in South Korea: Social Service Provision Through Resource Mobilization and the Birth of the Survivalist Residential Strategy, 1970–2015 (in Korean). PhD dissertation in Department of Sociology, Seoul National University.

Kim, Sang-Jo. 2007. Samsung Republic – A Government over the Government Produced from the Financial Crisis (in Korean). *Hwanghae Review* 56: 25–44.

Kim, Se-Kyun. 2013. The Launching of the Park Geun-Hye Regime and the Development Prospect for South Korean Society (in Korean). *Tomorrow-Opening History* 50: 79–86.

Kim, Seung-Gweon, Lee Sang-Heon, and Yang Hye-Gyeong. 1998. *Living Conditions and Welfare Needs of Unemployed Women and Their Families* (in Korean). Seoul: Korea Institute for Health and Social Affairs.

Kim, Sun-Yeong. 2011. *Loan-Recommending Society: Commodification of Credit and Social Jeopardy Seen Through the Issue of Financial Defaulters* (in Korean). Seoul: Humanitas.

Kim, Tae-Hoon. 2012. The 2012 Presidential Election, Analysis of Welfare Policy (in Korean). *Social Movement* 109: 71–86.

Kim, Taekyoon. 2008. The Social Construction of Welfare Control: A Sociological Review on State-Voluntary Sector Links in Korea. *International Sociology* 23 (6): 819–844.

Kim, Won. 2007. The Social Isolation of South Korea's Big Factory Unions: With a Focus on Hyundai Motors in Ulsan (in Korean). Unpublished paper.

Kim, Yeon Myung. 1993. The Impacts of the Cold War in the Korean Peninsula on the Welfare Systems of South and North Korea (in Korean). PhD dissertation in Department of Social Welfare, Chung Ang University.

Kim, Yeon Myung, and Park Sang Hee. 2012. Is It Public Welfare or Private Welfare? A Study on the Character of Social Welfare Corporations in Korea (in Korean). *Critical Social Policy* 36: 7–38.

Kim, Young-Soon. 1998. *The Crisis and Restructuring of the Welfare State: The Experiences of the United Kingdom and Sweden* (in Korean). Seoul: Seoul National University.

Kim, Yu-seon. 2014. The Size and Reality of Non-Regular Employment: The Result of 'the Supplementary Survey on Economically Active Population' (2014.8) by the National Statistical Office (in Korean). KLSI (Korea Labour & Society Institute) Issue Paper 2014–22. Seoul: KLSI.

Kinugasa, Tomoko. 2013. Reaping the Rewards of the Second Demographic Dividend. *East Asia Forum Quarterly* 5 (1). https://www.eastasiaforum. org/2013/04/01/reaping-the-rewards-of-the-second-demographic-dividend/

Koli, Ans, Rob van Tulder, and Carlijn Welters. 1999. International Codes of Conduct and Corporate Social Responsibility: Can Transnational Corporations Regulate Themselves? *Transnational Corporations* 8 (1): 143–180.

Kong, Tat Yan. 2000. *The Politics of Economic Reform in South Korea: A Fragile Miracle*. London: Routledge.

Koo, Hagen. 1993. The State, Minjung, and the Working Class in South Korea. In *State and Society in Contemporary Korea*, ed. Hagen Koo, 131–162. Ithaca: Cornell University Press.

———. 2001. *Korean Workers: The Culture and Politics of Class Formation*. Ithaca: Cornell University Press.

Koo, Yangmi. 2017. Korean Enterprises' Foreign Direct Investment to Vietnam and Changes in Vietnamese Industrial Structure and Regions (in Korean). *Journal of the Korean Geographical Society* 52 (4): 435–455.

Korea Broadcasting System, and Yonsei University. 1996. *White Book on Citizens' Consciousness Survey in South Korea, China, and Japan* (in Korean).

Korea Development Institute (KDI). 1998. Changes in People's Economic Consciousness in the One Year Under the International Monetary Fund (in Korean). Unpublished survey report.

Korea Economic Daily. www.hankyung.com

Korea Fair Trade Commission (KFTC). 2018. The Result of Analysis of the Operation Realities of Public Interest Corporations Belonging to Large Enterprise Conglomerates (in Korean). Press release, 29 June 2018.

Korea Herald. www.koreaherald.com

Korea High Education Institute. 2011. *A Country of Insane Tuitions* (in Korean). Seoul: Gaemagowon.

Korea Institute for Health and Social Affairs (KIHASA) and Korea Labor Institute (KLI). 1998. Summary of the Research Report on the Unemployment Situation and Welfare Needs. Unpublished internal report.

Korea Trade-Investment Promotion Agency (KOTRA). 2015. *Management Examples of China-Entering Enterprises: The Success Stories of the Thirty Seven Colors of Thirty Seven Firms* (in Korean). Seoul: KOTRA.

———. 2016. *2016 Directory of Overseas-Advanced South Korean Firms.* Seoul: KOTRA.

Korean Statistical Information Service (KOSIS). 2018. Average Age at First Marriage by Cities and Provinces, 1990–2017. http://kosis.kr/statisticsList/statisticsListIndex.do?menuId=M_01_01&vwcd=MT_ZTITLE&parmTabId=M_01_01#SelectStatsBoxDiv

Krugman, Paul. 1994. The Myth of Asia's Miracle. *Foreign Affairs* 73 (6): 62–78.

Ku, Inhoe. 2006. *Income Inequality and Poverty in Korea: Worsening Income Distribution and the Need for Social Policy Reform* (in Korean). Seoul: Seoul National University Press.

Kuk, Min Ho. 2012. *Developmental State, Welfare State, and Neoliberalism* (in Korean). Gwangju: Chonnam National University Press.

Kukinews.

Kukmin Daily.

Kwon, Huck-ju. 1999. *The Welfare State in Korea: The Politics of Legitimation.* London: St. Martin's.

———. 2005. Transforming the Developmental Welfare State in East Asia. *Development and Change* 36 (3): 477–497.

Kyunghyang Daily.

Labor-Business-Government Committee (Nosajeongwiweonhoe). 1998. Labor-Business-Government Co-Declaration (in Korean). 20 Jan 1998.

Labor Today. www.labortoday.co.kr

Lee, Cheol-Sung. 2016. *When Solidarity Works: Labor-Civic Networks and Welfare States in the Market Reform Era.* Cambridge: Cambridge University Press.

Lee, Gyu-Cheol. 2005. China's *Gonghui* Institution: The *Gonghui* Organization and Dealing Strategies from the Perspective of Foreign-Invested Firms (in Korean). *International Labor Brief* 5 (2): 79–84.

Lee, Hyeon Jung. 2012. 'The Parent-Child Suicide Pact' and the Concept of the Family in East Asia: A Cross-Cultural Approach of South Korea, China, and Japan (in Korean). *Korean Studies* 40: 187–227.

Lee, Hyun-Ju, et al. 2006. *The Structure of Poverty in Korea* (in Korean). Seoul: Korea Institute for Social Development and Policy Research.

Lee, Jang-Won. 2018. The Proceeding Situation and Assignment of the Regular Position Transition of Non-Regular Employees in Public Sectors (in Korean). *Monthly Labor Review* 160: 71–79.

Lee, JiEun. 2009. The Trend of the Leverage of Our Country's Households and Corporations and Its Implications (in Korean). *Korea Institute of Finance, Weekly Financial Brief* 18 (23): 8–9.

Lee, Myung-Bak. 2007. Korea 747. http://english.mbplaza.net/default/korea/?type=html/747_01&wgrp=42&m=2

Lee, Pyoung-Soo. 2015. Basic Law on Service Industry Development and Medical Privatization (in Korean). *Journal of the Korean Medical Association* 58 (2): 86–88.

Lee, Sang-Ho. 2018. Local Regions' Extinction in South Korea 2018: Focusing on the Trend of 2013~2018 and Population Movement in Non-Capital Region Areas (in Korean). *Employment Trend Brief, July* 2018: 2–21.

Lee, Sang-Young, Noh Yong-Hwan, and Lee Gi-Ju. 2012. Policy Issues and Directions for a Rapid Increase in Suicides in Korea (in Korean). KIHASA Research Report 2012–64, Seoul: Korea Institute for Health and Social Affairs (KIHASA).

Lee, Seung-Hee. 2010. Report on *Chaebol*'s Control of Media (Korean). *Economic Reform Report* 2010–12, Seoul: Economic Reform Research Institute.

Lee, Sophia Seung-yoon, Back Seung Ho, Kim Migyoung, and Kim Yoon Young. 2017. Analysis of Precariousness in Korean Youth Labour Market (in Korean). *Critical Social Policy* 54: 487–521.

Lewis, W. Arthur. 1954. Economic Development with Unlimited Supplies of Labour. *Manchester School of Economics and Social Studies* 22 (1): 139–191.

Lim, Hyun-Chin, and Jin-Ho Jang. 2006. Neo-Liberalism in Post-Crisis South Korea: Social Conditions and Outcomes. *Journal of Contemporary Asia* 36 (4): 442–463.

Lim, Young Il. 1997. *South Korea's Labor Movement and Class Politics in South Korea, 1987–1995* (in Korean). Masan: Kyungnam University Press.

Lin, Yi-Min. 2014. *Between Politics and Markets: Firms, Competition, and Institutional Change in Post-Mao China.* Cambridge: Cambridge University Press.

Los Angeles Times.

Mader, Philip. 2015. *The Political Economy of Microfinance: Financializing Poverty.* Basingstoke: Palgrave Macmillan.

Maeil Labor News, 6 Nov 2017. http://www.labortoday.co.kr

March, James, and Herbert Simon. 1958. *Organizations.* New York: Wiley.

Marshall, T.H. 1964. *Class, Citizenship, and Social Development.* Garden City: Doubleday.

Masina, Pietro. 2006. *Vietnam's Development Strategies.* London: Routledge.

Mason, Edward S., Mahnje Kim, Kwang Suk Kim, David C. Cole, and Dwight H. Perkins. 1981. *The Economic and Social Modernization of the Republic of Korea*. Cambridge: Harvard University Press.

Matthews, John. 1995. *High-Technology Industrialisation in East Asia: The Case of the Semiconductor Industry in Taiwan and Korea*. Taipei: Chung-Hua Institution for Economic Research.

Ministry of Finance and Economy, Republic of Korea. 2002. *Whitebook of Public Fund Administration, 2002* (in Korean).

Ministry of Labor, Republic of Korea. www.molab.go.kr

Mishra, Ramesh, Stein Kuhnle, Neil Gilbert, and Kyungbae Chung, eds. 2004. *Modernizing the Korean Welfare State: Towards the Productive Welfare Model*. New Brunswick: Transaction Publishers.

Morrissey, Oliver, and Manop Udomkerdmongkol. 2011. Governance, Private Investment and Foreign Direct Investment in Developing Countries. *World Development* 40 (3): 437–445.

Nam, Jeong-Lim. 2000. Gender Politics in the Korean Transition to Democracy. *Korean Studies* 24 (1): 94–112.

Nam, Seong-Il, and Lee Hwa-Yeong. 1998. An Analysis of the Characteristics of Recent Unemployment in South Korea: A Comparison of the Pre- and the Post-Foreign Currency Crisis (in Korean). Unpublished research report.

National Statistical Office (NSO), Republic of Korea. 1997. *Social Indicators in Korea, 1997*.

National Statistical Office (NSO). 1998. *Fifty Years' Economic and Social Change Seen Through Statistics* (in Korean).

———. 1999. Summary of the Household Financial Balance among Urban Worker Households in the Fourth Quarter and the Entire Year of 1998 (in Korean). Unpublished media release.

———. 2016. The Result of the 2016 Social Survey (Family, Education, Health, Safety, Environment), 15 Nov 2016.

———. 2018a. Year 2017 Birth Statistics (Final), 21 Aug 2018.

———. 2018b. The Result of the Survey of Household Conditions in the First Quarter of 2018 (in Korean).

Newsweek.

No, Jung-Gi. 2012. A Study on the 1987 Great Labour Struggle (in Korean). *Economy and Society* 96: 178–209.

Ochiai, Emiko. 2011. Unsustainable Societies: The Failure of Familialism in East Asia's Compressed Modernity. *Historical Social Research* 36 (2): 219–245.

Oh, Chang-Sup, and Choi Sung-Hyeok. 2012. The Empirical Study on the Cause of Low Fertility: Factors to Impact on Falling of Nuptiality and Rising of Age at First Marriage (in Korean). *Journal of Public Welfare and Administration* 22 (1): 91–125.

OhmynewsTV, 11 Oct 2017. https://www.youtube.com/watch?v=4V9Ylnb5ZWA

Organisation for Economic Co-operation and Development (OECD). 2017. *Preventing Ageing Unequally*. Paris: OECD Publishing.

———. 2018. *OECD Economic Surveys, Korea: Overview*. http://www.oecd.org/eco/surveys/Korea-2018-OECD-economic-survey-overview.pdf

———. Each year. Economic Outlook, Analysis and Forecasts. www.oecd.org/eco/outlook/

Palat, Ravi. 1998. Varieties of Crony Capitalism. *Hindu On-Line*, 22 Aug 1998.

———. 1999. Miracles of the Day Before? The Great Asian Meltdown and the Changing World-Economy. *Development and Society* 28 (1): 1–48.

Park, Chan-Jong. 2014. The Transformation of Debt-Economy in South Korea: Focusing on the State-Industry-Finance Relationship (in Korean). PhD dissertation in Department of Sociology, Seoul National University.

Park, Chang Gyun. 2009. The Trend of Household Debts and Financial Instability. Paper presented at the 500th Weekly Seminar of the Korea Institute of Finance, 11 Aug 2009.

Park, Jeong Seon. 2014. A Study on Supervision and Human Rights in the Residential Institutions for the Disabled (in Korean). *Korean Journal of Family Welfare* 44: 163–190.

Park, Jong-Hun. 1999. A Study of the Protection Mechanism of Middle Class Families against the Unemployment of Family Heads in South Korean Society (in Korean). Master thesis in Department of Sociology, Seoul National University.

Park, Keong-Suk. 2007. Meaning of the Discourses of Filial Piety Law in a Moral and Political Economy (in Korean). *Journal of the Korean Family Studies Association* 19 (3): 31–52.

Park, Mi Youn, and Cha Kyung-Wook. 2008. Retirement Planning and Private Education Expenditures of Households with School-Aged Children (in Korean). *Financial Planning Review* 1 (1): 131–156.

Park, Yoon-Young. 2002. A Study on Policy Making Process of the National Basic Livelihood Institution: Focused on Enactment of National Basic Livelihood Act (in Korean). *Korean Journal of Social Welfare* 49 (5): 264–295.

Parwez, Sazzad. 2015. Modified Labor Welfare Measures for Special Economic Zone & Implications. Munich Personal RePEc Archive. https://mpra.ub.uni-muenchen.de/63835/1/MPRA_paper_63835.pdf

People's Solidarity for Participatory Democracy (PSPD), Economic Democratization Committee. 1998. *White Book on Public Interest Foundations: Accusing Public Interest Foundations That Are Chaebol's Camouflaged Affiliate Firms* (in Korean). Seoul: Jijeong.

Pham, Ngoc Huyen. 2017. A Study on South Korean ODA to Vietnam. Master thesis at the Graduate School of International Studies, Ewha Womans University.

Pingali, Prabhu, and Vo-Tong Xuan. 1992. Vietnam: Decollectivization and Rice Productivity Growth. *Economic Development and Cultural Change* 40 (40): 697–718.

POSCO Research Institute. 2014. No Eggs in One Basket: Foreign Companies Leave China and Head Towards Vietnam. *POSCO Chindia Plus Quarterly* 15 (Summer): 10–33.

Presidential Committee on Ageing Society and Population Policy. 2018. The Roadmap of the Low Fertility-Ageing Society Policy for "the Improvement of the Quality of Life for All Generations and the Realization of the Inclusionary State" (in Korean). Report agenda, 7 Dec 2018.

Presidential Council for Future and Vision, Ministry of Strategy and Finance, and Financial Services Commission (Republic of Korea). 2010. International Seminar on 'Future Vision for Korea's Financial Industry: Takeoff in the Post-Crisis Era' (in Korean). Press brief, 3 February 2010.

Pressian. www.pressian.com

Rajkai, Zsombor, ed. 2016. *Family and Social Change in Socialist and Post-Socialist Societies.* Leiden and Boston: Brill.

Realmeter. www.realmeter.net, 17 Dec 2018.

Riskin, Carl. 1987. *China's Political Economy: The Quest for Development since 1949.* Oxford: Oxford University Press.

Rock, Michael T. 2017. *Dictators, Democrats, and Development in Southeast Asia: Implications for the Rest.* Oxford: Oxford University Press.

Rueschemeyer, Dietrich, Evelyne Stephens, and John Stephens. 1992. *Capitalist Development and Democracy.* Chicago: University of Chicago Press.

Sagunin. 2015. Who Are Entertainers That Have Been Sacked After Appearing in Advertisements of Money Lender Industry (in Korean), 12 Oct 2015.

Sen, Amartya. 1981. *Poverty and Famines: An Essay on Entitlement and Deprivation.* Oxford: Oxford University Press.

Seo, Bong Seob. 1997. Welfare Policies and Democratization in Korea (in Korean). *Korean Public Administration Review* 31 (1): 95–111.

Seol, Dong-Hoon. 2002. The Discrimination of Gastarbeiter and Their Civil Right (in Korean). *Citizen and the World* 2: 345–356.

———. 2014. The Citizenship of Foreign Workers: Stratified Formation, Fragmented Evolution. In *South Korea in Transition: Politics and Culture of Citizenship*, ed. Chang Kyung-Sup, 131–146. London: Routledge.

Seoul Institute of Economic and Social Studies, ed. 2014. *The Economic and Social Policy of the Park Geun-hye Government: The Disappearance of Economic Democratization and Welfare* (in Korean). Seoul: Hanul Academy.

Shin, Eui Hang, and Chin Seung Kwon. 1989. Social Affinity Among Top Managerial Executives of Large Corporations in Korea. *Sociological Forum* 4 (1): 3–26.

Shin, Kwang-Yeong. 2015. *Swedish Social Democracy: Labor, Welfare, and Politics* (in Korean). Seoul: Hanul.

Shujiro, Urata. 2008. The Creation of Regional Production Networks in Asia Pacific: The Case of Japanese Multinational Corporations. In *Multinational*

Corporations and the Emerging Network Economy in Asia and the Pacific, ed. Juan J. Palacios, 114–138. London: Routledge.

Shyn, Yong-Sang. 2008. The Impact of Household Debt Increase and Interest Rate Rise on Consumption Activity by Income Strata (in Korean). Korea Institute of Finance, *Weekly Financial Brief* 17 (35): 8–9.

Sisa Journal.

Skocpol, Theda. 1992. *Protecting Soldiers and Mothers: The Social Origins of Social Policy in the United States.* Cambridge: Harvard University Press.

Soederberg, Susanne. 2014. *Debtfare States and the Poverty Industry: Money, Discipline, and the Surplus Population.* London: Routledge.

Somerville, Jennifer. 1992. The New Right and Family Politics. *Economy and Society* 21 (2): 93–128.

Son, Nak-Gu. 2008. *Real Estate Class Society* (in Korean). Seoul: Humanitas.

Song, Baek-Seok. 2007. 'Samsung Republic Phenomenon' and the Limits of the Capitalist State (in Korean). *Korean Political Science Review* 41 (1): 57–79.

Song, Ho-Keun. 1995. *Korea's Company Welfare: An Empirical Research* (in Korean). Seoul: Korea Labor Institute.

———. 1997. *Market and Welfare Politics: A Study of Social Democratic Sweden* (in Korean). Seoul: Sahoebipyeong.

Song, Tae-Gyeong. 2011. *The Secret of Loan Heaven: The Truth Concealed Behind My Debt Pile* (in Korean). Seoul: Gaemagowon.

Song, Won Keun, Shin Hak-rim, Won-jae Lee, and Il-young Lee. 2016. *Chaebol* (Conglomerates) in Korea, *Chaebol's* Korea? (in Korean). *Quarterly Changbi* 44 (4): 449–476.

Sovacool, Benjamin K. 2010. The Political Economy of Oil and Gas in Southeast Asia: Heading towards the Natural Resource Curse? *Pacific Review* 23 (2): 225–259.

Standing, Guy. 2011. *Precariat: The New Dangerous Class.* London: Bloomsbury.

Stepan, Alfred. 1978. *The State and Society: Peru in Comparative Perspective.* Princeton: Princeton University Press.

Straughan, Paulin, Angelique Chan, and Gavin Jones, eds. 2009. *Ultra-Low Fertility in Pacific Asia: Trends, Causes and Policy Issues.* London: Routledge.

Taylor, Robert, Cho Young-Doo, and Hyun Jae Hoon. 2001. The HRM Strategies of Korean Companies in China: Localization of Management. In *Changing Economic Environment in Asia: Firms' Strategies in the Region*, ed. J. Bassino Andreosso-O'Callaghan and J. Jassaud, 77–90. Basingstoke: Palgrave Macmillan.

The Committee on Economic, Social and Cultural Rights, the U.N. Economic and Social Council. 2001. Concluding Observations of the Committee on Economic, Social and Cultural Rights on Non-Compliance with Reporting Obligations by States Parties: Republic of Korea, 9 May 2001.

The Economist. 2014. South Korea's Household Debt: Hole in Won, Korean Households Are Struggling under Mounting Debt, 31 May 2014.

The Economist Intelligence Unit. 2015. *integrAsian: How Asia's Economic Ties Are Changing the Business Landscape.* London: The Economist. https://s3-eu-west-1.amazonaws.com/papillon-local/uploads/5/7/Final%20 Integrasian%20Report.pdf.

The Government of the Republic of Korea. 2016. Country Partnership Strategy for the Socialist Republic of Vietnam (in Korean).

The Hankyoreh. www.hani.co.kr

Therborn, Göran. 1986. *Why Some Peoples Are More Unemployed Than Others: Strange Paradox of Growth and Unemployment.* London: Verso.

Thomas, Vinod. 2017. Demographics, Dividends, and Labor Productivity in Asia. *Brookings Report-Future Development,* 4 Dec 2017.

Thurbon, Elizabeth. 2016. *Developmental Mindset: The Revival of Financial Activism in South Korea.* Ithaca: Cornell University Press.

Turner, Bryan S. 2016. We Are All Denizens Now: On the Erosion of Citizenship. *Citizenship Studies* 20 (6/7): 679–692.

Um, Eui Hyeon. 2007. The Issues and Subjects of Non-Regular Labors' Problem: The Case of the Non-Regular Workers Protection Law (in Korean). *National Policy Studies* 21 (2): 71–106.

Wacquant, Loic. 2008. *Urban Outcasts: A Comparative Sociology of Advanced Marginality.* Cambridge: Polity Press.

———. 2010. Crafting the Neoliberal State: Workfare, Prisonfare, and Social Insecurity. *Sociological Forum* 25 (2): 197–220.

Wade, Robert. 1990. *Governing the Market: Economic Theory and the Role of Government in East Asian Industrialization.* Princeton: Princeton University Press.

———. 1998. The Asian Debt-And-Development Crisis of 1997–?: Causes and Consequences. *World Development* 26 (8): 1535–1553.

Weekly Chosun.

Weiss, Linda. 1998. *The Myth of the Powerless State.* Ithaca: Cornell University Press.

White, Gordon, and Roger Goodman. 1998. Welfare Orientalism and Search for an East Asian Welfare Model. In *The East Asian Welfare Model: Welfare Orientalism and the State,* ed. Roger Goodman, Gordon White, and Huck-ju Kwon, 3–24. London: Routledge.

World Health Organization. WHO; http://www.who.int/

Yang, Jae-Jin. 2017. *The Political Economy of the Small Welfare State in South Korea.* Cambridge: Cambridge University Press.

Yeh, Emily T. 2017. *The Geoeconomics and Geopolitics of Chinese Development and Investment in Asia.* London: Routledge.

Yeom, Ji Hye, Park Jong-Seo, Lee Sang-Lim, and Lee Min-A. 2010. *Strategies for Workforce Utilization in Times of Low Fertility, Population Aging, and Labor Shortage.* KIHASA Research Report, 2010-30-14. Seoul: Korea Institute for Health and Social Affairs.

Yoo, Kyeongwon. 2009. Analysis on the Issue of Household Debts: Focusing on Micro Data (in Korean). Institute for Monetary and Economic Research (The Bank of Korea), *Economic Analysis* 15 (4): 1–32.

Yoon, Hong-Sik. 2008. The Expansion of New Social Risks and the Base Draft of the Policy of the Lee Myung-Bak Government: Focusing on the Area of Women and Family (Welfare) Policies (in Korean). *Monthly Welfare Trends* 113 (March 2008): 23–27.

———. 2018. Aid-Welfare Regime in Korea, 1948–1961 (in Korean). *Social Welfare Policy* 45 (1): 115–147.

Yoon, Jin-Ho. 2005. The Causes for Income Bipolarization and the Direction for Policy Responses (in Korean). In *The South Korean Economy: Beyond Globalization, Structural Adjustment, Bipolarization*, ed. Seoul Social and Economic Research Center, 110–148. Seoul: Hanul.

Yoon, Jin-Ho, Yu-Sun Kim, Jang-Ho Kim, Dae-Myung Roh, and Jae-Eun Seok. 2005. The Direction of Labor and Welfare Policies for Allied Growth and Bipolarization Annulment (in Korean). Report Submitted to the Presidential Commission on Policy and Planning, Republic of Korea, November 2005.

Yu, Hong. 2016. Motivation behind China's 'One Belt, One Road': Initiatives and Establishment of the Asian Infrastructure Investment Bank. *Journal of Contemporary China* 105: 353–368.

Yun, Yeong-Ho. 1998. Tardy and Dull, the Structural Adjustment of Five Largest *Chaebol*: 'Mighty *Chaebol*' Head-On Contest against D.J. Reform (in Korean). *Shin Dong-A* 41 (11): 160–171.

Zhang, Juan, and Wenrong Ma. 2014. Reflections on "Women Returning to the Home" in Daqiuzhuang Village. *Journal of Chinese Education* 25 (1): 75–80.

INDEX

© The Author(s) 2019   215
Chang K-S, *Developmental Liberalism in South Korea*,
International Political Economy Series,
https://doi.org/10.1007/978-3-030-14576-7

CPSIA information can be obtained
at www.ICGtesting.com
Printed in the USA
LVHW072315170519
618114LV00008B/7/P